# Manipulating Parents

## Tactics Used by Children of All Ages and Ways Parents Can Turn the Tables

PAUL W. ROBINSON
*with* Timothy J. Newby and Robert D. Hill

Prentice-Hall, Inc., Englewood Cliffs, N.J. 07632

*Library of Congress Cataloging in Publication Data*

Robinson, Paul W.
Manipulating parents.

(A Spectrum Book)
Bibliography: p.
Includes index.

ISBN 0-13-552166-1

ISBN 0-13-552158-0 {PBK.}



A SPECTRUM BOOK



10 9 8 7 6 5 4 3 2 1

Printed in the United States of America



Prentice-Hall International, Inc., *London*
Prentice-Hall of Australia Pty. Limited, *Sydney*
Prentice-Hall of Canada, Ltd., *Toronto*
Prentice-Hall of India Private Limited, *New Delhi*
Prentice-Hall of Japan, Inc., *Tokyo*
Prentice-Hall of Southeast Asia Pte. Ltd., *Singapore*
Whitehall Books Limited, Wellington, New Zealand

# Contents

*Foreword* *vii*
*Preface* *xi*

**1**

Who Is Really Driving the Family Bus 1

**2**

The Parent's Bill of Rights 19

**3**

Subliminal Parent Training (Hidden Persuaders) 41

4

The Superthreshold Approach 54

5

The Incompatible
Response Approach 64

6

Tactics Used on Psychologists
and Social Workers 74

7

The Natural Method
of Parenting 88

8

How to Stop Them:
Three Ways to Get Rid of
Undesirable Dimensions in Children 113

9

How to Stop Them:
Three More Ways 129

10

Punishment 139

11

Four Ways to Get Them to Do What You Want 165

12

Sources of Help for Parents 190

13

Problems Requiring Professional Help 205

14

Types of Problems Parents Can Handle 218

15

Caring—The Family Adhesive 232

16

What to Do
with a Bad Apple 254

Index 267

# Foreword

Dr. Robinson's tactics for manipulating children *really work!* Grant Elementary School in Springville, Utah, had an unusually large number of hyperactive, uncooperative third grade children in 1979. The principal took all the unmanageable kids and formed one class. I was assigned to teach these eighteen children, many of whom were on medication for hyperactivity. The experience I went through for the next five months can be described only as a nightmare. Each day's class was filled with fights, yelling, throwing chairs, and comments like "Try and make me do that!". Many mornings I cried as I anticipated going to school. I often called in sick. The principal could get no substitute teacher who took my place to come back a second time. In January I told the principal I was quitting because I could not take it any more. He talked me into staying.

At that time, I heard about Dr. Robinson and skeptically went to him for help. He came out, observed, filmed my class, and then explained how we could manipulate those kids. With strong doubts I listened as he told me how to implement tactics which would re-direct their aggressive, anti-social hyperactivity into achievement-oriented, socially-acceptable activities. *And It Worked!*

Within three weeks we had subtely turned the tables on all my students and they were doing their schoolwork. In class they studied vocabulary words, read books, and helped each other learn. Many even asked to take schoolwork home. Never before had any of them asked for homework. The principal, the other teachers, and I could not believe our eyes. Eighteen previously unmanageable kids were now working together to learn and I was in control of the classroom. KBYU television came out and filmed a documentary which showed how the kids had acted and what they became.

Thanks to many of the tactics presented in this book, I now have confidence in working with problem children. I know how to out-manipulate children for their good and mine. A parent often has one or two problem children to work with. Imagine what coping with eighteen was like.

Cynthia Smith
Third Grade Teacher
Grant Elementary School
Springville, Utah

For many years Dr. Robinson has taken some of the more difficult problem children from our state foster parent program into his *own* home. The problems these children (mostly teenagers) have had includes being suicidal, incest cases, having strong character disorders, being defiant to parents, child abuse cases, law breakers, and drug users. He has taken in children of all colors, ages, and varying ethnic backgrounds. We have yet to see him fail with a child placed in his home.

Ed Solie M.S.W.
Director of Utah County Foster Care Program
Utah State Division of Social Services

As a child psychologist, I have been a colleague of Dr. Paul W. Robinson's for over ten years. It is not hard for a psychologist to fly into a city, give a talk on how to raise children, then fly out again. No one sees his children, or knows if he practices what he preaches. Many psychologists tell parents how to deal with problem children, but Dr. Robinson is the only one I know of who has the ability to take them into his home and show how it is done. I can tell you first hand that Dr. Robinson and his wife, Carol, effectively use the strategies and tactics presented in this book. I have been to their home many times. They have had children in their home from Puerto Rico, Canada, India and Russia, besides many born in the U.S. What they can do with problem children of all ages is nothing short of amazing.

Dr. Robinson is a rather unique psychologist in that he is both an applied psychologist and scientist. Besides being effective in treating behavioral problems, he has an outstanding record as a scholar and researcher.

He is the author of numerous professional journal articles and five college textbooks. One of his books was the number one selling college text in the nation in the field of experimental psychology.

Combining his skills as a scientist and applied psychologist, Dr. Robinson has studied hundreds of parent-child problem situations, identifying many principles and strategies that slip by the average psychologist. In this book he provides insights and strategies parents can use to cope with children that cannot be found anywhere else. And he does so in a storytelling manner that readers will find interesting and enjoyable. Any parent or teacher who is serious about learning how to effectively deal with children should have a copy of this book.

Dr. Larry C. Jensen
Child Psychologist
Professor of Psychology
Author

A special thanks to Deedra Newby and Debra Hill for their patience and support while this was being written.

# Preface

Have you ever been shopping and seen a young girl manipulate her mother by crying and screaming until she received the candy she wanted? Do you know a twelve year old who gets whatever he wants from his parents by creating uncomfortable situations? Perhaps you have a niece or nephew who gets on your nerves, but you dare not reprimand the little troublemaker for fear of offending your relatives. Or possibly you feel your children are getting the best of you and you are not sure exactly how they do it or what you can do about it.

Each of us was a child once, and all of us manipulated our parents. We intentionally picked certain times and places to ask to use the car or to hit mother up for a new dress. We often avoided a punishment we deserved by denying we had anything to do with the broken window. We even did many of the things our children do that we now find so distasteful. We cried, threw tantrums, demanded our right to do whatever we pleased, and avoided going to bed. In high school we often hid our activities by doing one thing and telling our parents we were doing something else, or we frustrated our parents by just doing what we wanted with little concern for their feelings.

Now that we have passed through the veil that separates childhood from parenthood we find ourselves on the receiving end of those manipulative tactics. As parents, grandparents, aunts, uncles, teachers, and neighbors we frequently find ourselves being coerced and maneuvered by the younger generation who often manipulate us without our realizing what is being done. And there are numerous other times when we are aware of their intentions but are not sure how to deal with them.

Parents are uncomfortable for three main reasons when it comes to dealing with manipulative children. First, parents have difficulty recalling the tactics they used to manipulate their parents. Most of us went through childhood without taking notes. At the time we did not consider that someday we would be in our parents shoes and that it would be valuable as parents to have kept a record as to what we did at different age levels, and why we did it. Unfortunately, we went through our youth preparing to be adults, but few of us were adequately preparing to be parents.

Second, a result of mass media is that present-day children are more sophisticated in the ways of manipulating parents. Children are the main audience of television programs and commercials, and many programs deal with problems of effectively coping with parents. These programs also show children the more effective techniques they can use to sway their parents.

Unfortunately, many such programs are not as beneficial to parents. On television the programs showing children doing inappropriate acts, such as lying, running away, stealing, or being inconsiderate, typically end with the child realizing the wrong and telling the parent he or she is sorry and wants to change. Few parents can identify with such endings because very few children ever react that way. Television programs generally have heart rendering endings, but they are quite unrealistic. The mass media have done a great deal to make children more effective manipulators while giving parents little help in properly handling manipulating children.

Third, present-day parents are confronted with so many conflicting opinions on what they should be doing that they lack the confidence needed to assert ourselves as parents. We find ourselves wondering if we are doing the right things. Did I reprimand my daughter too harshly? Did I really try to understand my son's position? Am I pushing my children too hard in life? Should I let my child cry it out, or go give her love and affection? What is the proper way to get rid of tantrum behavior in my son? How do I handle a conniving child who manipulates his brothers and sisters? Some child-rearing experts advocate letting children grow out of such tendencies. Others claim you should be stern and put an immediate stop to such actions. There are almost as many different theories on child-rearing as there are different breakfast cereals.

*Manipulating Parents* is a book to help the present-day parent deal with the problems a parent faces when children try to manipulate them. The first part of the book (Chapters 3–6) identifies the main types of tactics children use to get what they want from parents. Some of these tactics are quite subtle and are accomplished without the parents realizing what is going on. Other tactics are obvious attempts by children to mold and manipulate their parents. These chapters also advise the reader as to which types of parents are most susceptible to certain tactics. Suggestions are included as to how to spot when certain tactics are being used on you.

The second section of the book (Chapters 7–14) identifies a variety of strategies parents may use to counteract the tactics used by children. Chapter 7 points out that if children can successfully mold and manipulate parents, parents should be capable of doing the same to children. The fact that parenting can be fun and rewarding besides being effective is also discussed. Chapters 8 and 9 identify six basic strategies parents can use to handle existing undesirable behaviors in children who have already established disruptive and unacceptable behaviors. Chapter 11 explains tactics parents can use to mold the child from infancy to adulthood without having to resort to the stronger tactics needed to handle children with established behavioral problems. Chapter 10 deals with the controversial issue of punishment. The facts and fallacies surrounding this issue is addressed in hopes the reader will gain a better understanding of what punishment is, when to use it, and when not to use it.

Chapter 12 tells the parent about a variety of places they can go to get help in properly raising their children. Some of these places provide services for children that parents cannot provide; others simply make raising children a little easier on the parent.

Throughout the book are discussed many child behavior problems that the parents can effectively deal with themselves if they are aware of the proper strategies. There are a number of behavior problems, however, that the parent should not try to deal with themselves. Certain problems require the skill and expertise of a trained psychologist. Chapter 13 points out many of these types of problems and briefly explains some of the approaches psychologists use to handle them.

The third section of the book (Chapters 15 and 16) addresses some side issues parents often ask about. How can I get my child to care about my feelings? When is it too late to change a "problem" child? What problems do adoptive children present to parents? Are there successful programs for problem children that I can get help from?

Several themes the reader should consider will be encountered throughout the book. First, the term *manipulate* is used again and again. When you read the title, *Manipulating Parents,* you probably were not sure whether it meant children manipulating parents or parents manipulating children. That title was intentionally chosen because the book is about both. The word *manipulate* may seem rather strong and negative. Although there are several different definitions of it in the dictionary, the one this book means to portray is "to manage or utilize skillfully." The book explains the skillful techniques children use to get what they want from parents, and it also emphasizes how parents can manipulate (skillfully utilize methods for molding) children. The second is closely related to the first. Although children do manipulate parents for bad reasons, such actions indicate that what the child is doing is wrong—not that the child is bad. I am convinced that children are not born with "bad blood." Children simply learn incorrect ways of dealing with society, and these inappropriate actions can and should be corrected. Along with this is the idea that parents have the right and obligation to manipulate their children in such a way that the child learns the socially acceptable methods for dealing with other people. Although both children and parents can manipulate for good and bad reasons, the book focuses on bad manipulative tactics used by children and good manipulative tactics parents can use to help the child develop properly.

The third theme running through the book is that the best way to deal with children, even problem children, is to rely on your natural instincts. Although psychologists continually build more sophisticated theories and explanations as to why children behave the way they do, Mother Nature instilled a rather simple but complete plan of life on this planet that even children can implement. More mothers and fathers are looking to psychologists and social workers for help in outwitting the younger, weaker, less mature, and less intelligent youth who is successfully manipulating his/her parents. This book points out many natural child-rearing techniques which any parent has the ability to employ. Most of these techniques are illustrated with actual case histories, and, we hope, provide greater child-rearing insight to the reader.

# 1

# Who Is Really Driving the Family Bus?

## GETTING A CLEARER VIEW OF THE ROAD

I wish I had a nickel for each time a psychologist has said to himself, "If only Mrs. Jones or Mr. Johnson could sit in my chair and listen to the problems other parents have, I'm sure it would give them insights as to what to do with their child." The often quoted statement, "You can't see the forest for the trees" is certainly true when it comes to raising children.

Ever notice how easy it is to spot problems other parents are having? I have met many parents who have good solutions as to how their neighbors could better handle their kids. Oftentimes we are better at spotting how the neighbor's children are manipulating their parents than we are at seeing what our children are doing to us. And one of the reasons we are able to spot other parents' mistakes so often is because we can get a clearer view of what is going on in that family from our more distant vantage point.

Not too long ago my family was camped at a picturesque spot in Yellowstone Park. After a short time a family with young teenagers pulled into the spot next to ours. As the parents set up camp, the children went about doing whatever fit their fancy. The father pulled the tent from the Volkswagen bus and proceeded to set it up while his wife set out the support equipment on the picnic table. During the next two days the parents spent most of their time meeting the desires of their children. On the second day the children disagreed as to whether father should take them fishing or back to Old Faithful Lodge. During some bickering while getting into the van the father interjected, "Now look! Who is really driving the family bus anyway? You guys or me?" To my wife and me the answer was obvious. The actions of this man's children left little doubt in our minds as to who really ran the family. I am sure that father would have gained a great deal of insight if the mirror image of himself could have left his body and sat with us for two days and observed his children and himself interact.

This book is an attempt to help parents become better at dealing with their own children by letting them indirectly sit in the psychologist's chair and listen to how children manipulate other parents. This book is mainly a compilation of child-parenting situations and reflections that I and many of my psychologist colleagues have experienced, or have been told about by parents. Almost all are actual case histories and true stories which show where children have successfully manipulated their parents, or parents have successfully manipulated their children. I hope these stories will help you spot how your children are manipulating you and give you some ideas on how to better cope with children in the future.

It should become apparent as you read through the book that the child who manipulates his parents is viewed from a somewhat unconventional perspective. Children who manipulate parents are not *wrong.* Children who throw tantrums to get their way are not *wrong.* A child who ignores the instructions of a parent is not *wrong.* A girl who does not help her mother keep the house clean is not *wrong.* The child is not *wrong*—the things he or she does are *wrong.* Children who create problems by manipulating their parents to get what they want may be doing things we parents feel are unacceptable and inappropriate. However, they have simply found ways of getting what they want in ways parents dislike. They are not wrong. What is wrong is that conditions prevail which allow these children to get away with unacceptable behaviors.

Children who manipulate parents may be wrong in exactly what they are doing, but they are successful in accomplishing things they set out to do. That is why they do it. We parents might not consider crying, biting, yelling, bickering, complaining, and other forms of inconsiderate actions as success, but that is exactly what they have become for many manipulative children. They can use such behaviors to manipulate parents to get what they want. A young boy cries and father lets him stay up, although the boy was told to go to bed. A young girl bites an older brother to make him leave her alone. A teenager complains about having to help do the dishes; so mother does them alone. These examples illustrate successful behaviors used to manipulate parents and siblings. Let's look briefly at four children who were very successful at manipulating adults.

## STORIES OF SUCCESS

*Danny, the Independent Five-Year-Old*

Danny, a good-looking, sandy-haired boy of five, got up from his chair and headed for his coat hanging on the classroom wall near the door.

"What are you doing Danny?" asked Miss Anderson, the kindergarten teacher at Park Elementary School.

"I'm going to get my coat."

"Why are you getting your coat?"

"I'm going home."

"It's only five after ten, and *we* don't go home until just before lunch."

"I do" Danny retorted as he walked out the door.

*Harold, the Four-Year-Old Manipulator*

"Guess what Harold did this morning?" my wife asked one evening at the dinner table.

Harold is the four-year-old son of Lee, a doctor who lives three houses down the block. Lee and his wife are both college graduates who have some rather novel ideas concerning raising children.

"What?" I inquired.

"Lee was putting up an acoustic tile ceiling in his basement party room last night. He left the ladder and hammer in the room because he finished so late. Early this morning Harold climbed the ladder and used the hammer to pull tiles down."

"Wasn't Harold the one who started the fire by putting a piece of Tupperware on the stove and turning it on one morning a few weeks ago?" I asked.

"Yes."

"What did they do about it?"

"Well, nothing," my wife replied. "You see, Carrie (Lee's wife) feels both of those incidents are her fault, not Harold's. Every morning Harold and his brother get up at 5:30 to watch cartoons. And ever since last year when Harold caused the bathroom to flood when he tried to flush a roll of toilet paper down the toilet she has been getting up at 5:30 to keep an eye on them. According to her the Tupperware and tile incidents only happened because she failed to get up and be with them."

*Lee Ann, the Head-Strong Teenager*

Richard J. was a rather successful and wealthy presidential executive of a large corporation situated near a small town in Ohio. He and his wife had one child, a seventeen-year-old daughter, Lee Ann. Lee Ann was an attractive, forceful, and active teenager. She had often taken the family car without permission. She was involved in two accidents before her license was taken away. In that last accident she ran into a utility pole early one morning on her way to cheerleading practice. She had fallen asleep at the wheel.

Richard came home one day and announced the family was going to Hawaii to get away from it all.

"I'm not going unless Pam comes too," Lee Ann quipped.

The next day Richard bought a ticket for Pam, Lee Ann's best friend.

After arriving in Hawaii they all went to a quaint resort which was designed in bungalow style. Upon finding out all four were to stay in the same multiroom bungalow, Lee Ann demanded that her father rent a separate bungalow for her and Pam.

He did.

Richard and his wife came to check on Lee Ann and Pam as they were settling in their own bungalow. Lee Ann said, "Now mom and dad, we won't want people to know that we are with you two, so when we pass you around here, please act like you don't know us."

They did.

*Todd, the Pest*

"By the way, Paul," Phil said to me at one of our few neighborhood parties, "I've got a problem with my brother's family—more specifically with his four-year-old son. His christened name is Todd, but all his neighbors have more appropriately labeled him 'Atilla the Hun.' He does whatever he wants. He takes what he wants from smaller kids, and screams when adults try to reprimand him. Even my cat is a nervous wreck because of him. My cat likes to sleep on the throw rug next to our couch. When the cat is sleeping Todd climbs up on the arm of the couch and jumps down on its tail and feet.

"A while back, Todd pulled three leaves off one of our large indoor plants. My wife said, 'Rosemary, your son just ripped three leaves off this plant!'

" 'Don't worry,' she replied. 'I'm sure he won't put them in his mouth. That plant isn't poisonous, is it?'

"He pesters grownups incessantly," Phil continued. "Rosemary says he is just a mature child for his age who is developing his skills of getting adult attention."

"Do you think she is right?" I said, answering a question with a question.

"Well, there is no doubt he is good at getting attention," Phil replied. "If you don't look at him when he grabs your arm and talks to you, he hits you in the groin."

What you have just read is four success stories. Actually, they are four incidents about four different children who have learned to do pretty much what they want and use adults as they see fit. These four incidents actually happened and are a small sample of the millions of successful incidents recorded each year by children who expend a great deal of effort training their parents.

Now, you might not consider these success stories. They might sound to you more like examples of children who have failed to learn proper ways of acting. I must confess that for years I shared that view. Day after day I would hear parents recount such incidents happening with their children. And day after day I would see these incidents as unfortunate family problems. Like most psychologists I viewed these poor misguided children as needing professional help to get them on the proper track.

As time passed, however, it slowly dawned on me that there was always one person in each situation who viewed such incidents as successes rather than failures. Though my meddling often resulted in the child learning to obtain his wants in a manner which better pleased his parents, actually he had felt rather comfortable in the way things were going before I entered the picture. While my conversion to the idea that these were success stories was slow, there was one particular incident which helped me crystalize my new view.

A friend and colleague of mine purchased a registered pup whose breed was noted for retrieving water fowl. One day after the dog had reached maturity, Dave began training him to fetch a stick. Part of the training included placing a piece of marshmallow on the end of the stick to be retrieved. After a while the dog seemed to be getting the idea. It wasn't long, however, until the dog refused to retrieve the stick unless one-half marshmallow was the reward. Then he wouldn't perform unless a whole marshmallow was given each time. After a substantial number of marshmallows had been given (plus six blueberry muffins which he found the dog also liked), Dave gave me a call to complain about his dog. "You can't believe how dumb this dog is. He just lays there, looking at me. I can't get him to do a thing now. The guy that sold him to me gypped me. I'm going to sell him."

Those words reminded me of something a father had said about his son just two days earlier, "He just lays around the house. I can't get him to do a thing."

"That dog turned the tables on Dave," I thought. "He did to Dave what we in psychology call 'shaping.'" He trained Dave to gradually give him more for his efforts. It was apparent that the dog and the boy had each trained an adult to satisfy their needs. The boy had reached the ultimate of getting everything he wanted without having to fulfill any of the demands of his father. Given time, the dog had a chance to do the same to Dave. I then got in my car and went to purchase a very smart dog from someone I was sure was willing to make me a good deal.

## A CHILD'S APPROACH TO PARENT REARING—DOING WHAT COMES NATURALLY

For quite some time the incidents of that dog and boy continued to reappear in my thoughts. I kept asking myself how they did it. How did they learn to employ some rather successful and seemingly complicated psychological tactics? After all, I went through long years of training to learn how to manipulate a person's behavior with these tactics. If these incidents had been accomplished by another adult I wouldn't have been so worried. Even without professional training, an adult might do it by reading books on the subject.

But how do you explain a young boy doing it? And even more puzzling than that—how can a dog do it? The more I pondered this puzzle, the more it became apparent. What they were doing was implementing strategies with which Mother Nature had endowed them. They were simply acting *naturally*. While I and my professional colleagues had spent years in universities learning how to manipulate man's actions, they had learned through direct experience what to do. Through trying this natural reaction in one situation and trying that natural tendency in another situation they learned how to effectively manipulate behavior. And what was so irritating, was that they did it without having to spend any time learning the technical jargon required of psychologists.

I found it difficult to accept the idea that someone could effectively deal with, and even manipulate, other people by just sharpening the natural inclinations they were born with. After all, the field of psychology has been trying to gain a better understanding of man and his actions for over one hundred years. And each year the theories as to exactly how it's done get greater in number, and more complex. Could it really be possible that raising a child does not require parents to have a social worker, juvenile officer, and psychologist on call? Perish the thought!

Being a research-oriented psychologist, I decided to find out if that might be possible. The question became: how to study the problem? I could observe successful parents who didn't use psychologists and see how they did it. But one problem would be, had they read about how to do it from books? A second problem was finding enough successful parents to observe. Successful parents are a vanishing breed. The solution seemed to be to study successful children. There was little possibility of them having learned their tactics from books or specialized training; and the number of successful children is increasing every day.

This approach of studying the children and their successes might seem a little unusual. It is like a detective studying successful

criminals to find ways of reducing crime. My plan was to study the different ways children go about manipulating parents. I hoped that identifying the tactics children use would lead me to answering the question of how parents might become more effective.

## EFFECTIVE PARENTING—THE NATURAL APPROACH

On several occasions I have asked parents "What value is there for having children in a marriage?" One husband, a truck driver in his late thirties, once replied, "It brings the husband and wife closer together."

"How is that?" I asked.

"It gives them a common enemy," was his answer.

Unfortunately, many perceive more fact than fiction in what he said. Oftentimes parents see their children as the enemy who must, somehow, be outflanked. Childrearing is like a war where superior weaponry is needed. In the initial years of confrontation, parents feel they have that superiority in terms of greater reasoning power and maturity. Typically, it is towards the teenage years that parents feel compelled to bring out the social worker and psychologist reinforcements as more complex strategy seems required.

In such situations, we psychologists are more than willing to lend a helping hand by introducing parents to our latest psychological models for training children—complete with the latest technical words and diagrams. Often the parent then feels like the Indochinese soldier who is given a new jet plane and has no idea of how to get it off the ground.

Parents should not blame themselves if they find that the childrearing approaches advocated in a variety of books do not seem to work in their situation. I have had that happen many times myself. Wanting to be a diligent parent and up-to-date psychologist, I read most, if not all, the "How to do it" books on childrearing.

My interest in the dynamics between parent and child began long before I entered the psychological profession. As a teenager I had the opportunity to experience what I felt were two different worlds. On the one hand I was a member of a religiously oriented family of five children. I had the good fortune of being adopted by a man who exemplified honesty and integrity. During my years in school I was somewhat active in athletics, student government, and Christian youth groups.

On the other hand, there were a few somewhat socially deprived young men in my home town with whom I became acquainted. During my years of association with these fellows, all of them spent time in jail for a variety of offenses, from drunk driving and disorderly conduct to robbery. One of the young men's father was in prison for running a car-theft ring, among other things. He and his midnight employees would steal a car, strip it, and fence the parts.

Through these fellows I learned of a world of teenage gang fights and other socially inappropriate activities. Having the misfortune of being with two of them one night when a gang fight broke out, I became a strategic observer of what happens when fifteen- to seventeen-year-old individuals use fists, brass knuckles, chains, and pipes to debate social values. However, my victorious associates and their friends kidded me about my "strategic observations" since there were no windows at floor level in the car from which I was observing.

Although I was president of some Christian youth organizations, I'm sure my Bishop had some doubts about my activities, because on two occasions I was able to find out for him who committed certain robberies. I was, however, simply a person who had a friendship with fellows labeled by most as juvenile delinquents. My only personal misadventure with the law came when I was with two of these fellows one night cruising Main Street in my car. Having been stopped by two policemen for an unusually loud car, a status symbol for teenagers of the '50s and '60s era, one of my "friends" made a comment regarding the police officer's family ancestry. We all were then invited to stay the night in Portland, Oregon, compliments of the city.

While most people, even many of my other friends, viewed these fellows as delinquents, I frankly saw no great character disorders which distinguished them from other kids our age. However, all three did poorly in school and quit coming, except when forced to. The fellow whose father was in prison would like to have played sports but was not able to because of poor grades and citizenship. On one occasion he broke into a service station because he was hungry. He was a good mechanic, yet he took nothing but candy and gum, although tools and new car parts were also there for his taking.

Although more of my experiences are discussed in a later chapter, the point to be made here is that I saw little real difference between them and the rest of us teenagers. They liked people caring about them, and they wanted to enjoy life—some very natural feelings it seemed to me.

When I went away to college I decided to make working with such people my profession. (Even my wife teases that I seem to bring home stray kids like boys bring home stray dogs. My wife only gave birth to two children, yet we currently have thirteen people around our dinner table at night.) I selected psychology as my field of study and became particularly interested in psychological research. The theories of behavior which I became familiar with awed me in their complexity. I was soon taken by the conviction that if I studied these theories well, I would be a master at human control techniques. Believing wisdom increased with length at a university, I launched my career teaching at universities and doing volunteer work on the side. Over the years I ran into far too many situations where the theories and child-rearing approaches I was taught in school left something to be desired.

As time passed and I reflected on incidents like the dog controlling his owner and the boy controlling his parents, plus my own teenage experiences, I began looking less at psychological ideas and started looking more at kids. My wife and I began filling our home with children, hoping we would learn more from them as to what we should do. Thanks to the proceeds of one of my earlier books, we built a large home and began adding to the family. We had two children, adopted some, and took in foster kids from the state. We ended up with children of all colors from a variety of countries including Puerto Rico, Russia, Canada, and India. Some had no special problems while others were brought here with suicidal tendencies, strong sociopathic character disorders (a technical psychological term which means nobody has been able to do anything with them), incest problems, and child-beating cases. Most of these children were young teenagers when they arrived in our home.

One of the many things my wife and I learned was that most psychological ideas presented in books can work. The question is when and how. Reading a "how to raise children" book and then raising kids is like an army drill instructor teaching his recruits by the book about what to do in combat when the instructor has never experienced battle himself. Obviously the manual has the important parts, but experience is valuable in putting the parts together correctly.

A second point we learned was that kids often do a better job than parents with manipulating. While parents often subordinate the value of raising children to their desires for success in their jobs or hobbies, manipulating parents and other adults is the job and hobby of most kids. Children concentrate on parents more than parents concentrate on children.

The main intent of this book is to point out to parents that effective childrearing can be accomplished by using some rather elementary and natural techniques which are the day-to-day arsenal used by almost every child. We are going to illustrate how children go about manipulating parents in a very natural way without the help of psychologists; *and* they do it without being able to physically "make" parents behave. This second point is quite important to remember. It emphasizes that manipulating someone else doesn't require superior force or reasoning power.

Parents do not need psychologists to be successful parents. In fact, they don't even need books. However, we hope this book may be of value in that: (1) it will unveil many effective and often disguised techniques that children use on their parents; (2) it will provide many cases to help parents more precisely identify the actual problem situations with which they are involved; and (3) it will illustrate a variety of training tactics that parents may turn to their effective use. Keep in mind raising children should be one of the most challenging and enjoyable experiences in life.

## THE PARENTS' BATTLE CRY—"HELP"

The wise person looks for help in solving problems. Looking for help is not a sign of weakness, but a sign of wisdom. Teenagers are particularly successful in manipulating parents because they get help from their friends. Have you ever heard "But Mother, all the other kids' mothers let them do it."? Teenagers meet almost daily at public schools and learn from each other what to do to influence their parents. One of the greatest advantages most teenagers have over their parents is that parents are more isolated in our society. Parents seldom get together. Parents are more effective in situations where they do get together and discuss their children. With all their other social responsibilities, however, it is often impractical. Books and psychologists may often help, as in the case of Ann.

For two weeks Ann had been bringing her four-year-old son, Troy, to the local grade school. Troy was one of several preschool volunteers participating in a psychological study aimed at a better understanding of how children make decisions. One day while Troy was being tested, Ann, in an apologetic manner, asked if we could talk for a few minutes. She was an unusually attractive woman in her middle twenties. Her slender frame was stylishly dressed, although her long brown hair was not so fashionably arranged. I had talked to her and the other parents several times in the past. Ann had always appeared somewhat timid and nervous, though friendly.

"I lost my husband a little over two years ago," she began, "and I have raised Troy by myself since just before his second birthday. I've tried hard to be a good mother. I love Troy very much. It has become too much for me though, . . . and I feel I'm losing my mind. I talked to my clergyman and told him I felt I needed to give Troy up for adoption. He advised me to seek some psychological counseling before making such a decision. I feel the world closing in on me and I'm not sure I can stand up to the pressure for myself, let alone for Troy and me both."

Having difficulty keeping her composure, she continued. She was the only child of a rather well-to-do family. Having no brothers or sisters, she had never been required to care for children while she was growing up. Her father was a strong, self-confident person who had made most decisions for her before she married. The fellow she married was much like her father. She felt secure with him and enjoyed her marriage. Prior to having Troy, she was somewhat apprehensive about having a child, but she felt comfortable with the idea because of the security and love her husband provided.

When he was killed, her world started falling apart. Her husband left her financially secure so she had no money worries. It was Troy. He began demanding her time to such an extent that she felt she was losing her identity. She found herself devoting all her time to Troy. After almost a year, she came to the conclusion that she could not make it alone. She had felt comfortable when married and decided to marry again. Attempts at dating produced more anxiety than consolation, however. Any romantic intentions a suitor brought with him as he came to pick up Ann for a date were quickly dispelled by Troy who would cling to one of his mother's legs, often ruining her nylons, and yelling "Please don't go mommy. Don't leave me!" On several such occasions, Ann would get nervous, lose her composure, and cry.

During the next few talks we had it became apparent that Ann sincerely felt she was not a fit mother and could not give Troy what he needed. Believing she had failed him, she decided to put him up for adoption and, if possible, try to pull her own life together.

I began explaining to her that I felt she was wrong—she did have what Troy needed. And if she would work with me, I was confident we could satisfy both her's and Troy's needs without an adoption. I gave her a packet of material and told her to take it home, and during the next week record the number and length of the times Troy demanded her attention. Somewhat reassured that help was forthcoming, she left my office. She returned one week later with the packet. I questioned her about the week's happenings. She recounted incidents where Troy would scream and yell unless she sat next to him while he colored. As in the past, if she locked her bedroom door to get some rest during the day he would go into the kitchen and run a pan back and forth over other pots and pie tins on the shelves, until the racket made mother appear.

After hearing the incidents we looked over the records she had kept. "My goodness," I remarked, "you have been averaging eight hours a day directly attending to the wants of your child. That is nine times more than the average mother spends on a child his age! It is obvious that you mean a great deal to him. Without a father, or brothers or sisters, or children his age close by, you are the focal point of his life. You are of great value to him, and he is manipulating you to get as much of a good thing as he can. Contrary to your feelings, you do not owe him that time. Mother Nature never intended parents to fit into the lives of their children, the opposite is true. Children should fit into the lifestyle of the parents. But we will talk about this at a later date."

I went on to explain to her that we were going to arrange it so he did not demand so much of her. We were not going to let him manipulate her as he was. She was going to be a better mother while spending less time with him, and more time on her own goals, and end up with a more independent child.

I mentioned that we were going to use a technique called *extinction* to get Troy to stop demanding so much of her time. I said to her, "Beginning tomorrow I want you to start refusing many of his requests for your time. Respond to his basic needs of eating, dressing, and so on, but do not let him interrupt *your* activities. If

he wants you to be near him when he colors, tell him to wait until you are done housecleaning, sewing, drawing, reading, or whatever else you are involved in. We want him to learn that you are not going to come to his every beck and call. We want him to learn to do more things on his own; and let you satisfy some of your own wants and desires.

"There is one thing I must caution you about, however. When the procedure of extinction is started, the yells, screams, and other forms of tantrum behaviors will actually increase for a while before they begin to drop."

I diagrammed for her what to expect. Figure 1 shows what typically happens when extinction is employed. The first condition in the figure (labeled baseline) is the amount of demands put on Ann before extinction was begun. This is the daily information she was asked to keep track of for that first week. The second part of the figure (Day 8 on) was what I drew to show her what would most likely happen. I explained that Troy's demands would increase in number and frequency for a few days. "Don't worry," I said. "That is a good sign. It tells us that what we are doing is having an effect on Troy and that it is going to work."

I pointed out that this increase in yelling and so on, is natural.

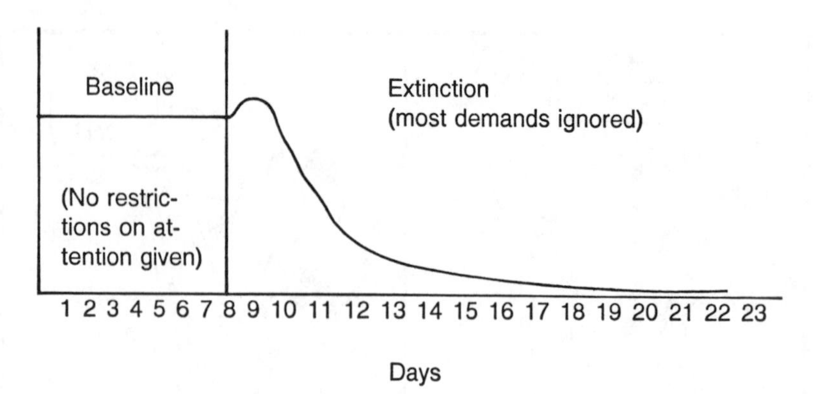


For example, people typically do more than just slightly turn a door knob when they unexpectantly find the door is locked. They give that little extra jiggle and turn to make sure the door is actually locked and is not going to give in to their efforts.

"These next few days are going to be very trying for you" I continued, "but once they are over your life will become more enjoyable day by day. Do not hesitate to call me, even at my home, if you need help."

The following evening she called my home and said, "He is kicking me in the leg! What shall I do?"

Now Ann, being a rather timid individual, was not prone to spanking or other forms of discipline. Any mention of such discipline had been met by a cool reserve from her in my office. But all of us have our limits, and I felt Troy had now brought Ann to hers.

"Spank him!" I replied. "Let him know that such actions will not be tolerated by you."

And she did.

To make a long story short, things went as expected, though not quite as quickly. Within a couple of weeks, however, Troy's demands on his mother had drastically declined, and were continuing to drop. Six weeks after extinction was begun Ann came in and enthusiastically reported that she had taken Troy on a shopping spree with her and she thoroughly enjoyed it. "I can't believe it" she said. "I really enjoy Troy now. Would you believe it? I've gone out twice, with no tantrums by Troy. It was great. I no longer feel inadequate as a mother . . . or a person." Ann married within the next year, and at last report was expecting.

While Ann's child was not a teenager, her case nicely illustrates several important aspects of childrearing.

*Manipulating Parents Is Natural.* The tendency of a child to manipulate parents is a natural consequence in life. It is natural for individuals to try to manipulate those dimensions in life which hold the key to greater success and enjoyment. Employees often try to manipulate bosses, through favors, praise, and extra effort, to get pay raises or easier jobs. Wives manipulate husbands. Husbands manipulate wives. Parents are the holders of almost everything that is of value to their children, particularly young children. We should not be surprised when they try to get all they can from us. We can control it by being aware of the process, however.

*Parenting Doesn't Take Time.* Being a good parent does not require all of your time. In fact it often takes less time than what most unsuccessful parents are giving now. This is an important point discussed in detail later on.

*Go for Help.* Do not isolate yourself in raising children. You need to seriously look at what other people do. Just as your kids watch and see what other kids do to be successful, watch other parents. Look at their kids and adopt tactics from parents who are successful. Look close enough to be sure what it is about those parents that makes them successful. Not only observe, but ask for help. Ask for advice. Your kids do! Keeping parents apart and uninformed is one the best tactics a child can use. An effective extension of this idea is used by children separate the parents so they are not in agreement with, or do not communicate well, with each other. Besides, help from parents and family is cheaper than books and psychologists.

*Children Can Manipulate Unconsciously.* Contrary to what many parents feel, a child can manipulate his parents without consciously recognizing what he or she is doing. Look how easy it is for a parent to wreck his/her marriage without realizing it. Troy meant no harm.

His mother was the most valuable thing in his life; and he simply wanted as much of a good thing as he could get.

*Parents Raise Children Unconsciously.* Few of the things a child learns from his parents comes from direct and intentional instruction. A father may take a few minutes to tell his son to obey the law. The child watches his father speed many times; and notes his father's derogatory words about the police as he receives a ticket. What a parent *tells* his child is a small fraction of what he *shows* his child.

*You Do Not Owe Your Life to Your Child.* Mother Nature nicely arranged life so an individual should be able to have experiences for self-development. Raising children should add to one's life, not take it over. There are many challenges in life besides childrearing.

*Raising Children Should Be Fun.* Ann began experiencing something many parents do not. Raising kids should be enjoyable. Do not let your children build your prison, let them help you get more out of life.

*Little Things Mean a Lot.* There are a great many little things in childrearing that makes the difference between a successful and an unsuccessful parent. For example, many parents have tried to use the technique we call "extinction," but fail. Often they give up when the screams and yells start to get worse. Knowing that it naturally occurs, and that it is a good sign, could be the difference between succeeding or failing. Just as a small amount of salt and pepper with other seasonings can make the difference between a good and great steak, so do little things often make the difference in childrearing.

# 2
# Parents' Bill of Rights

## PARENTS ARE PEOPLE TOO

Two women were sitting next to each other in the doctor's waiting room. One woman, five months along, was going through her first trial of pregnancy with some apprehension. This young prospective mother turned to the second woman, who was eight and one-half months, bulging with the look of motherhood and said, "Aren't you troubled, pushing all that weight around?"

"Yes," replied the woman about to have her second child. "But I'm not half as troubled as I will be when that weight is out and pushing me around."

The attitude of the second woman exemplifies the feeling more and more parents are experiencing. That fresh and crisp fragrance of potential parenthood which flowed in the nostrils of many young couples years ago has been replaced by concern and worry. Seldom do you hear parents recount experiences of joy and happiness they are having with their children. Instead, the air is full of stories concerning teenagers in cars running people off the road, people being mugged by gangs of youngsters in parks, and parents being killed by their children. Just recently in the news two girls, nine and thirteen years of age, burned their parents to death in a mobile home because the girls didn't get their way. An eight-year-old boy on the East Coast tried to rob a bank at the drive-up window. And in most of the cases the parents are blamed. Parents are accused of being too permissive. On the one hand, parents have become victims of their children, while social agencies of the government continually charge parents with physical and mental abuse. No wonder the thought of raising children has become repugnant. It seems as though married couples have little to gain and much to lose by bringing children into the world.

The remainder of this book focuses on the techniques children use to get the upper hand with their parents. It is also going to show how these techniques, plus others available to parents, can make child-rearing an enjoyable and challenging experience. The game of life is one which pits one generation against another. It's a fascinating and unique game in that people of all ages can play; and one does not need to be the most intelligent or mature to win. And, contrary to most games, everyone can win.

Throughout the book the reader may find many rather serious situations presented in a seemingly light-hearted manner. This is not intended to make parenting appear to be a joking matter. I'm convinced Mother Nature provided a sense of humor as a salve for keeping parents and psychologists from having nervous breakdowns.

Before we begin talking about tactics used by children, perhaps it is a good idea to explain the rights of parents. All too often they are not sure what their rights are. That is, what should they expect from raising children? With these rights in mind it may be easier for a parent to tell when a child had steered the "family bus" off Mother Nature's intended course, and when a parent's rights have been violated. All too often the rights of children and society are championed with parents becoming the forgotten citizens. It is important to remember *parents are people too!*

While parents have many rights, there are seven that need to be particularly kept in mind. The Bill of Rights for Parents is listed below.

## PARENTAL BILL OF RIGHTS

Parents have the right to:

1. Raise children
2. Preside in the family
3. Enjoy their children
4. Manipulate their children
5. Expect service from their children
6. Have their own lifestyle
7. Make mistakes in childrearing

### The Right to Raise Children

This first right of parents seems so obvious that the reader may wonder why it is listed. Keep in mind that twenty years ago an unmarried man and woman living together was socially and even legally unthinkable. Twenty years ago men wearing necklaces and having hair as long as women was absurd. Abortion was not acceptable. I believe all parents would rise up in anger if they only realized how much their right to raise children has eroded in the past ten years. Over this time the position taken by the U.S. government and state social services is that children are, in fact, wards of the government. Government has the right to step in and determine the best interests of children over objections of parents. Some laws have passed, and some are pending, which strongly restrict the rights of parents. For example, underage girls are already allowed to have abortions without parental consent—*or knowledge.* All children now have the legal right to counsel to challenge their parents' rights to do many things such as put them in hospitals or institutions. Laws are being legislated which will allow children to take their parents to court for spanking them; or for moving them from one city to another, as when a father or mother changes jobs.

Lately, we have heard of court cases where women are suing men they lived with, but did not marry, for large portions of their wealth. How would you like your thirteen-year-old son to sue you for your financial holdings plus your future earning power because he felt you neglected him or disciplined him incorrectly? Sound too fantastic? Don't bet against it.

I believe this first right of parents must be kept with broad powers maintained by parents. Obviously, some parents are neglecting and abusing their children. A large portion of the children I deal with are victims of such abuse. But turning parental powers over to social agencies and the courts certainly won't solve the problems. More is said about this matter in a later chapter dealing with legal rights.

### The Right to Preside in the Family

Parents, not children, have the right to preside in the family. Without fail, Mother Nature places offspring under the watchful eye of the elders. I cannot think of any species in the animal kingdom where the developing young are allowed to preside over the parents—except for man.

Bud and Shirley lived in an average neighborhood near a large city on the West Coast. They were well-liked by all who knew them. Bud worked at a brewery and was a real handyman. Anybody needing help with home fix-it problems called on Bud for help. Many years ago they had purchased an acre of land and built their own home. Using some skills he had acquired, Bud built a ranch-style home out of an attractive type of cinderblock. Bringing the used hops home from the brewery, Bud and Shirley used them as fertilizer on their flower beds. The landscaping of their yard was the envy of the neighborhood. Their children were also the talk of the neighborhood.

They had three children, Alex, seventeen, Joan, fifteen, and Jimmy, twelve. All three children seemed to have minds of their own (a catchy phrase meaning they did what they wanted). While being pretty smart, none of the three did very well in school. They did not seem to care. They worked on assignments when nothing more interesting was around. Teachers' attempts to stimulate them did not seem to work. When Alex was caught flushing cherry bombs down the school toilets at age eleven, the principal got very upset over the incident, but Alex just seemed to take it quietly in stride. When Alex was twelve, all three children climbed into the attic of the house when their parents were gone. Although they had been warned many times before by their parents not to do such things, they took blankets and candles in the attic for their little "clubhouse." A fire somehow started, and had it not been for some quick-thinking neighbors, the results could have been disastrous. At age fourteen Alex and his sister took one of their mother's best sheets, made it into a sail, and attached it to a soapbox car that Bud had helped Alex make a year or two earlier. On a very windy day Alex and Joan were successfully navigating their "sail car" down a public street when their mother saw them and angrily retrieved her sheet. When Alex was fifteen, all three children decided to take a neighbor's car for a joy ride late one night. Bud paid for the damages and no legal action was taken.

"Our lives have just been one problem situation after another," Bud said in a frustrated voice after recounting a dozen different instances to me. "Shirley and I have tried to be good examples for them. We have tried to guide them but they will not listen. Many times they act as if they don't even care whether Shirley and I exist. In the past they have not really been obnoxious and demanding; most of what they did seemed prankish. But now they are demanding things. Alex feels we should get him a car, and Joan feels she should be able to bring any guy she wants to the house and have the right to drink and use drugs. I will be so glad when they are married and gone so I can get rid of this fear of not knowing what is going to happen next."

There is a natural tendency for many children to manipulate parents so their wishes come first. In many cases children act as if their parents are pawns to be used for their wishes. Alex, Joan, and Jimmy showed little concern for the feelings of adults around them. Teachers, principals, and neighbors were there to be used. Their parents were there to provide for their wants.

Parents, and other adults for that matter, should not feel guilty for claiming the right to preside over all members of their household. Often, parents find their children questioning the right of parents to rule the home. Children say such things as:

"You owe it to me. You brought me into this life."
"You don't understand my problem."

"I can do what I want, and you do not have the right to stop me."
"Why can't I do it my way?"
"I'm old enough to make my own decisions."

With technology changing so fast, we parents often find ourselves questioning whether our attitudes and feelings are outmoded. We worry whether we are doing the right thing. It is important for us to remember that the pains and pitfalls of growing up have not basically changed. While cars and styles change, teenage broken hearts feel the same. Losing a friend feels the same. Teenagers are no smarter at knowing the value of money than you and I were at their age. And most important, they need the guidance and counseling as much as we did—though they argue against it, as we did.

Too often I see parents who are gas station attendants, farmers, store clerks, carpenters, waitresses, and secretaries who feel inferior to doctors, lawyers, and executives in providing proper guidance for their children. Keep in mind no profession corners the market on giving children proper guidance. In fact, some of the greatest advice I have heard given to children came from people who never completed high school. Some of the most effective people I've seen work with children are grandparents who learned the lessons of life in the trenches while raising their children and the children of others.

All parents have walked life's road farther than their children. And all parents, irrespective of occupation, have had the experiences their children need to learn from. Parents should accept with more confidence their right to make decisions for their children. Don't be intimidated by your children's claims that they can decide for themselves. It is your family. You started it and you have the right to preside.

## The Right to Enjoy Child Rearing

There is a special relationship that appears as if by magic when an infant joins his parents in experiencing life. With a special feeling that Mother Nature instills, Mother and Father tend to the needs of the infant. Placing their wants second to the child's, the parents lose sleep as they care for the fussing child throughout the night. Mother endures the inconveniences of feeding the child several times each day and night. Mother after mother tends to the wants of her year-old child while coping with the morning sickness and nausea caused by the unborn waiting to enter the channels of birth.

For the first few years the parents unselfishly give up a major portion of their lives for the child while getting little more than smiles and self-satisfaction in return. Few parents begrudge their sacrifices to the child. They do not expect the child to repay their service day by day, because during those first two or three years the child is dependent on the sacrifices of his/her parents.

Children are not capable of meeting life head-on when they enter the world. They need a buffer between themselves and those everyday pitfalls in society which would end their life quickly if someone were not there to smooth out the way. Parents are those buffers. Besides providing food and shelter, parents keep the child from swallowing drain cleaners and razor blades. They protect children from dangerous objects like knives, scissors, lawn mowers, and garbage disposals. They protect children from being taken advantage of by other people. They protect them from making bad decisions in life due to lack of maturity.

Oftentimes the child uses the parent selfishly. After the parent has fed, clothed, and cared for the child in his formative years, the child manipulates the parent to continue that role when, in fact, the child should be learning to carry his own weight. Kids whine and throw tantrums to get their way with parents. They manipulate parents to do all the house chores by complaining when asked to help or by ignoring parental requests. They want parents to buy candy for them every time they go to the store. They want Father to fix their tricycle right now. Mother is expected to stop her conversation with other adults to listen to her child. The teenage daughter wants the rent money to buy a new dress for the dance. The children do not want to be bothered setting the table or washing dishes. Mother can do that. Mother and Dad are expected to let them dress any way they like, and not complain about the loud music saturating the house.

Over the years parents have somehow been convinced they

should put up with the selfish demands of their children. "They are just going through a phase, and they will grow out of it." "They are searching for their identity. It is natural."

While it is true that what the children are doing is natural, the idea that parents should put up with it is wrong. Mother Nature has endowed all of us with the motivation to gain our desires in life with the least effort possible. A man in the midst of digging a ditch will try to think of an easier way to complete the task. A mother with a food budget will try to get the most she can for her money, not the least. It is no wonder then that a child will try to get out of doing chores around the house, but still draw the benefits from living there. These are natural tendencies. It is not a phase in life that we try to get the most for the least. Infants do it, teenagers do it, and we adults most certainly do it. We adults are somewhat different from children in that we have learned restraint in our demands. We learn people will avoid us if we are constantly asking for favors but not returning them. Most people will not put up with our turning on a radio in a movie theater. Bosses fire us if we come to work only when we feel like it. Store merchants demand cash for merchandise, and do not give in to begging.

As the child's buffer, it is the right and responsibility of the parents to teach them that society expects them to work for what they want and to be considerate of others. Children are inexperienced and make many wrong choices if left to their own desires. They eat snacks before meals. They do not prepare for the future; they spend now. They often put their immediate desires ahead of concern for others. Children will skip school when given the choice, instead of choosing an education which they will need in the years to come.

It is interesting to note that most of the parent–child conflicts are a result of children not wanting to do what, in the long run, will better prepare them to enter society. They complain about parents trying to get them to work. The daughter gets upset when mother says she should turn her radio down or help with the dishes. Children cry when the parent does not get them the toy they want.

"Why do I have to go get Dad the paper?"
"Why should I have to do dishes?"
"Why can't I stay up late on school nights?"
"Why should I share my things?"
"Why should I clean my room?"
"Why can't I say what I please, and swear if I want?"

It may surprise the reader to know there are many parents out there that seldom hear such questions. (Keep in mind I said seldom.) Some children get Dad the paper without complaining. Some children go right to the sink after dinner without being told. Some children go right to bed when told to do so, without complaining. And the children who act this way are generally good students in school, have many friends, love their parents, and are loved by their parents. These children are usually better prepared for life, and are more well-received in society.

Children who learn to listen and serve their parents make not only the parents' lives more enjoyable, but usually theirs also. Parents have the right to enjoy their children, to have their children do what they say, and to have their children carry their weight in the family. Too many parents worry about infringing on the rights of their children.

## The Right to Manipulate Children

"What right do I have to manipulate my children?" This is a question psychologists are being asked more and more. Parents not only have the right but the obligation to do so. Mother Nature set it up for many animals that they were endowed at birth with almost everything they ever need to know. Young salmon hatch from eggs with no parents to teach them. Their inner instincts with which they are born are all they have to see them through life. They are genetically wired inside to make their way to the ocean, and several years later return to their place of birth to spawn.

The same is not true for mankind. The newborn infant cannot survive without constant care from parents. The infant needs to be clothed, fed, and protected. And as the child grows he needs something else—he needs to learn. Mother Nature did not prewire him to know how to handle different situations; this he must pick up through experience. This experience may be first-hand experience—things he encounters himself. Or, the experience may be indirect, such as listening to what has happened to others.

Children must learn to communicate, to walk, to express anger, to ride a bike, to drive, and to be considerate of others. These may sound like things children can do without much help. However, we find that the environment a child finds himself in plays a significant role in how he develops. An extreme example of this is illustrated by the Wolf Children of India. Several years ago, two young girls, eight and two years of age, were found living with a pack of wolves in an eastern province of India. A Reverend Singh ran an orphanage in that area. He found and captured the two girls, naming them Kamala and Amala. (The Reverend Singh wrote a book entitled *The Wolf Children of India* which includes pictures.) Both girls ran on all fours in such a manner that their knee joints did not function properly. They initially snarled and growled at people, preferred raw to cooked food, and preferred sleeping on the bare floor instead of a bed. Reverend Singh and his wife spent many hours trying to civilize the two girls. Kamala, the oldest, soon learned to like it at the orphanage. She learned to talk and even pouted when other kids did not include her in their games. Amala never did learn to like being around people. She stuck close to her sister, trying to get her to leave. After a while Amala realized Kamala liked it where she was. Amala then began withdrawing from Kamala and everyone else. Pretty soon she did not seem to care whether she ate or not. Her desire to live continued to fade. Within two years after being brought to the orphanage, Amala died. The girls, raised by animals, show not only that the environment can greatly influence what we become, but also that children have a great ability to adapt to their surroundings.

Most parents are comfortable with the idea that they should help their children learn to do such things as walking and talking. But what about teaching them what to like, or how to act? Do we as parents infringe on our children's rights when we want them to be quiet, or to be considerate of others, or to be patient? Does disciplining my children stifle their creativity or harm their self-images? Should I not try to manipulate and change them so much, and be more considerate of how they feel? Do I demand too much from my children? Perhaps a better understanding of the parents' role in manipulating children can come by answering these questions.

Should I teach them what to like and how to act? This question is really asking whether parents have the right to teach their children social values. The answer is—absolutely! No one has a better right, nor have social service agencies of any kind been found to do a better job than most parents.

The parent-to-child system of passing on social values is the natural way. It generally places an adult with every newborn child in a one-on-one learning environment twenty-four hours a day. Imagine how expensive it would be for governmental agencies to provide that kind of service to its future generations. And keep in mind, the adults provided by agencies would not have the natural concern or self-sacrificing attitude that Mother Nature instills in most parents.

Do we parents infringe on our children's rights when we have them conform to our values? Few topics have been talked about more between parent and child than what most people refer to as the generation gap. "That's old-fashioned." "You don't understand. You are from an old generation." "Your values are out-of-date." These are the type of statements parents hear when teenagers try to avoid doing what their parents want them to do. And such statements from our children generally get us to relax our demands on our children because we are sensitive about the issue. In such confrontations between parent and teenager, the parents are in the position of trying to do what is right in the long run for their child. The child, on the other hand, is motivated to go somewhere or do something that will give him immediate enjoyment. Seldom does the child consider the long-term benefit of his day-to-day actions. That is one of the reasons Mother Nature places children under the management of parents.

Unfortunately, science and technology are progressing so fast in our day and age that parents begin to wonder. Transportation has changed dramatically since the turn of the century. Electronic technology has advanced so far that most of us don't understand how dozens of telephone conversations can be transmitted by means of light along a single plastic fiber with the same diameter as a straight pin. We can see the physical dimensions of life have changed dramatically, so we begin to accept the idea that socially our values are outdated too. But is that really the case?

Not too long ago a noted psychologist was addressing the national convention of the American Psychological Association and said that if four scientists (a chemist, a medical researcher, an electrical engineer, and a psychologist) were resurrected from a hundred years ago, only one of the four, the psychologist, would still be able to intelligently converse with present-day scientists in his field. Most areas of science like chemistry, medicine, and electricity have advanced so far that scientists of a hundred years ago would not be able to intelligently talk to present-day scientists. With all of psychology's sophisticated theories and ideas, the basic problems and issues confronting childrearing today are the same as those one hundred years ago. The problem handled by psychologists one hundred years ago are not that different from the problems present-day psychologists deal with. A child growing up thirty years ago needed love and affection as much as a child growing up today. The importance of having friends has not changed much.

We psychologists must accept some of the blame for making parents feel behind the times. We have not been wise in all the advice we give out. Fifteen years ago we chastised parents for being too Victorian in terms of sex. "Get sex out in the open," we said. "Talk to your children more about it. Freely discuss sexual issues. This will not cause an increase in sexual activity in teenagers. A better understanding of sex will delay many from participating before they are ready to handle it. The teenage pregnancy problem will be helped if we talk about it."

Now we have to admit we were wrong. Teenage sexual activity did not decline with that approach; it took off like a forest fire. And now that we have society so involved in our mistake the only advice we can give to help parents cope with the situation is to use the pill or abortion. It is unfortunate that we did not originally ask ourselves what real information there was that increasing sexual involvement would enhance a teenager's life. The actual fact of the matter is, there is no sound psychological research to support that idea. One of the side problems of this issue is that we adults have become so infatuated with sex ourselves that we have increased our sexual activites. Psychologists are people too, and now have books written on how psychologists can go about having sexual relations with their patients—for therapeutic reasons, of course. It is interesting to note that studies show this psychologist-patient sex therapy is almost exclusively used when the patient is quite attractive. Perhaps some good old Victorian values would be better for all of us.

Several years back, psychologists advocated that parents should be more submissive in child-rearing practices. "Children can determine for themselves what is good and bad," we said. An example often given to parents concerned eating habits. If day after day a child is placed before all sorts of food (including cakes, candies, vegetables, fruits, and meats) the child will come to select a balanced diet. It was argued that children would do the same in terms of social values. Children, while committing some annoying and antisocial activities, would, in the long run, straighten themselves out.

Again, we psychologists find ourselves in a position of being wrong. A generation of such child-rearing practices sadly points several things out to us that Mother Nature already knew. When given the choice, kids play rather than work, daydream rather than do math problems, think of themselves before others, and strive for short-term pleasures rather than striving to work for long-term goals.

In Mother Nature's scheme of things parents have the obligation to manipulate and mold their children. It is not the parents' job to turn their child into something specific like a pianist, carpenter, doctor, or butcher. They are there to oversee the child's training in honesty, fairness, consideration, planning, dependability, patience, responsibility, desire to succeed in life, and happiness. Often the learning of these virtues requires a child to do what he doesn't want to do. A child may have to mow the lawn instead of play with friends, share what he has with other children, sit quietly when he wants to be rowdy, wait his turn in the lunch line, or earn spending money. The parents must be in a position of authority to help the child learn to handle such situations; like a piece of clay the personality of the child needs to be manipulated and molded so that he may one day be successfully on his own.

## The Right to Expect Service from Children

Parents have the right to expect service from their children. No child has the right to a free ride in the family. There are many things which have to be done. Money must be earned, housing is required, organization is necessary, and many jobs such as cooking, cleaning, sewing, and washing need to be done. Parents should not shoulder the complete load. Responsibilities should be distributed throughout the family as children get older. Three- and four-year-olds can pick up toys and clothing around the house. Five-, six-, and seven-year-olds can empty wastebaskets, make beds, set the dinner table, and clean up their rooms. Eight-, nine-, and ten-year-olds can clean bathrooms, vacuum rugs, wipe dishes. Eleven- and twelve-year-olds can weed gardens, wash dishes, shine shoes, feed pets, clean windows, and clean out fireplaces. Teenagers can wash and clean cars, wash clothes, iron clothes, fix meals, baby-sit younger brothers and sisters, and help younger children practice schoolwork at home. All children can learn to reduce the workload by keeping their own things picked up and by putting games, books, and other articles back in their rightful positions.

Most parents fail to tap one of the best family resources—a work force. There are reasons why. Children often complain and throw tantrums when asked to help around the house. (We husbands often do the same things when it is time to do dishes.) Parents frequently feel it is easier to do it themselves than to go through the hassle of trying to get their kids to help. It also takes time to train children to help and some parents would rather do it themselves.

I know of many parents who effectively recruit the services of their children. There are a number of ways to do it. Let me illustrate how it works around our house. We have what we call a duty roster posted in the family room of our home. On the roster are the names of all the children and the duties they each have for the week. On Monday nights we have a family meeting where duties are assigned and family activities for the week are planned. The duty roster (like the one on pages 34 and 35) is then posted. Each day the children recheck the chart to see what their jobs are for the day. Most of them check it as soon as they get home from school, for that is when jobs such as cleaning windows, vacuuming floors, cleaning bathrooms, cleaning cars, and the like are done. Everyone must clean up his room before going to school in the morning. Each evening after the children are in bed, my wife, Carol, checks off what jobs were and were not done by each child. Every Monday at our family meeting they receive their allowances, minus money deducted for each job not completed. Children under twelve-years-old get an allowance which is figured by multiplying twenty cents for each year of age. (A six-year-old gets $1.20.) This money is for things they see during the week that they want, such as gum and pencils. After a child turns twelve, his allowance is larger. Carol and I calculated how much money each child over twelve needs per week for personal necessities (for example, nylons, shampoo, razor blades, cologne, aftershave) and entertainment. This amount is given to them, and they buy their own things each week. This approach is used to help them learn to handle money and become more independent. A child can miss two of the daily jobs each week. More than two incomplete jobs results in the loss of the whole week's allowance.

The charts work particularly well for younger children from four to seven, who check it every day and enjoy seeing the checks which indicate that they did their jobs. Children who can't read go to the chart and ask the other children what has to be done, unless their jobs don't change from week to week as is usually the case. Carol does not keep reminding them that they need to do their jobs. Such coaxing tends to have them wait for reminders before doing their work.

Parents can do a variety of things to stimulate their children to help carry the family load. First of all, give them a sense of family responsibility. Explain, and re-emphasize as often as necessary, that everyone in the family needs to pitch in and help. If they say they don't like to help, remind them that you also do not like doing many things that have to be done for the family. Be firm but considerate in emphasizing your point. Second, do not give in to continuing complaints. Third, make sure the children keep the necessity of helping in perspective by withholding privileges such as not going out to play until the work is done. By combining suggestions two

## DUTY ROSTER

| | Job | Mon. | Tue. | Wed. | Thur. | Fri. | Sat. | Comments |
|---|---|---|---|---|---|---|---|---|
| **Tammy Butler** | Clean up room | | | | | | | |
| | Vacuum | | | | | | | |
| | Dishes | | | | | | | |
| | Fold clothes | | | | | | | |
| | Cook | | | | | | | |
| | Put away clothes | | | | | | | |
| | Keep articles up | | | | | | | |
| | Clean Windows | | | | | | | |
| | Clean Cars | | | | | | | |
| **Marta Rivers** | Clean up room | | | | | | | |
| | Put away clothes | | | | | | | |
| | Keep articles up | | | | | | | |
| | Vacuum | | | | | | | |
| | Bathrooms | | | | | | | |
| | Sweep Garage | | | | | | | |
| | Clean Windows | | | | | | | |
| | Cook | | | | | | | |
| | Dust | | | | | | | |
| **Kristy Graves** | Clean up room | | | | | | | |
| | Put away clothes | | | | | | | |
| | Keep articles up | | | | | | | |
| | Vacuum | | | | | | | |
| | Clean windows | | | | | | | |

| | | | | | | | | |
|---|---|---|---|---|---|---|---|---|
| | Dust | | | | | | | |
| | Sweep Garage | | | | | | | |
| | Cook | | | | | | | |
| | Dishes | | | | | | | |
| **Michael Robinson** | Clean up room | | | | | | | |
| | Feed/water rabbits | | | | | | | |
| | Put away clothes | | | | | | | |
| | Keep articles up | | | | | | | |
| | Clean windows | | | | | | | |
| | Dust | | | | | | | |
| | Water bushes | | | | | | | |
| **Kit Robinson** | Clean up room | | | | | | | |
| | Put clothes away | | | | | | | |
| | Keep articles up | | | | | | | |
| | Clean windows | | | | | | | |
| | Water horses | | | | | | | |
| | Dust | | | | | | | |
| | Water bushes | | | | | | | |
| **Shawn Robinson** | Clean up room | | | | | | | |
| | Put clothes away | | | | | | | |
| | Keep articles up | | | | | | | |
| | Feed/water birds | | | | | | | |
| | Empty wastebasket | | | | | | | |
| | Feed ducks | | | | | | | |
| | Water bushes | | | | | | | |

and three, complaints about helping soon fade. Fourth, start early in training. Children three and four are not too young to learn.

Keep in mind it is not absolutely essential to start young. In our home, teenage foster children are constantly being added to the family, and are expected to pull their weight. And they do. Fifth, let them know you appreciate their help and continue to emphasize that pulling one's weight is a natural part of living, and it is expected by society.

It is important to remember that the more service parents require of their children, the better it helps the child prepare for life on his own. And the more you do for the child (for example, cleaning his room, making his bed, letting him throw his clothes around, not having him help with the cooking) the less prepared that child is for life later on. Can parents demand too much service from their children? It is possible, but not very probable. Children who have family jobs around the house rate their parents higher than children who do not have such responsibilities. This is true even for children who average two hours of chores a day.

## The Right to One's Own Lifestyle

Should I be a buddy to my child? Should I give my child outdoor experiences such as camping and fishing? Should I give my child piano lessons to develop her artistic talents? Should I learn to like the type of activities my children like? Should I put up with the music my kids like to listen to?

When asked questions like these I often surprise many parents by answering "If you want to." In effect, all of the questions mentioned above are based on the implication that "I as a parent should fit my life in with the lives of my children." I am not sure who started this idea about parenting. I suspect it is just one of several prevailing ideas in society that has been slipped in on us by our children. As children, we spent the first eighteen years or so as apprentices to our parents. We were then given the legal right to do what we wanted with our lives. If we wanted to become sailors, we could. If we wanted to see the world, we had the right to earn such a trip. If we wanted to sit around and watch football games on weekends, we could. No laws compel us to change our lifestyle to properly raise children. What parents should be asking is "How do we help our children fit themselves into our lifestyle?"

Several years back Evelyn, a woman in her middle thirties, lost her husband in an industrial accident. She had three teenage children ranging from thirteen to seventeen years of age. Within a year after losing her husband she found her life was completely taken up in serving her kids. While the family ate breakfast and dinner together when Hank was alive, she now made three separate breakfasts and three separate dinners to fit the changing lifestyles of her kids. She found herself washing clothes more frequently as her children became more lax in picking up their clothes. The children's needs for money rose dramatically with Hank's death. Being a "good mother" she spent more and more time on her children. She felt she owed it to them.

What Evelyn experienced from her children was something quite natural. Without meaning to, the children imposed more on their mother after their father died. Mother felt an obligation to do everything she could for her kids. And her children received more of a good thing. They ate when it fit their fancy, their clothes were kept ready for them, and money would appear whenever the demand was made. Evelyn's life was soon completely taken up serving her children.

Concerned over her welfare, Evelyn's sister approached me to get some advice. "Isn't there something wrong?" she asked. "It doesn't seem normal—how much she has changed for her kids."

"It's more normal than you might imagine," I told her. "Somewhere along the way most parents have gotten the idea that they are not good parents unless they put their children as the focal point of their existence. They feel obligated to get their teeth straightened, to send them to summer camps, to sign them up for piano lessons, and to put them in little league baseball. Most mothers spend a large portion of their time carting the kids around to schools, dances, movie theaters, doctor appointments, and all sorts of other activities. Most family vacations are centered around the interests of the children."

It is important to remember parents have a right to their own lifestyle. Their lifestyle should allow them the freedom to work toward the things they feel are of value. Children should experience fitting themselves into their parents' lifestyle. Later, when they are grown, they have the right to become whatever they want. But their apprenticeship under other, more mature humans, is an important part of life. During this part of life they are allowed to see life, and even try it, without having to worry about a place to sleep or something to eat. The only price Mother Nature expects them to pay is to follow and listen and obey. And when they come of age they can do what they want.

Parents are presently in that stage of life where they can do with their lives what they will. And children do not have the right to take away the parents' chance at self-fulfillment.

## The Right to Make Mistakes

According to Christian theology there has only been one person who ever walked this earth that did not make mistakes. Other than that one person we have all made mistakes, and will continue to make mistakes as long as we live. Keeping this in mind should make raising children a lot easier. So many parents hesitate doing various things with their children for fear of wrecking the child. Actually, Mother Nature endowed us with a great deal of psychological resiliency. Unlike baking cookies or making a casserole, it is almost impossible to spoil a child by making a few mistakes. Most of the psychological experiences a child has leave semipermanent rather than permanent effects. Like pencil marks on paper, many of the effects of children from parental mistakes can be erased. If a child is punished for something he did not do, it is possible for him to get over it. If parents are too permissive with their children, that can be corrected. If a parent unjustly criticizes or yells at his child, it does not produce an irreversible effect.

Don came in to discuss his twelve-year-old son, Pat. "For almost twelve years I have been spending most of my time trying to make a success of my bus company," Don informed me. "And now that it is financially stable I began to spend time with my son, only to find out he is a big sissy."

Don was a good-sized man who played on the defensive line of a football team at a large university during his college years. His son, Pat, was larger than most classmates. Somewhere along the line Pat had several bad experiences where other children had threatened to beat him up if he did not do what they said. It had happened so often, and the fear of being hit had grown so much inside Pat, that he avoided hard, physical contact games. Even nine-year-old boys could threaten Pat, and he would do what they wanted.

With great concern in his eyes Don asked if there was anything that could be done. Or was it too late? After explaining to him how adaptable and changeable children are, we began devising a program to help. We set about having someone teach him to box. By gradually mixing in more difficult but successful boxing triumphs with experiences of getting hit, Pat came to realize that being hit was not as painful as his fears had built it up to be. Within a year Pat was a pretty good fighter, and he no longer was easily intimidated.

There are two things for parents to keep in mind about making mistakes. First, the longer you continue to make mistakes before correcting them, the more difficult it is to change the child. The stronger bad habits are in children, the more difficult they are to eliminate.

The second point relates to a rather interesting phenomenon in psychology. It is perhaps best explained by giving a hypothetical situation. Suppose you had two women who had both just lost their husbands. One woman had always worked to help the family finances while the second woman had always been financially well-off and just stayed around the house. Which of the two women would most likely experience the more severe case of traumatic shock from losing her husband? The woman who was financially well-off would. Assuming everything else is equal, we find nervous breakdowns and other severe emotional disorders are more likely to happen to people who can physically afford to have them. A woman who gets petrified of bees may freeze when encountering one in her home, yet not freeze when one appears in her car as she drives down the road. In the car she cannot afford to freeze; at least not until after she can get the car stopped. In the same sense, the working woman has too many responsibilities for psychological trauma from her husband's death to set in. The main point to be made for parents from these examples is that children with no responsibilities around the home are more prone to be affected by parental mistakes when they are made, than children who have family responsibilities. A son who loafs around the house is more likely to be emotionally upset by his father suddenly yelling at him that if that son had other things on his mind to cope with at the same time.

# 3
# Subliminal Parent Training (The Hidden Persuaders)

## HOW DID IT HAPPEN?

Seeing things differently than they really are is a common experience. The magician uses his sleight of hand to produce a fifty-cent piece from behind the ear of a wide-eyed child. The father pitches dimes at a small glass plate at the carnival to win a duckling for his daughter, a seemingly easy task that results in very few winners. The flashing lights on the theater marquee produce the illusion of moving lights. The magician, the father, the theater marquee, are all situations which are designed to make things seem physically different from what they really are. People often try to affect the decisions and opinions of others by making things seem different than they really are.

How many of us have met the salesman who convinced us we couldn't live without a certain home appliance, only to find out later that we might not be able to live because of the payments? I still recall the first salesman who entered our apartment in the university housing complex for married students. With a self-confident smile he demonstrated the only vacuum cleaner in the world with the power to suck the chrome off a trailer hitch. After a forty-five minute demonstration during which he vacuumed up such common carpet items as two inch nuts and bolts, sand, and a large glass of milk, he left our home minus one vacuum cleaner, but holding a contract for which I had to pay thirty dollars a month for eighteen months. Then, thirty dollars was a large amount of money for a struggling college couple in the sixties. And to this day I am still not quite sure how he did it.

Such instances of one person putting something over on another are common. We often find ourselves the victim in rather obvious con games. Ed, a psychologist friend of mine, is no exception. Ed's car door on the driver's side had been damaged by someone who had not watched where he was going. After getting several repair estimates, he sent them to his insurance company. They mailed him a check to get the repair work done. Within a few days after receiving the check, a rather short middle-aged man knocked on his door and offered to repair the car door for a sum of money which was half that received from the insurance company. Seeing the possibility of coming out ahead financially, Ed said "yes." The man set to work immediately, first removing the inside panel, and then pounding out the dent.

After covering the dented area with some sort of compound, the man reapproached Ed. "Wait until this compound dries," he said, "then go down to the paint shop at the address on this card. They will sand it down and paint it." Ed then paid the man the amount of money agreed upon, and he left. "I became suspicious," Ed said as he continued recounting his experience, "when three days later the compound still had not dried. I drove to the address listed—there was no paint shop."

These subtle ways of getting what you want from other people are what psychologists call subliminal tactics. Roughly translated, subliminal means "without being aware." If someone gets you to do something without you realizing all that is being done, you are the victim of subliminal tactics. Subliminal tactics are most frequently used in situations where an individual cannot be forced to comply. A salesman cannot force you to buy, so he uses subliminal tactics. A wife is not strong enough to make her husband do what she wants, so she uses subliminal strategies. Children often use subliminal strategies to manipulate their parents. There are a variety of ways children go about using *subliminal tactics* (or hidden persuaders as some like to call them).

### Ask for More—Settle for Less

Back several years ago there was a great deal of concern aroused in movie goers when it was reported that some movie houses had been flashing the words "Buy Popcorn" on the movie screen for a fraction of a second several times during each film. This type of commercialism was called *subliminal advertising* and was supposed to cause people to go to the refreshment stand without realizing they had been manipulated. The concern over subliminal advertising has died down over the years.

I recalled the idea of subliminal advertising, however, at a movie theater recently when I watched a young girl about five years old use a modified version of it.

"I want some popcorn," the girl demanded.

"No," replied the mother, deeply engrossed in the plot.

"I want some popcorn, some root beer, and some red licorice!" the girl countered.

"Now look," the mother said, turning toward her daughter. "You can have some popcorn. But you cannot have anything else."

"Okay," she replied.

The mother then set out to buy the popcorn, confident she had won the battle. That girl had just manipulated her mother. Not receiving her initial request, she then demanded more. Her quick reply of "Okay" to her mom made it apparent that she had reached her intended objective. That little gal had just employed a tactic which all labor unions are familiar with—ask for more than you want, and then settle for what you initially intended to get. This strategy is effective on parents because it makes us feel as if we have won. We do not allow our children to get all they want, yet we show some consideration by fulfilling a portion of their wishes.

### When the Hand Is Quicker Than the Eye

There seems to be several different ways grade-school children go about getting parents to purchase items in the store. On several occasions I have sat down with groups of grade-school children and asked them how they get what they want from their parents.

"I like going with my mom to the grocery store," six-year-old Jeffry reported. "When Mom ain't looking I put things in her cart, and she buys 'em."

"Doesn't she notice them when she gets to the checkstand?" I asked. "And doesn't she put them back?"

"Sometimes she sees them, but she don't look a lot of times."

"Does she put them back when she sees what you have done?"

"No, she just looks at the woman counting them up like she's not sure what to do. And then keeps 'em."

## When the Hand Is not Quicker Than the Eye—Repeating Tactics Pays Off

"You don't even have to sneak the things in the basket," one lad piped up. "Just put them in there."

"What does your mother do when you do that?" I inquired.

"She says 'don't' and puts most of them back."

"Most of them?" I asked. "Doesn't she put all of them back?"

"No. When she puts things back, I put more in. After a while when I see she has left enough of the things in, I stop."

"How often can you do this to your parents?" I asked the group.

The answer, as with most of the groups I talked to, is *almost all the time.*

"Do you think your parents understand that you do this to them?" I asked.

"Well, they kinda do," replied one little blonde girl. "But, they forget easy. And a lot of times, they don't know."

## Molding Unconsciously—the Unsuspecting Parent

One Saturday afternoon my wife and I took our family over to another psychologist's home for an afternoon swim and backyard barbecue. While Larry was imitating the Galloping Gourmet with his new outdoor barbecue, our wives were busy making salads and drinks. I stretched out in a reclining lounge chair as Larry and I talked shop.

As most people are aware, different psychologists do different things. Whereas I spend most of my time studying how children (and other animals) learn, Larry is a marriage counselor.

Our conversation centered around the way one person goes about manipulating another person without the other knowing it. As we talked, I watched my two boys and his daughter playing with the garden hose. Having little interest in the deep pool, these two- to four-year-old kids came across the hose and began a game where one child was chasing the other two in an attempt to squirt them. Noticing that the water spigot to which the hose was attached was next to my lounge chair, I said "Hey Larry, I'll bet I can manipulate your daughter without her realizing it."

"In what way?" he replied.

"I'm going to turn off the water and teach her to shake the end of the hose up and down ten times to turn the water on," I proposed.

Larry accepted my challenge so I set to work. My plan was to turn the water off until Cindy shook the hose once, then I would turn it on for fifteen seconds. I would gradually require her to shake it two, three, four times, and so on, until she shook it ten times to get the water on.

I lay down in the lounge chair and slid my hat down over my eyes to give the impression I was asleep. The chair was in such a position that the kids could not see my hand on the knob. I turned the water off.

Cindy stopped chasing the boys and looked at the hose. Then she looked over toward me. With both hands on the hose she then drew the hose right next to her face and looked down the inside of the hose.

Now, psychologists are people too, and like other people we are not totally above temptation. So when she looked down the hose, the same thought went through my mind that would go through yours . . . so I turned the hose on.

"Paul," Larry called out in a somewhat chastising manner as he tried to keep from laughing.

"Okay, okay. That was just too tempting," I replied as Cindy wiped the water off her face.

Seeing no connection between her father's voice and what

she was doing, Cindy began checking along the hose to see why it wasn't working. As she walked she inadvertently shook the hose. I turned on the water. And she began chasing the boys again. After a few seconds I turned it off again. It was only a few moments later that she shook the hose again. It came on.

As a few minutes passed she learned that shaking the hose brought the water back on. Within ten minutes Cindy was well under my control. When I turned off the water she would vigorously shake the hose up and down until ten shakes had occurred, then off she would run, squirting and laughing.

"Why, that is amazing," Larry said! "I'm impressed. How did you learn to do that?"

While I did learn that kind of shaping technique in college, I had to admit to him that the idea came from watching my neighbor's thirteen-year-old son do essentially the same thing to his two-year-old brother.

### Using Diversions

*Mother Gets a Nap.* Two years ago my wife, Carol, and I adopted a four-year-old girl named Kamala. She came from an orphanage in southeast India. Although her young life included many dreadful experiences (including a person's attempt to drown her to get rid of her) she arrived at our home with a cheerful and vibrant outlook on life that most children in America could not match.

Over the months she put on weight to the extent that it began to worry us. My wife decided to curtail her eating, so she regulated quite closely what Kamala ate at meals, and cut out her in-between-meal snacks.

Although we watched her carefully she continued to gain weight. She gained more weight than the weight of the food she was allowed to eat. My wife and I began suspecting each other of giving her food when the other was not around. The answer to the mystery started to unfold one day as one of her friends was playing with her in her room. My wife walked in as Kamala was sharing some sugar-coated breakfast cereal with her playmate. When Carol questioned Kamala about how she obtained the cereal, Kamala gave somewhat vague and conflicting answers.

When I arrived home that night we continued the questioning.

The answer revealed to both of us just how sharp kids can be. Each day after coming home from kindergarten and having lunch, Kamala would say "Let's take a nap Mommy." Carol and Kamala would then lay down. Only Carol would go to sleep, however. After Carol was asleep, Kamala would get up and go into the kitchen. She would get out some zip-lock sandwich bags and fill them with Cheerios, Sugar Smacks, nuts, candy, and anything else she could find. She stashed over one dozen bags in a variety of places throughout the house. When hungry, she would simply go to one of her caches of food when no one was looking. I'm not sure when she started doing this, but I suspect attendants at the orphanage take afternoon naps.

*Jeffry the Helper.* Jeffry was a curly-haired six-year-old who was one of mother's best helpers. He came late in the family. His brothers and sisters ranged in age from thirteen to twenty-two. Whenever mother was cleaning the house, Jeffry was there. Whenever his older brothers were cleaning their room, Jeffry was there. In fact, he cleaned rooms all by himself. One day a neighbor lady commented to Jeffry's mother about how nice it was that Jeffry always shared his allowance and bought ice cream and candy for all his friends. "Jeffry receives no allowance," replied his mother. With a more watchful eye the parents soon found out the source of Jeffry's riches. He would snitch money from banks, wallets, purses, and jewelry boxes while helping. Confronted with his deeds he confessed he learned his trade from an older sister whom he observed helping mother on several occasions.

*Malcom the Horsetrader.* Malcom was a twelve-year-old boy who lived in a housing project near a middle-class subdivision. He and three other boys his age were some of the most pleasant young men to talk to. They were often found talking to various neighborhood fathers as the men worked on weekly chores of washing cars, cleaning out garages, and cleaning up yards. On many occasions, Malcom and his friends would be interested in trading or selling items. One day their tactics were uncovered.

"Say, where did you get that Mitchel 300 fishing reel with the dented swivel?" one man said to his neighbor. "I thought I lost that last year."

"I bought it for two dollars from Malcom" was the reply. Malcom and his friends had been the source of many small and unnoticed thefts throughout their part of town.

Diversionary tactics are a popular approach for many children in situations where parents are generally the ones who run the home. It is an approach that is popular for use on neighbors and relatives who don't generally give in to other strategies. It's an approach that takes more skill and finesse than the strategies discussed in the next two chapters. It usually takes time and effort to set up, but until caught, the profits are often higher than what tantrums and other forms of irritating actions can produce. Diversionary tactics are the main tactics used by children who eventually find themselves in serious trouble with the law.

In many cases, teenagers use diversionary tactics to get to do things they know their parents would object to. They often say they are going to a dance when in fact they are out drinking. One creative teenager set up a small still in his basement. He led his parents to believe he was just keenly interested in chemistry.

### Setting Up Your Parents—Divide and Conquer

One of the most effective strategies used by children is to drive a psychological wedge between their parents. While it may provide short-term gains for a child, it is the cause of far too many men and women splitting up their marriage. It generally starts when parents have different philosophies about things such as childrearing. One believes in spanking; the other does not. One believes in being firm while the other believes in being permissive. These types of situations lead to instances where one parent lets the child do something that the other parent would object to. "Now don't tell mommy I let you stay up late." "Don't tell daddy we went shopping."

One such situation occurred in the east when three daughters of a large department store manager divided their parents. Walt was a successful man who had different ideas about childrearing than his wife. While his girls were quite young they learned to talk mother into doing things (for example, stay up late while dad worked late, not come home from friends' homes until late, get mother to overspend on clothes for them) that father would not budge on. Little disagreements between husband and wife became big disagreements. The girls did nothing to help. In fact they tried to keep their parents from enjoying each other. As the girls entered high school their desires for cars and clothes were met with the help of their mother. One day Walt did not return home from work. His wife has not heard from him since.

### Setting Up the Divorced Parent

*Killing with Kindness.* Situations where children pit one parent against another include where divorces have occurred previously. Children often dislike the idea of their father or mother remarrying.

Daloris was a woman in her early thirties who had been divorced for the first time four years ago. A little over a year later she remarried. Her new husband, Tony, had two daughters from his prior marriage, twelve and fourteen years of age. Daloris and Tony's marriage was in trouble. Although both of them felt they had been working hard to overcome problems, the problems seemed to be increasing. There were not so many major fights occurring as there were ever increasing feelings of uncomfortableness each were experiencing with the day-to-day problems in running the household. After looking closely at the situation and visiting the home a few times, the reason for the problems came to the surface. The two girls disliked their father remarrying, and had set out in a subtle and systematic way to create dissension between Tony and Daloris. Using the philosophy that you can catch more flies with honey than vinegar, both girls had acted sweet and helpful. On the sly, however, they planted seeds of uncertainty. Among many acts, they took the wedding rings from Daloris's first marriage out of her jewelry box and placed them in a semiconspicuous place on Tony's dresser. They listened through doors to personal communications and led Daloris to believe Tony was sharing confidences with them. Feeling somewhat hurt, Daloris began alienating herself from Tony and believing more and more what the girls were saying. Daloris soon found herself taking out her feelings on her husband; Tony found himself finding more consolation and comfort at home in talking to his daughters. The daughters' plan was working beautifully, and would have succeeded except for one thing; they became so involved in Daloris' and Tony's lives that they came to feel the heartache each was going through. When the marriage was going under, the girls confessed their role in getting the trouble started, and expressed their unhappiness in what had resulted. Most remarriages where children set out to submarine the new family are not that fortunate.

*The "Dad Lets Me Do This" Approach.* Remarriage situations provide children with a means of getting what they want that few resist. Brad was a ten-year-old fourth grader whose mother remarried about a year ago. The divorce had been uncontested; both parties wanted to go their own way. Brad's new father got along with Brad quite well. There were times, however, when he felt himself giving in to many of Brad's requests. "My dad lets me stay up past 10:30," Brad would say when trying to get his stepfather to give him more time. "My dad said I could get a pocket knife like this big one." "My dad don't care if I don't come home right after school." "I know what Brad is trying to do" his stepfather said. "But I find it hard to not let those comments influence my decisions. I find myself getting upset with Brad because I end up letting him do what I would not if he were my real son."

Few, if any, remarried parents have not found themselves experiencing the same thing as Brad's stepfather. Remarriages are such natural setups for this type of action from children, that we should not let ourselves get upset when it happens. The important thing is that we do not allow those subtle pressures to work. And most parents know what should be done.

## TYPES OF SUBLIMINAL TACTICS

The fundamental principle behind most parent training is to get the parent to allow the child to do something he desires, but which the parent often finds objectionable. In most of life's situations the parent and child both want the same thing. Both like to go play in the ocean. Both like to do exciting things and have fun. Where both like the same thing, few children try to manipulate the parent. The problem comes when what the child considers exciting, fun, or desirable does not coincide with the parent's view. The subliminal training of parents is typically tried by children who have come to the realization, either through experience or example, that their parents cannot be directly intimidated into letting them get what they want. They have to resort to one of several indirect tactics. These tactics include: (1) diversions, (2) shaping, (3) and propagandizing.

## Diversions

Diversions are often employed by adults in situations where they are under the control of someone else. A man may tell his boss he cannot come to work because he is sick when he is actually going fishing. Knowing her parents can stop her, a teenager may tell her parents she is going over to Betty's home when she is actually going out drinking. In some cases, diversions are used to spare the feelings of yourself and others. You may not be totally under the control of someone else, but you do not want to create an uncomfortable situation. The wife tells her husband she has a headache.

## Shaping

Often parents are shaped and molded by their children slowly and subtly in such a way the parents are unaware of what is happening. One good example concerned David, a twelve-year-old boy, who had a morning paper route. He had to be up by 4:30 in order to finish his route by seven. He started off waking his father up on rainy days to take him. Then cold mornings became included. After getting dad that far he began to wake him every morning, often complaining how hard it was to peddle his bike. Eventually Dave had his dad delivering papers while he stayed in bed. David's success at getting his father to do the route by himself lasted for over six months before his dad overheard him bragging to his friends about his accomplishment.

Tammy worked something similar on her mom. She signed up for a sewing class in junior high. Initially she worked on her projects, asking help from mother infrequently. Later, Tammy relied more heavily on her mother to help. The last two projects for Tammy's class were done completely by her mother with coaxing from her daughter. Many parents are easy victims for children because parents hate to see a job half done. Some children, however, consistently start project after project and the parents finish them.

### Propagandizing

Influencing people by making things sound different than they really are is something society calls propaganda. It is an effective technique to influence people's attitudes. Man's innate tendencies to want to believe what is heard make us susceptible to this strategy.

Propaganda is used by children because we, as parents, find these techniques difficult to cope with. The student tells the teacher he missed the test because he was sick. The child tells the parent she received a "D" because the teacher doesn't like her. The teenage son makes up a story to his parents when he is going out with his friends to drink. The girl caught shoplifting complains she did it because her family is too poor to buy her nice clothes so she feels bad at school. Telling us the teacher gave her a D because of personality conflicts places a seed of doubt in parents so we are not so quick to reprimand. Few children are foolish enough to say "I received a D because I goofed off all the time in class." And the same is true for adults. Few men tell their boss they are going fishing to get a day off.

## TYPES OF PARENTS SUSCEPTIBLE TO SUBLIMINAL TACTICS

Through the years husbands and wives learn more about one another. They learn what makes their mate happy, and they learn what makes their mate sad. They learn to cue off those subtle little things a marriage partner does. A wife may know her husband is upset at a party while no one else senses it. A husband may sense his wife is mad at a class reunion when no one else realizes it.

Often we use this knowledge about our mate to help us get what we want. The wife knows the right moment to tell her husband she bought a new dress. And children learn to do the same thing.

A teenage son learns not to ask father for the car until after mother has filled Dad with roast beef and he is settled into his easy chair. Through years of living with other people you learn their strengths and weaknesses. And few individuals can spot parents' weaknesses better than their own children. In fact, in most families where children use subliminal techniques, the children are more perceptive at noting the weaknesses of a father than the wife is. And they are more perceptive in spotting mother's weaknesses than father is.

Children are mirrors of their parents' strengths and weaknesses. By watching children, psychologists (and most observant people for that matter) can tell a great deal about the parents and what goes on in the family. When I see children using subliminal techniques it tells me several things about them. (Keep in mind what I say may not always be true, but is generally true.) First, it tells me the parents rather than the children run the household. Children trying to skirt around or circumvent parents indicate their awareness that the mother and/or father are the powers that be in their lives. These parents usually run a better-than-average family in terms of organization. They are viewed by their children as being consistent in what they do, and as having concern for their children. While many teenagers today could care less about what their parents feel or do, this is not generally the case for children who are using subliminal strategies. Oftentimes they use these strategies so parents' opinions of them will not change. For example, they don't want their parents to know they are out drinking, or that they were out in parked cars when the parents are against such activities.

The subliminal strategies are generally more sophisticated than the ones described in the following two chapters. Children using subliminal strategies are much more aware of what they are doing. They are generally good students in school, or should be. They usually show less rebellion and get along better socially than most children. Their above-average ability in creativity is often displayed in the exact strategies they use. Although subliminal strategies are often used by children, some, like Harold in the next chapter, use much more direct methods.

# 4
# The Superthreshold Approach

## THE DIRECT METHOD—GOING FOR WHAT THEY WANT

Harold was the son of a doctor. At a tender young age he developed a successful approach of dealing with his parents that gave them fits. He just did whatever he wanted. At age three he was going to the bathroom in the middle of the night when he became infatuated with a roll of toilet paper. He unwound the whole roll into the toilet and repeatedly flushed the clogged toilet for the satisfaction of watching the water overflow the bowl, run across the bathroom floor, and seemingly disappear into the hall carpet. Although he was given a strong scolding, he repeated the incident the following night.

One afternoon a next-door neighbor heard a banging on the side of his home. Upon rounding the corner of his house, there was Harold with a hammer. He had broken the handle of the water spigot protruding from the man's home and was in the process of doing the same thing to the whole pipe.

"What the hell are you doing," the man angrily charged.

"Just hammerin'," Harold replied.

As the man was in the midst of giving Harold a Scotch blessing, Harold's mother came on the scene and scolded the man for yelling at her son as she took Harold back on her property.

Another time, Harold's father had set the garbage cans on the curb for the weekly collection, and Harold and a playmate spotted some bottles in the trash. They threw the bottles in the air and watched them crash in the middle of the street. They then proceeded down the sidewalk doing the same thing with bottles found in the trash cans of others on the block. A year or so later Harold got up early, around 5:30 A.M., as he often did to watch cartoons on TV. For some unexplained reason he placed a Tupperware bowl on the stove and turned it on. After that incident his mother always arose at 5:30 so she could watch Harold and his younger brother and keep such incidents from recurring. Harold's parents' philosophy on childrearing centered around the idea that too much parental intervention in a child's world stifles proper psychological development. They firmly believed that any form of physical discipline would be detrimental to Harold's mental health.

Whenever Harold's parents were questioned about his actions they would reply "He will grow out of it." And he did—to some degree. Upon entering school he encountered many children who did not share his parents' philosophy. Some of his kindergarten classmates became upset when he took toys and school supplies from them. And many of these classmates physically expressed their philosophies. Harold seemed to grow out of his phase of doing what he wanted when he wanted by the end of his kindergarten year. It is interesting to note that although he had learned to be more considerate and cooperative at school, he continued going through his "phase" for several more years at home. Children seem to go through phases at a quicker pace when their environment makes it more rewarding (and perhaps less painful) to do so.

Harold used a rather direct approach on his parents. The direct approach is one of several approaches psychologists classify as superthreshold approaches. The term superthreshold means *above threshold* or *above the awareness level.* The child makes no effort to hide his or her intent, so the parent is aware of what is being done.

An ever increasing number of children use the rather direct

approach in going for what they want. Many teenagers seem to ignore warnings of parents and make long-distance phone calls which the parents end up paying for. Oftentimes young children stay up past bedtime and create a scene when mother or father remind them it is time for bed. Parents are frequently seen searching in shopping malls for their child who has taken off to look at what he or she wants. Children who use this strategy for manipulating their parents often make replies like:

> "Oh, I forgot you told me not to use the phone."
> "I did not mean to cause a problem."
> "I just turned around and could not see you Mother."

The children who make such statements usually have parents who do use physical discipline on them, though sparingly. Over time the children learn that many unacceptable actions are tolerated by parents if you have an excuse. Children (like Harold) whose parents do not use physical discipline are less prone to make up excuses. Doing what they want generally does not result in much more than a mildly unpleasant scolding, so they seldom need excuses to avoid a stronger consequence.

## WEARING PARENTS DOWN

Have you ever seen a young child squirming in his mother's arms until she puts him down? Sure. We all have. What that child learns when he finally reaches the floor is that persistence often pays off with parents. "Although Mom and Dad tell me 'No' or try to resist my efforts, they will eventually give me my way if I keep at it." Few of us have not fallen victim to this approach at one time or another. A young son may beg and beg and beg to get a BB gun. Finally his persistent request overcomes any reluctance about his ability to properly handle such a toy, and his parents purchase the gun. A daughter continually talks about all her friends having a certain hairstyle until mother concedes. While shopping, a young child repeatedly asks for some ice cream until mother becomes tired of saying "No."

There is an inherent aspect of this strategy that makes it difficult for parents to deal with it. When a parent gives in to this approach there is usually a feeling of relief. The child has created an uncomfortable situation by repeatedly asking for what is wanted. That uncomfortable feeling then disappears for the parent as he or she gives in. The feeling of relief is a false one, however, for while the short-term effect of giving in may make the present situation more satisfying, the tendency for the child to create such situations grows in strength. And the next time the child is prone to be even more persistently annoying as the parent is challenged. As is often the case in life, quick, short relief may result in greater problems further down the road.

## OVERPOWERING PARENTS

Leon was employed as a maintenance man in a steel plant, and had been for over twenty years. He was a small-framed man who never created problems for anyone. He and his wife, Louise, had two sons who were older teenagers and quite a bit larger than their father. For years the boys had created problems for their parents. While growing up they would throw tantrums to intimidate their parents. In fifth through tenth grades they repeatedly stole money out of their mother's purse and stole from their father's wallet at night. On one occasion they intimidated their mother into making out a check for thirty dollars to them. On later occasions when that was not successful, they forged and cashed checks on their parents' account. Although neighbors and friends repeatedly tried to get Leon and Louise to file charges against their boys or get some type of help, they refused. They had a strong fear their boys would leave them completely; and that fear was more dominating in their minds than all the things their sons did to them.

Ellie was a large-boned, heavy-set teenager who lived with her mother and younger brother. At the age of thirteen a neighbor woman caught her stealing her garden hose and gave her a scolding. That evening Ellie painted "Mrs. Allen is a bitch" on the walk in front of the woman's home. At age sixteen Ellie was trying to force her mother to give her a large amount of her welfare check when another neighbor close by stepped in and stopped her. Holding a grudge over the incident, Ellie waited until the man took his family on vacation. Breaking a window in the now vacant home, she put three cats and six pigeons loose in the house and boarded up the window so they could not get out. Ten days later the man returned to find all those animals dead and a bad odor in the home. The whole neighborhood slept easier after Ellie left home at age seventeen.

It is estimated that one out of seven teenagers use some form of physical intimidation to get what they want from their parents. Years ago it was mostly boys, but the number of girls employing this strategy has risen sharply during the past decade. A large portion of the foster girls brought to our home have either hit their own mother or the foster mothers they have had before coming to us.

## THREE "FACES" OF PARENTING—A CONSEQUENCE OF SUPERTHRESHOLD TACTICS

There is an interesting side effect that happens to parents whose children employ the superthreshold approach. Ever notice how the parents of a rambunctious and headstrong child often seem to blame everyone but the child for his actions?

> "If Billy had had a lock on his bike, my Jimmy would not have taken it."
>
> "My daughter would not be a problem in your class if you ran the class properly."
>
> "My Terry would not cut across your lawn if you did not provoke him by complaining about him."

Each of us have run into such parents, and find ourselves asking "How can that parent be so blind as not to see that their child is the problem?"

In 1978, Carol and I were working with law enforcement officers to apprehend teenagers who were involved in drug trafficking. We were accidentally confronted by two nervous girls, thirteen and fourteen years of age, who had a pillowcase containing money and jewelry items. Due to the suspicious nature of the situation, we confiscated the pillowcase and drove the girls to their home. It was about ten o'clock in the morning. That evening I went back to the home and asked the father if he was missing any money or jewelry. He said "No." I explained the situation and he said I must be mistaken. His girls were obviously not the ones I had brought to his home that morning. He said, however, he would talk to his girls when they returned home.

Three hours later he called, somewhat embarrassed, to say it was his girls. They apparently had stolen some money he and his new wife had stashed, plus the wedding rings and jewelry from his wife's previous marriage. They had also taken some items from close neighbors. I said he could come pick up the items in the morning and try to work things out between his daughters and the neighbors. In the morning when he arrived only my wife was home. His attitude had changed drastically. He seemed bitter and defensive while implying the civil rights of his daughters might have been violated. "Why did that man act so ungrateful?" my wife asked me later that night. "We were just trying to help him."

The answer to my wife's question involves a psychological defense mechanism which few people realize they use. How each of us feels about ourselves is very important psychologically. For us to have good mental health, we need to visualize ourselves as competent, successful, and able to effectively cope with the world around us. Whenever something happens in life with which we do not successfully cope it creates a psychological uneasiness within us which typically stays in our mind until we successfully deal with the problem. However, the inner mind can only take being in this uneasy state for a limited length of time. If the person does not handle the situation through outside action and remove this psychologically traumatic situation, the mind will interject a psychological defense mechanism to make it seem as if the problem is no problem.

This psychological defense mechanism is like shock which may set in right after someone has been in a car accident. In one particular case a man was thrown from a car as it missed a turn in the road. Somewhat stunned, he was helping get people out of the car when someone showed him in a mirror that he had a small piece of his skull missing. At the sight of his head, he fainted. Right after the accident he had gone into shock. This shock is a physiological defense mechanism which blocks pain from the individual for a short while. This generally gives the person a better chance to get his or her wits about them and handle the emergency.

When a seemingly serious psychological problem is not solved by a person after a span of time, a psychological defense mechanism, like shock, steps in and distorts the real situation to get rid of the mental pressure the unsolved problem creates. Suppose, for example, a child does things which his parent disapproves of time after time. Initially the parent tries to correct the child, but in the long run is unsuccessful. This creates a psychological trauma in the parent. To protect the mental health of this person, his or her mind removes the guilt of unsuccessfully handling the child by psychologically distorting the situation so their child is not the problem. And when the trouble is not due to the child, then the parent no longer has to blame him or herself for being inadequate as a parent.

Parents whose children successfully use the superthreshold approach generally go through three different phases (or "faces" as I like to refer to them) in reaching the point where they come to the distorted perception that their child is not the problem. During the first phase of this process the parent is generally appreciative to people who point out the wrong things their child does. During this phase they realize their child is the source of the problem and take steps to change the child. During the second phase the parents still realize their child is causing problems, but do not appreciate people pointing the shortcomings of their child out to them. At this point their inability to cope with their child plays on their mind. They have generally tried several things to correct the child but nothing is working, and their optimism that something will work is fading. Psychological distortions are gradually being introduced by the mind itself to cope with the problem.

In the third phase the unconscious deception is complete. Whenever confronted by police or neighbors about their child's actions, they may strongly lash out while claiming innocence on the part of the child. In the early part of this phase this psychological distortion may dissipate from the mind of the parent a few hours after the incident. As time goes on, however, the distortion stays with the parent continually. Once the child is grown and on his own reality about those earlier situations often returns at a time when the truth can no longer hurt the parents.

These three phases of parenting with superthreshold children was nicely illustrated in a family that immigrated to the United States from South America. Manuel and Anita moved to Utah with four children ranging in age from eight to fourteen years. Manuel was a skilled tradesman who spoke fluent English who was hired at a technical school to work with Spanish-speaking students. He was a religious man who strongly believed in the Christian philosophy of life. During his first few years in this country he was considered by his neighbors as quite helpful and friendly. That seemed to change as his next to youngest son, Bernie, grew older.

When Bernie was eleven, Manuel received a telephone call from the manager of a local golf course. Manuel was politely informed that Bernie had been caught stealing from lockers in the clubhouse. After picking up his son, Manuel thanked the man and set off for home with some discipline in mind. Bernie was much like Harold, discussed earlier in this chapter. Bernie had somewhat of a devil-may-care attitude. He was really no problem around the house, and generally did whatever caught his fancy.

Over the next two years items began disappearing from around the neighborhood. Bicycles, gas cans, fishing gear, and lawn mowers were missing. Manuel's patience with his neighbors grew thin when different missing items were traced to Bernie. His attempts at correcting Bernie's behavior had repeatedly failed. Bernie would seem to behave himself for a while, then get caught with someone else's bike. At age fifteen Bernie and two of his friends were caught by the police stealing batteries out of cars parked on the street at night. Manuel seriously argued to juvenile court officers that Bernie was a good boy who was an innocent bystander who was with his friends who were really the ones doing the stealing. He also claimed the police had been out to "get" his son for quite some time. Over the course of four years Manuel and his family moved to different neighborhoods three times because of what he called problems his neighbors created for his family.

## TYPES OF PARENTS SUSCEPTIBLE TO SUPERTHRESHOLD TACTICS

There is not a parent who hasn't experienced this technique. As the infant comes home from the hospital, parents become sensitive to this approach. When the child cries, the parents move quickly to satisfy its needs. Although the initial tendencies for the child's crying are based on physiological needs that have to be met, it isn't long until the child learns that parents will come whenever the crying starts.

As time goes by, parents start to resist the child's crying demands. In response, the child cries louder, hits higher notes, and learns to intersperse crying with silence because parents are less affected by a monotonic sound like old-time police cars. Notice that new police cars have sirens which put out a sound which oscillates up and down. Many parents learn to refrain from giving in to such pressure, while others choose to give in to the crying.

Because all children start out using this natural technique, it is not surprising to find it is one of the most popular strategies for children less than five years old. And because all parents accept it as a rather natural tendency for children, it is not surprising that so many parents allow it to continue. While all parents allow it to happen to some degree, there are certain types of parents who are more prone to let even their teenagers get away with it.

Some parents are very self-confident and sure of themselves. They are not threatened by their ten-year-old doing what he wants. In many cases the father recalls that he himself was a little wild and unruly, and sees no reason not to allow his children to be the same. While such parents do give in to the demands of their children, they see nothing wrong in doing so. In cases such as this, the unruliness is often somewhat restrained, for these parents tend to have limits beyond which they will not be pushed. Children quickly learn these limits and either stay within them or subtly try to expand what they can get away with. Children with such parents have a tendency to push other children, neighbors, and relatives further than their own parents. Neighbors and relatives are hesitant to confront such parents who are generally quite assertive and outgoing.

A second type of parent susceptible to this approach is the more frail and shy type of parent. These parents are the type of individuals who do not complain when being overcharged at a store. They do not like to cause trouble and avoid confrontations whenever possible. Children learn to spot when their parents are timid and may begin to exploit this as a weakness. Most timid parents realize what is happening but are fearful that if they put their foot down, their children will either leave home or get physical right back.

Such parents do not realize the power they have. They do not realize that demanding, overbearing children rate their parents quite low. When such parents become more assertive, children actually tend to appreciate and value their parents more. This does not mean the children immediately become more submissive. On the contrary. At first they get mad and more overbearing, but this mood will change if the parents stand firm.

It was mentioned earlier in this chapter that parents whose children successfully use superthreshold tactics often go through three different attitude phases. This can happen with both types of parents who are most prone to these types of tactics when they are unsuccessful in controlling their children. An interesting point is that parents who have gone through all three phases often come back to reality about their children once the children have left home and the parents are no longer confronted daily with their failure.

# 5
# The Incompatible Response Approach

## SETTING PARENTS UP

More common than subliminal or superthreshold techniques is what psychologists call the incompatible response approach. The incompatible response approach basically involves putting parents in a situation where only one or two choices are possible, and conditions are arranged so the choice the child wants is most likely the one parents will choose. With this approach the child is really doing what is often referred to as setting a person up. For example, Tammy may want to go to Anita's house to listen to records, but knows dad will most likely tell her no if she asks by herself. She then takes Anita with her to ask dad, because she has learned from past experience that he, like most parents, feels more intimidated when other people are around when such decisions are made. Not wanting to be viewed as an ogre by friends and neighbors, dad says yes although he would not have if Tammy had approached him by herself.

Parents can be set up in a variety of ways. And that is why the approach is so popular. All parents have several issues they are sensitive about which makes them vulnerable. If a parent is conscientious about wanting his or her child to have everything the Jones's have, the child may say "I need a new dress–all the other girls are getting them" or "All the other kid's parents let them stay up after ten thirty." Adopted children often use the tactic "You don't let me because I'm adopted." This type of comment has a way of affecting parents.

The basis of the incompatible approach is "find the parents' emotional weaknesses and use them to your advantage." In one instance that might be exploiting the parents' desires to not make a scene when guests are around. In another instance it might entail making the parents feel they do not really love the child if they do not succumb to what the child wants.

## Everybody is Doing It

Oftentimes our children sense that we parents want to be fair with them in letting them do what other parents allow. They can also figure out that we parents are not keeping up with what is actually going on around us. Knowing this, we often find ourselves giving in to pressure from our children.

A few years back, a mother (let's call her Mrs. Jones) in her late thirties made arrangements to rent a party room in a teen center built by a citizens' group in a town of nearly fifty thousand people. The teen center had basketball courts, a swimming pool, outside tennis courts, and a medium-sized party and game room. The party room had a soda fountain and a place where all types of games (for example, pool, scrabble, electronic pocket games) could be checked out. It also had a jukebox and a dance floor, with couches and stuffed chairs around the walls.

This party and game room could be rented for private teenage parties. Mrs. Jones reserved the place for her daughter's thirteenth birthday party, on a Thursday night in November. A custodian walked past the door to the room about ten thirty. Seeing no light coming from under the door, yet hearing music, he walked in. Turning the lights on, he found Mrs. Jones half asleep in a chair and the young teenagers involved in what might be called a blind man's version of "I'll show you mine, if you show me yours."

In discussing the situation with the mother, it became apparent that she was somewhat the victim of the line "Everybody is doing it." For quite some time her daughter had used this line on her mother. By referring to the sex education films she had seen at school and talking over the birth control pill issue, she had convinced her mother that such activities were quite socially acceptable to other parents. Mrs. Jones came from a family very conservative on the issue of sex, married late in life, and was divorced. Her few encounters with men after her divorce helped reinforced the comments of her daughter that she was behind the times on the role of sex in life. Having almost no personal social life, and living mainly for the daughter she loved so much, her decisions were easily influenced by her daughter's claim "Everybody is doing it."

Although Mrs. Jones' situation is somewhat of an extreme example, most parents have at one time or another allowed their judgment to be swayed by their children, in essence, saying the same thing. Children may get guitars, cars, or new clothes, using this approach. They may also get to stay up late, stay out overnight, and get involved in certain types of activities that parents typically prefer they would not get involved in.

### You Like Her Best

Ever hear a child say "How come Cynthia always gets what she wants, but I don't?" Playing on the idea of sibling preferences by parents is another common incompatible response approach. No parent ever treats two children exactly the same. There are a number of situations in which one child is being reprimanded while the other is not. Or one may need a new coat when the other does not. With literally dozens and dozens of such occasions occurring, it is no wonder a child is able to pick out a few where one might honestly feel some favoritism was being shown.

Rare is the parent who is not sensitive to such accusations. One of the most sensitive issues of parenting is being fair. No parent likes to be thought of as being otherwise. Rivalry between brothers and sisters because of believed inequities in parental attention is one of the most popular psychological topics. Almost every book on childrearing talks about sibling rivalry and its role in the family.

Soon after our first child was born, Carol and I applied to adopt another boy. It was not long until a caseworker came to visit us. She came back two or three times and asked what, I felt, were some unusual questions. Being a psychologist, adoption proceedings and interviews were not completely foreign to me, but many of the caseworker's questions seemed out of the ordinary. They seemed unusual, that is, until I realized what the caseworker was worried about. It became clear from her questions that she felt I was adopting a second child so quickly after the first in order to carry out some psychological experiment and compare the behavior of our own newborn son to the behavior of our son-to-be.

I became somewhat irked at the caseworker once I realized what her concerns were. I then began to talk as if her concerns were correct. Putting her on, I mentioned how I planned to treat them differently and see how it affected them. I said that the child we were adopting would obviously be intellectually inferior to our real son, but our son would help him the best he could. Her eyes seemed to widen as I talked. When she left it was apparent she was concerned.

Two days later I had lunch with the director of the adoption program who was a professional friend of mine. "You should have heard the horror story your caseworker brought back to the office with her after talking to you and your wife," he said with a grin. "When I told her I knew you quite well and was sure you were pulling her leg, she became embarrassed, then mad."

I then told him of my experience with her and said that I had been a little upset that someone would think a psychologist would seriously adopt a child to experiment on him. The incident points up the fact that preferential feelings for one child over another is a major issue in psychology; and one that children can learn to use to their advantage.

### Putting Parents Over a Barrel

Audrey was eleven years old and the only daughter of a stockbroker. Having a stockbroker father, appearances meant a great deal to Audrey's family. A look of success helped his business, whereas any hints of financial reversals obviously affected potential investors. Keeping up appearances became the key to Audrey getting her way with her parents. On one occasion Audrey's father was telling of a successful investment when Audrey innocently piped up "Does that mean we can go back to using butter now instead of margarine?" She had just paid her dad back for not getting her way the day before when she talked back to her mother. Whenever her parents disciplined her, Audrey retaliated by doing something in front of friends and business associates. After being disciplined for not cleaning her room, Audrey told a neighbor her mother got mad at her for no reason, just because the family was having money problems. One day she wore socks with holes in them to school and told her teacher she had no lunch money because mother would not give it to her. Most of the time Audrey did get what she wanted. "She keeps putting us over a barrel," her Dad remarked. "She threatens to do such things if we will not give her her way."

There are a number of cases where children are able to place parents over a barrel because of something parents have done. Stephanie was sixteen years old and had a stepfather. Her mother had been divorced and had remarried when Stephanie was twelve. Stephanie was a high-strung girl who had fought a lot with her mother. The stepfather tended to support the mother in the mother–daughter disagreements until something happened. After foolishly expressing a biological urge with the daughter, the stepfather found himself over a barrel. The girl was willing to keep the incident quiet as long as the stepfather gave her good reason to.

### Setting Up Divorced Parents

While few children are not adversely affected by divorce, there are many children who attempt to use the situation to their advantage. Divorce typically produces a situation where two parents end up competing for the affection of their children. Having been together on the average for over ten years prior to divorce, both parents have tendencies to blame the other, and neither have complete trust in the former mate. Children who are manipulators could not ask for a better situation. The problem is compounded even more because at least one of the parents usually remarries so the child can work the new parent the same way the original parents were used. One of the main problems in marrying a divorced parent where children are involved is that children often get their way by saying such things as "My real dad let me do this" or "My real mother always lets me have these." Communications between divorced parents have usually deteriorated to the point that most children are never confronted on such claims. Such comments by the child create situations parents feel uncomfortable to deal with. Typically, divorced parents give in rather than make an issue about the situation.

It is important to remember that children in such situations are aware of what they are doing. Generally, children in divorce situations rate parents *and* stepparents higher when they do not give in to such tactics.

## You Don't Love Me as Much Because I Am Adopted

Do not be surprised when your adopted daughter or son turns to you while being disciplined and says something to the effect that "You don't love me as much because I'm adopted." Whenever anyone, no matter how young, is experiencing an unpleasant situation because of someone else, they have a tendency to want to strike back. A six-year-old girl being reprimanded by her mother may turn to her mother and say "I hate you." When husbands and wives get into arguments, either may end up getting their feelings hurt, and then it is natural to try and hurt the other person in return. If a wife with artistic talent, yet poor cooking skills, embarrasses her husband in front of guests, he may end up making a comment about some earlier cooking fiasco she has had. He most likely will not make any comments about her artistic skills. We do not compliment people who have hurt us. Compliments do not help us get even. We search for something about our mate that will hurt and we come up with comments like:

> "I hope our children do not turn out to be as inept as you."
> "Why don't you grow up and quit being a mama's boy?"
> "Why don't you learn to dress with some style?"
> "You're just a dumb, stupid blonde."
> "Why did I marry a dumb Frenchman?"

To really hurt our mate we make much more personal comments about particular intimate situations in which we claim they are inept.

Children learn to do essentially the same thing. Often in frustration, while being reprimanded, they say things to hurt their parents. And they find their parents' soft spots. They find those comments to which their parents are sensitive and often learn to use these issues as a lever to manipulate their parents.

One of the most common complaints heard by foster parents from their foster children when they are being disciplined is "You don't love me because I'm not really yours." They learn that such comments not only have the effect of reducing discipline, but they may also be used to increase the likelihood of getting something they want. We foster parents are sensitive about such remarks because we want to be fair.

Adopted children often learn to use the same tactics on their parents. A large number of adoptive parents having difficulty with their children report this problem and want answers on how to handle it. Some adoptive parents have the idea that this indicates they are lacking as parents. The answer to adoptive parents as to how to handle such situations should be apparent with the following statement. *The more sensitive adoptive parents and society are to the issue of adoption, the more frequent adopted children tend to use this tactic.* Adopted children have no innate tendency to bring up the issue of adoption. Through experience, adopted children may learn that their parents are sensitive about this issue, and once they are aware of that, they may use that sensitivity to get their way by placing their parents in an incompatible response situation.

## FINDING PARENTAL SOFT SPOTS

The phrase "incompatible response situation" seems like quite a mouthful to most readers. The meaning of the phrase is straightforward. If two items do not go together, we say they are incompatible. If two people cannot get along living together, we say they are incompatible. The phrase "incompatible response situation" refers to getting someone to do or agree with something that is against (or incompatible with, as Webster would say) their typical inclinations. So when a child arranges conditions so the parents agree to something they are typically not in favor of, we call that action by the parents an incompatible response. Those parents have done something that, barring extenuating circumstances, they would not normally do.

When children use this tactic on their parents they create certain circumstances they expect will influence the decision of their parents. As mentioned earlier, this tactic is most often used by older children. Effective use of this tactic requires a person to be quite familiar with the person on which it is being used. And it requires some thought. The longer a child lives with his or her parents, the better the parents are understood and the older and smarter the child becomes. Knowing the parents better, and growing wiser with the years, older children are more effective in identifying the circumstances that will affect the different kinds of parental decisions they want to influence.

As the years pass, children come to identify those soft spots we parents are sensitive to. They learn such things as:

"Father gives in more when my friends are around."

"Mother gives in when I cry."

"Both my parents are sensitive to my threats to run away."

"Both my parents get concerned when I say they don't love me."

"Mother will do almost anything to keep dad from finding out what she did to the car last spring."

"Father will do almost anything to keep Mom from finding out what he did."

"My parents don't want other people to think certain things about them."

"Dad always gives in when I ask while he is busy dealing with someone else."

"Mother is more agreeable when she is in a good mood.

Such items of information are parent soft spots. They are weak links in our armor which are often exploited by the manipulative child. The soft spots a parent can have are almost limitless, so all of them cannot be identified here. The point is that all of us *have* soft spots, and our children can and do learn to use them to influence our decisions.

The idea of our children doing this to us should not be alarming. We use such tactics on each other, don't we? Husbands use this approach on wives. Wives use it on husbands. And we all use it on our friends at one time or another. The tendency for our children to do it is natural. Being a natural tendency, we should not blame them for doing it. We should, however, make a positive effort to insure such approaches do not pay off for our children. When the incompatible approach does not work on a parent, the child will quit using it.

## TYPES OF PARENTS SUSCEPTIBLE TO INCOMPATIBLE RESPONSE TACTICS

There are several reasons the incompatible response approach is so commonly used. Because it is such a natural tactic all people are susceptible to it. Every person has soft spots which can be exploited by others. No matter what your age, where you live, what your nationality is, or what your socioeconomic status in life is, you have soft spots. And there are dozens of ways soft spots can be exploited.

Although every parent is susceptible to this approach, there are certain types of parents more susceptible than others. Parents in a hurry are particularly vulnerable to this tactic. When you are on the go, you are less prone to sit down and evaluate the choices placed before you. Children easily recognize this and may be quick to capitalize on it. Parents stongly concerned about being fair with their children are more susceptible. Concern for being fair often breeds parents who are more considerate of another person's point of view. Parents trying to be fair are victimized with this approach more than parents who exert stronger authoritarian figures in their family.

Natural parents, foster parents, divorced parents, adoptive parents, single parents; all are susceptible in some degree to this strategy. Of the three strategies mentioned that children employ, this is perhaps the easiest one for parents to cope with. Chapter nine discusses alternative tactics that parents can successfully use to cope with children who use this type of strategy. Chapter nine also explains how you can use this approach to your advantage.

# 6
# Tactics Used on Psychologists and Social Workers

## USING SOCIETY AGAINST THE PARENT

Before the reader gets the idea that parents are the only victims of manipulative children, it is perhaps of benefit to point out that psychologists, social workers, and the juvenile court system are not immune to being manipulated. Although we professionals in child care are more successful in dealing with child-rearing problems we can by no means claim perfection. In fact, some of the things manipulative children have done to us professionals would make even the most abused parent take heart.

Many manipulative young members of society have been successful in using society against the parent. This chapter includes true case situations where teenagers have fooled social workers into helping them succeed against their parents. Individuals have been successful in getting overzealous psychologists to help them by overstepping their professional bounds. And there have been numerous cases where teenagers have been successful in getting many professionals (including social workers, psychologists, and juvenile court officers) fighting each other as they go on their merry way.

This last type of situation is well illustrated by a recent incident close to my own home town. In 1978 two sixteen-year-old boys with a long history of manipulating their parents and taking advantage of most other people they came in contact with, found themselves in a situation where they could not only take advantage of some weaknesses in society, but also successfully propagate a major confrontation between professional people with different philosophies on childrearing. Although the parents of both boys wanted them enrolled in a private school designed to help such young men, the boys succeeded in getting a civil liberties group to file suit against the school, thereby allowing the boys to be placed in less controlled settings where they could violate other peoples' rights.

Karl was sixteen years old when the courts in his state decided to send him to a private residential school. He was a head-strong boy who became quite physical and hard to handle when he wanted his way. He showed little self-control and broke into private homes on different occasions to take what he wanted. In the spring of 1978 he was sent to the school geared to help parents remodel teenagers who take advantage of other members of society.

In August, 1978, Eddie was enrolled in the school. Eddie's mother was divorced, and even though Eddie was not as difficult to handle as Karl, Eddie's mother realized she needed to get help if Eddie was to become a responsible adult. Eddie, like Karl, was heading down the road to juvenile delinquency. His mother hoped the school would provide the guidance, discipline, and encouragement Eddie needed to finish his high school requirements so he could join the armed forces when he came of age.

Two weeks after Eddie and Karl met they ran away from the school. Within twenty-four hours both were picked up by the police and taken to the local office of the State Division of Social Services. At the office the two were interviewed by Joan, a social worker. Telling some hard-luck stories, they convinced Joan they were misunderstood by their parents and mistreated at the school. Taken in by the two young men, Joan contacted a local civil liberties group who leaped at the chance to legally represent the boys against the school. Ms. Adams, the president of the local chapter of the civil liberties group, filed a complaint against the school charging the school with violating the rights of the two boys by opening their mail while looking for drugs and putting the boys in "time out" rooms when they acted out. Ms. Adams petitioned the juvenile court not to return the boys to the school which the parents had chosen for them. Feeling she was a better judge of what the boys needed, Ms. Adams argued for the boys to be placed in foster homes. In response to her requests, the Division of Social Services placed the boys in a minimum security detention home.

During the first night at the detention home, the boys escaped, stole a car, and sped away. They broke into private homes and stole a variety of items including guns. Over the next few months they went on a minicrime spree which took them to Las Vegas, Los Angeles, and up through California to San Francisco. They were later returned to Salt Lake City were Ms. Adams' request to put them in foster homes was honored. They ran away from the foster homes several times. During these stays in foster homes Karl attacked a teacher who dared to verbally reprimand him for not doing his schoolwork. The teacher was seriously injured.

In court, Ms. Adams argued that the school physically abused the boys and had one boy testify that Mr. Davis, one of the owners of the school, had not only hit him, but kneed him in the face. While the boy's story that he had earlier recounted to Ms. Adams convinced her of physical brutality, the cross-examination revealed a somewhat different picture. It seems that Mr. Davis encountered the boy and a friend as they were beating up a school attendant. The two young men had lured the attendant into their bedroom on some pretext, knocked him down, then were choking him while he was on the floor. Mr. Davis quickly shoved and kneed the boy who had a strangle hold on the blue-faced attendant.

Eddie's mother was subpoenaed to testify on the case. During her testimony, she expressed strong dismay that her son had not been allowed to stay in the school. She commented that the court battle had taken two years. Now her son was eighteen years old and had an even bigger police record. It was too late now to help straighten him out. "What am I supposed to do now with my son?" she asked the court.

The jury acquitted the school of any wrongdoing, but there were more negative results from the case. The school decided to reduce the number of such boys in their program. Although the juvenile courts have now referred several such unmanageable boys in trouble with the law, the school has recently declined to take them in.

While the jury acquitted the school of any violations, the judge in that case ordered that the staff quit opening mail, restrict any discipline procedures which resulted in aggressive boys in "time out" rooms, and to no longer use lie detectors with the boys. "Such procedural restrictions make it much more difficult to help some of our boys," said the director of the school. Opening mail not only helps us stop drug and pornographic traffic into the school, but it also helps us stop some of these fellows from getting outside help to run away. On the run, of course, they could rob and pillage other members of society. The lie detector was used as a diagnostic tool to help us discern whether a boy was being helped to deal with others without resorting to lying and expressing the benefits of a reputation of honesty. Once these aids were no longer available to us, we realized we could no longer control such boys or assure the safety of the less physical young men at our school, so we will no longer accept such cases."

"With facilities such as yours no longer accepting such hard-to-handle boys, where do you feel the courts will now place them?" I asked the director.

"They must put them in a more prisonlike facility or place them in less controllable foster home settings," was his reply. "And I'll bet more of them end up in foster homes that cannot provide the exceptional controls they need."

While the two boys played an integral part in producing the court case, they cannot receive all the credit for what happened. Their main concern was not to successfully prosecute the school. They showed no strong interest in improving the social system they found themselves in; they were simply interested in manipulating the system. They realized the school had the ability to watch them closely from then on and not allow them to sneak out of the school and rob homes. Being returned to a minimum security home was their main desire. Upon getting what they wanted they immediately stole a car and went on their way, leaving the civil liberties group with court action pending against the school, but no plaintiffs with which to prosecute the case. They had successfully manipulated concerned members of society and left them holding the bag.

### The Social Worker as a Pawn

Social workers have become an integral part of mental health programs. Among other things, they are caseworkers who work as a liason between foster parents and state social service divisions. They help in the juvenile court system by working with children who have gotten in trouble with the law. Their case loads are generally so large that they can spend little more than an hour or two a week helping each child and the child's family. Because of this, most of their time is spent talking to their cases. With so little time social workers are often vulnerable to making wrong decisions. Children can become good actors. And they often put on airs necessary to manipulate the social worker.

One such case of manipulating a caseworker involved a young social worker who was working with some foster parents who had a twelve-year-old hyperactive boy who talked almost continuously to his foster mother. He had been placed in three different foster homes, and both of the first two finally had social services come pick him up because he was so persistent at trying to get his way and liked to physically intimidate younger children in the families.

He had been in the third foster home for three months when the social worker was first assigned to work with the boy. She faithfully visited the family, talking to both the boy and foster parents on each visit. While the foster parents showed no desire to give up on working with Brian, they did report that he was an excessive talker who tried their patience on many occasions. Julie, the social worker, enjoyed her talks with Brian and felt his problem might be that none of the families had given Brian the attention and understanding he needed.

Around Christmas time the foster parents, the Bensons, planned on going to California for two weeks before school was out. Because states and not foster parents are legal guardians of foster children, foster children are often not legally allowed to leave the state they are in. In such situations the foster child is usually put in a special group home until the foster family returns. Instead of placing Brian in a special group home, Julie asked that Brian be placed with her and her husband for the two weeks. Julie believed she could make great strides with Brian during that time. She made the mistake of telling the foster parents this as the Bensons dropped Brian off at her home on their way out of town.

Upon their return the Bensons stopped to pick Brian up. Brian seemed none the worse for wear as he jumped in the car, but Julie was visually much more quiet and reserved as she talked briefly to the Bensons. When Mrs. Benson asked how it went, Julie gave the short reply, "We made some progress." During Julie's next visit the truth came out as Mrs. Benson asked about a water incident Brian had mentioned. It seems as though no matter how much time Julie spent with Brian, it did not quench his tendency to be persistent and ask questions. He talked to Julie as she made breakfast; he talked to her while she washed the dishes. He talked all the way to school, and continued on the return trip. He talked to Julie's husband while he read the paper, and repeatedly interrupted television programs with his questions. Each night he responded to their request for him to go to bed by explaining he always stayed up until he got tired because he could not sleep without being tired first.

After ten days Julie became frustrated with Brian's lack of response to her attempts to reduce his talking. Julie and her husband were beginning to get a true picture of what being around Brian was like. The water incident had occurred on Tuesday when Brian brought home a gold-looking necklace which had a butterfly made out of thin gold wire. Brian informed Julie that his teacher had told him to take the necklace home and solder on one wire wing which had broken off. On the journey home he asked Julie many questions such as whether she thought it was real gold, and what she meant by gold plating. Somehow the issue of 14 karat gold came up and he wanted to know what karat meant. Later that afternoon Brian tried to get Julie's husband to solder the wing on because his teacher had said it had to be done the next day. Julie's husband did not respond to his request, so Brian went rummaging through the home workshop. He picked out a large soldering gun and some solder and began doing it himself. He was stopped by Julie's husband who said such soldering work required a special jeweler's soldering gun and silver solder which he did not have. Brian was told it would have to be taken to a jeweler, at which time he asked where the closest jeweler was and when they could go get it done. Later that evening while doing the dishes, Julie became so frustrated at Brian's continuing questions and comments about the necklace that without thinking she reflexively took the pot she was cleaning and poured the water over Brian's head.

Mrs. Benson smiled as Julie embarrassingly recounted the incident. Julie had learned something we in the childrearing profession often forget. *Don't give advice until you have stood in the other person's shoes.* Many parents get upset at teachers, principals, social workers, and psychologists who tell them what needs to be done with their child when the advice giver appears to have little understanding as to what their problem is really like in the daily trenches. Mrs. Benson had the satisfaction few parents have of letting the therapist stand in her shoes for a while.

When social workers develop an incorrect picture of what is going on, children often capitalize on the situation. Myrna was a social worker in a town of thirty thousand people nestled in the Rocky Mountains. She was new in town, and one of her first assignments was to go to the county detention center where a fourteen-year-old girl was being held after running away from her parents who were living in the same city. About ten o'clock in the evening Myrna talked to the tearful girl as she recounted how her parents were always mad at her, no matter what she did. The next day Myrna set up a meeting with Donna, Donna's parents and the arresting policeman. During the meeting, when the conversation drifted toward the idea that Donna, rather than her parents, was at fault, Donna would get up and walk out of the room. Over the next three weeks the same results occurred. In private meetings with Myrna, Donna would talk about her parents and said she found it hard to talk with them around.

It was eventually decided that Donna needed to be placed in a foster home. She was brought to my home where she began to try to work the system. She intentionally set out to distort the picture for her parents, for Myrna, for her new social worker that visited her at my home, and for myself. She tried to produce dissension by telling little untruths to each of the parties involved. To her parents she said Ed, her new social worker, implied her parents were insensitive. To Ed she said Myrna had told her several things suggesting he was old-fashioned in his ideas. Mixing half statements that each person actually had said with falsehoods she made up, she soon created a situation where all parties became suspicious of the others.

To stop the problem, I called a meeting with all persons concerned. As Ed, Myrna, Donna, her mother, and I met together, we unraveled the falsehoods Donna had been planting. We also discussed Donna's misdoings, and what was to be done in the future.

After the two-hour meeting, Donna's mother and Myrna came to me and said "How did you do that?"

"Do what?" I replied.

"Donna has never sat through a meeting about her problem," Myrna said."She always gets up and leaves. Yet she sat there and not only admitted what she did, but offered suggestions about what should be done to correct the problem."

"That's right," her mother added. "How did you get her to sit there and not leave?"

"She just knew what would happen if she tried to leave," I replied. "The children here soon learn such tantrum behavior is not rewarded. We have weekly family council meetings where all the children are expected to participate. If one child is taking advantage of another, the problem is discussed in front of both parties. The kids soon learn it is better to stay and participate in decisions than leave the decision of punishment for wrongdoing up to the rest of the family."

Donna learned to manipulate social workers and her parents by not allowing them to directly confront her with false statements she made. The parents and social workers were manipulated by Donna because of their honest sensitivity of not wanting to hurt her feelings. Getting upset and acting hurt when they blamed her or brought up things she supposedly had said, Donna would masterfully manipulate the situation. Because of the work load, the social worker did not have time to spot and solve the problem as I did. Donna had learned to systematically take advantage of social workers that tried to help her.

## The Psychologist as a Pawn

Manipulative children use psychologists and psychiatrists as pawns, as parents and social workers are used. I could recount a variety of cases where psychologists were the victims of manipulative children, in situations like the social workers were. There is a problem, however, that psycholgists are often susceptible to that parents seldom realize. That problem deals with psychological testing. One of the main functions of psychologists is to administer psychological tests. Parents want to know how bright their children are. School teachers want mental handicaps their students have identified through psychological testing, and oftentimes psychologists are called upon to give psychological tests to individuals convicted of crimes to determine whether they knew what they were doing.

In 1964, Dr. Jeffry studied the use of psychologists in criminal cases to determine the sanity of criminals. One of the cases he reviewed dealt with a boy named Kent who had committed housebreakings, robberies, and rapes. Kent's lawyer was interested in freeing his client on the grounds that Kent was not responsible for his actions. The following are excerpts of the testimony of three psychologists.

Psychologist A testified that she had administered the following tests to Kent: the Wechsler Memory Scale, the Bender-Gestalt, the Rorschach, the Thematic Apperception Test, the House-Tree-Person Test, and the Szondi Test. From this evidence, she diagnosed the defendant as schizophrenic, chronic undifferentiated type, characterized by abnormal thoughts, difficulty with emotional control, deficient in common-sense judgment, and lacking in close relationships with other people. She considered these as indicative of psychosis and that the crimes of housebreaking, robbery, and rape, of which the defendant was accused, were products of the mental disease. The cross-examination of the psychologist went as follows [1]:

**Q:** What did the House-Tree-Person Test reveal?
**A:** The major finding was a feeling of withdrawal, running away from reality, feelings of rejection by women.

---

[1] From Jeffry [1964, pp. 838–843]. Copyright 1964 by The American Psychological Association. Reprinted by permission.

**Q:** And the results of the Szondi?

**A:** This showed a passive, depressed person who withdrew from the world of reality, with an inability to relate to others.

**Q:** Wasn't the Szondi Test made up around 1900, or the early 1900 period? And wasn't it made up of a number of pictures of Europeans who were acutely psychotic?

**A:** Yes, that is true.

**Q:** And this tells you something about his personality?

**A:** Yes, you can tell something about the person from his responses to the photos.

**Q:** And the House-Tree-Person Test—you handed the defendant, Kent, a pencil and a blank piece of paper. Is that right, Doctor?

**A:** That is correct.

**Q:** And you asked him to draw a house?

**A:** Yes.

**Q:** And what did this tell you about Kent?

**A:** The absence of a door and the bars on the windows indicated he saw the house as a jail, not a home. Also, you will notice it is a side view of the house; he was making it inaccessible.

**Q:** Isn't it normal to draw a side view of a house? You didn't ask him to draw a front view, did you?

**A:** No.

**Q:** And those bars on the window—could they have been Venetian blinds and not bars? Who called them bars, you or Kent?

**A:** I did.

**Q:** Did you ask him what they were?

**A:** No.

**Q:** What else did the drawing reveal about Kent?

**A:** The line in front of the house runs from left to right. This indicates a need for security.

**Q:** This line indicates insecurity! Could it also indicate the contour of the landscape, like a lawn or something?

**A:** This is not the interpretation I gave it.

**Q:** And the chimney—what does it indicate?

**A:** You will notice the chimney is dark. This indicates disturbed sexual feelings. The smoke indicates inner daydreaming.

**Q:** Did I understand you correctly? Did you say dark chimneys indicate disturbed sex feelings?

**A:** Yes.

**Q:** You then asked Kent to draw a tree. Why?

**A:** We have discovered that a person often expresses feelings about himself that are on a subconscious level when he draws a tree.

**Q:** And what does this drawing indicate about Kent's personality?

**A:** The defendant said it was a sequoia, fifteen hundred years old, and that it was diseased. This indicates a feeling of self-depreciation. Also, the tree has no leaves and it leans to the left. This indicates a lack of contact with the outside world—the absence of leaves.

**Q:** Don't trees lose their leaves in winter Doctor? If you look out the window now, in Washington, do you see leaves on the trees? Perhaps the defendant was drawing a picture of a tree without leaves, as they appear in the winter.

**A:** The important thing is, however, why did the defendant select this particular tree. He was stripped of leaves, of emotions.

**Q:** You then asked him to draw a person?

**A:** Yes.

**Q:** And he drew this picture of a male?

**A:** Yes.

**Q:** And what does this drawing indicate about Kent?

**A:** The man appears to be running. This indicates anxiety, agitation. He is running, you will notice, to the left. This indicates running away from the environment. If he had been running to the right this would indicate entering the environment.

**Q:** How about the hands?

**A:** The sharp fingers may indicate hostility.

**Q:** Anything else?

**A:** The head and the body appear to be separated by a dark collar, and the neck is long. This indicates a split between intellect and emotion. The dark hair, dark tie, dark shoes, and the dark buckle indicate anxiety about sexual problems.

**Q:** You then asked Kent to draw a person of the opposite sex. What did this picture indicate?

**A:** The dark piercing eyes indicated a feeling of rejection by women, hostility toward women.

**Q:** Are you familiar with the occasion upon which a Veterans' Administration psychologist gave this House-Tree-Person Test to fifty psychotics, and then gave fifty normal subjects the same test, and then a group of psychologists rated them?

**A:** No, I am not familiar with that research.

Psychologist B testified that he administered the Wechsler-Bellevue, the Graham Kendall, the Rorschach, and the Symonds Picture Story

Tests. He also testified that he had diagnosed the defendant as schizophrenic, undifferentiated type, and that mental illness had produced the alleged crimes. The cross-examination went as follows:

**Q:** Did you administer the Szondi Test Doctor?

**A:** No, I don't happen to think much of it. The tests assume a schizophrenic looks a certain way, and we have evidence this isn't so.

**Q:** What responses did you receive from Kent on the Rorschach, the ink blot test?

**A:** Wolf, butterfly, vagina, pelvis, bats, buttocks, etc.

**Q:** And from this you concluded the defendant was schizophrenic?

**A:** Yes, that and other things.

**Q:** You gave him the Wechsler Adult Scale?

**A:** Yes.

**Q:** On the word-information part of the test, the word "temperature" appears. What question did you ask the defendant?

**A:** At what temperature does water boil?

**Q:** You gave him a zero. Why?

**A:** Because he answered 190 degrees and that is the wrong answer. The right answer is 212 degrees F.

**Q:** What question did you ask about the Iliad?

**A:** I am not sure; I believe I asked him to identify the Iliad or who wrote the Iliad.

**Q:** And he answered "Aristotle?"

**A:** Yes.

**Q:** And you scored him zero?

**A:** That's correct.

**Q:** Now you asked the defendant to define blood vessels, did you not?

**A:** Yes.

**Q:** And his answer was capillaries and veins. You scored him zero. Why? Aren't capillaries and veins blood vessels?

**A:** I don't know. The norms don't consider the answer acceptable.

A third psychologist testified he saw the subject once at jail or the receiving home for an hour and a half; that he administered the Rorschach and started the Human Figure Drawing Test. The test was interrupted when the defendant's father was announced, and Kent became very upset and highly emotional.

He diagnosed the defendant as schizophrenic, undifferentiated type. He thought productivity existed: that is, the schizophrenia produced the housebreakings, robberies, and rapes. The test showed severe thinking disturbance, an inability to control impulses, and disturbed sexual feelings. His cross-examination went as follows:

**Q:** Why did you see the defendant, Kent?
**A:** Because of a call from Mr. Arens.
**Q:** Are you a member of the Washington School of Psychiatry?
**A:** No.
**Q:** The defendant made one drawing for you, right Doctor?
**A:** Yes, that is right.
**Q:** After the announced arrival of his father?
**A:** Yes.
**Q:** Do you use the House-Tree-Person Test?
**A:** Never.
**Q:** Does it have validity?
**A:** Yes.
**Q:** You do use the Szondi?
**A:** Five or six times.
**Q:** When did you stop using it?
**A:** At the fifth administration, about nine years ago.
**Q:** What does this drawing that Kent made for another psychologist indicate to you?
**A:** The transparency of the picture—that is, seeing through the figure to something beneath—suggests pathology.
**Q:** Do you usually diagnose on the basis of one Rorschach administered twice within an hour?
**A:** Frequently.
**Q:** What else in the drawing is significant psychologically?
**A:** The irregularity or sketchiness of the lines may suggest tension and anxiety. The attention paid to details—to the belt, bowtie, and pockets—indicates a little-boy-like quality about the defendant.
**Q:** Is it significant that the figure is running left, and not to the right?
**A:** To some people, yes. I don't place any significance on it.

Note that the testimony of the psychologists is somewhat conflicting. They disagree as to what the value of different tests are. One psychologist saw Kent only once for an hour and a half and was willing to testify that Kent was mentally unbalanced. These three psychologists do not represent psychology as a profession, for the profession's ethics expects psychologists to use tests properly. No test or portion of a test tells a psychologist exactly what a person is like. Lines of contour, types of houses, actions of people drawn, may vaguely suggest but *never* prove an individual has certain tendencies. Psychological test results must be weighed carefully along with interviews and background research on an individual. When psychologists lower their evaluative standards by doing quick evaluations, they can become pawns to vested interest groups around them.

## FINDING WEAK LINKS IN OUR ARMOR

From the previous cases cited in this chapter, it should be apparent that parents are not the only victims of manipulative children. Psychologists, psychiatrists, and social workers can be manipulated also. While we professionals have a great deal more schooling on the subject of childrearing, we have weak links in our armor that children often learn to manipulate to their advantage.

# 7
# The Natural Method of Parenting

## IF THEY CAN DO IT, WE CAN DO IT

One evening a group of local foster parents were having a meeting to compare notes as to what problems and solutions each had for the children in their care. The major portion of the meeting was taken up by each of the foster parents recounting incidents where their children had successfully manipulated them. One parent told of a fourteen-year-old foster child who repeatedly stole money from the other children, and how their many attempts to catch him at it failed. Another parent told how one of their children was a master at starting a fight between other children in the family. She could accomplish this without the other children realizing they both had been baited into a fight. The girl starting the fight would take sides in the argument; then later remind the person she sided with that she had been her friend. This would net the girl special favors in return.

A new foster parent sat quietly throughout the meeting listening intently to what was being said. She listened as I pointed out to the parents that these children had learned to manipulate us, yet they had no special education or training to develop these skills.

"During the natural course of their life they have picked up their ability to effectively manipulate their parents," I remarked.

"Well if they can do it, we can do it," the young lady blurted out with a boldness that surprised even herself. Feeling somewhat uneasy about making such a statement, the woman related how and why she and her husband became foster parents. Not being successful at starting a family of their own they decided to take in foster children. Taking in two children in sixth and eighth grade they soon found themselves unable to cope with the problems these two boys brought into their home. While this couple was far from a total failure, they soon began to question their own abilities to provide what the boys needed. They seriously wondered whether they had the necessary psychological training to properly mold and manipulate the children to be successful members of society. In fact her attendance at our meeting was her last stop before quitting the foster care program.

"Now that I realize my kids do not have any special training, yet successfully manipulate me, it is apparent that all I need is what I already have available. I just have to learn to use it better than the children do," she concluded. Her words, "If they can do it, we can do it," stuck with me because they are so true. Many parents draw the same conclusions this mother did. Many of us begin to doubt our ability. We often tell ourselves that we perhaps lack what it takes to deal effectively with our children as they seem to get the upper hand. This feeling of inadequacy is somewhat the result of psychological jargon.

> "The first duty of a parent is to lay a proper emotional foundation for the child."
> "Establish a working rapport with your child."
> "In a civilized world we should deal with our child on a higher mental plane."
> "A well-rounded child comes from an understanding parent."

These kinds of statements are made repeatedly by psychologists. They often cause insecurity in parents for they do not understand exactly what we mean by such comments, and if they do not know what the phrases mean, how can they possibly accomplish what they are told needs to be done? This dilemma leaves them with feelings of inadequacy. These feelings leave the parent asking, "How can I mold my child if I cannot do those things childrearing experts say are necessary?"

The answer to the previous questions is *You do not have to understand those phrases to effectively raise your child.* In the first place no two psychologists will give you the exact same definition of "emotional foundation," "rapport," "higher mental plane," or even the term "understanding." Such terms are couched with personal meanings to such an extent that the psychologist using the term may be able to effectively deal with children through these phrases; but the terms help the parent little. In the second place (and most importantly) many children (and some parents) who have never heard such phrases are very effective at manipulating other people. They do not know how to develop a proper emotional foundation, or deal on some higher mental plane. They simply work with what Mother Nature provides. They develop the knowlege of what to say to put mother in a good mood so they can use the car. They develop the ability to manipulate mother so she gives them a cookie or something else they want. They pick up the skill of winning arguments. They learn what to do to get mother to do the dishes instead of them. They learn what it takes to get money from father. They learn to manipulate teachers into giving a higher grade. They learn how to get more with less effort. And they do it without talking to one psychiatrist or psychologist!

And what is wrong with the skills they develop? All the things just mentioned can be good things to know how to do. Learning how to put someone in a good mood is not bad. Learning how and what to say to people so they will do things for you is not bad. Learning ways to get people to give you money is not bad. One of the main problems we parents have is thinking the idea of manipulating is inherently bad. Manipulation is nothing more than the skillful arrangement of conditions to get someone to do something. Teachers should be skillfully arranging conditions at school so children learn their academic subjects. Parents should skillfully arrange conditions so children become contributors rather than freeloaders on society. Manipulation can produce many good results. The problem is simply that children often learn to use effective manipulatory techniques to take advantage of parents and others. Skills for manipulating parents may be, and usually are, good skills for children to learn to later successfully live their lives. It's mainly how the child uses the manipulation that concerns us with problem children.

Once we parents acknowledge strategies for manipulation are not inherently bad, it is easier to realize that our world's success is based on the proper application of many of the same manipulative techniques children use on us. If they can learn to effectively use valuable psychologically based manipulative tactics, then we parents can learn to use these same manipulative tactics for the betterment of our parent-child relationships without necessarily addressing the often confusing ideas about proper emotional foundation, higher mental planes, and the like.

After realizing manipulation is an integral part of human living, and that many children learn to become effective manipulators, it is not hard to realize that Mother Nature has endowed our system of life with a way for us to effectively manipulate each other (be it for good or bad intent) that is so beautifully simple that even young children can grasp the principles involved. And once we have realized this, the statement "If they can do it, we can do it" takes on greater meaning. It should help us appreciate that not only is it possible for us to learn to use some rather simple and valuable manipulative skills, but also that these skills are as effective, if not more effective, than psychological strategies which are based on some rather intellectual sounding words, phrases, and philosophies of learned men. If our children can do it, we parents can also.

## DOING WHAT COMES NATURALLY

Suppose a parent is sitting at a table which has a spoon on it. There are at least two ways to lift that spoon off the table. First the parent can use the "natural method" of taking his or her hand, grasping the spoon, then lifting it off the table. A second way, a way which most would call an unnatural or possibly "supernatural method" is to use some form of levitation where the parent mentally wills the spoon to lift from the table. Now most of us have seen such feats of levitation, at least on television, and realize, although we do not understand how, such things are possible. We all would probably admit that the natural method of lifting the spoon accomplishes the task as well (though less sensationally) as the higher mental plane approach of levitation. We also realize that most of us would use the natural method, seeing it is quite unlikely we have the ability or could master the ability to levitate.

This example of lifting the spoon has many similarities to childrearing. With childrearing there are also at least two ways to do it. One is based on what some refer to as the psychological approach, whereas the other is based on the more natural (and less exciting) approach of dealing with each other's behaviors. With the psychological approach, the psychologist tries to get inside the mind of the child and figure out what the child meant by what he did. Instead of taking the actions of the child at face value, the psychologist searches for the hidden meaning of the act. "Did the child throw the tantrum because he was just mad; or because he has a strong feeling of psychological rejection?"

Some psychologists (and even some parents) may be effective in dealing with children using this approach. On the other hand, many psychologists and parents use the more natural approach that children use of responding to exactly what was said or done without looking for hidden meaning. If a child steals, the psychologist (using the natural approach) arranges conditions so the child learns not to steal rather than viewing stealing as a symptom of some more complicated psychological problem. While trained psychologists claim success using either of the two approaches, the proportion of parents who can effectively use the psychological approach is about as large as the proportion of parents who have the ability to levitate spoons. And discovering that the psychological approach shows *no* superiority over the more natural approach in dealing with childrearing, this book focuses on the natural approach Mother Nature endowed us with.

Over the next few chapters I shall discuss an approach to parenting that can be successfully implemented by any parent (or child for that matter). It is what I refer to as a *natural approach to parenting* because its success does not require the parent to have any special training over and above the training Mother Nature has given parents through everyday experiences. The natural parenting approach is based on identifying the natural strategies even children can learn through experience to manipulate their parents. This book takes those natural ingredients of life and explains how parents can employ them to mold and manipulate their children in ways that make the parent and child more happy and successful in life.

One of the first things to consider when taking the natural approach to childrearing is those natural conditions which should exist in the home. Before the parents set out to change the problem behaviors in one of their children, they should realize that problems do not come from thin air. They are generally the result of something present in the home setting. Parents may successfully employ some of the manipulative tactics explained in Chapters Eight and Nine only to find the problem behaviors returning some time later. Most psychologists working with state Social Services have been successful in changing the problem behavior in teenagers, only to see the remodeled child later return to his or her old ways after returning to their families. A good example of this was the case of Willie.

Willie was an eight-year-old boy who was taken from his mother because of parental neglect. Willie lived alone with his mom, who social services was quite sure was involved in prostitution. She was up most hours of the night, had many different men to her apartment in the evenings (with Willie present), and usually slept until one or two in the afternoon. Willie had to make his own meals and shoulder the responsibility of getting himself to school (which he did not do most of the time). At school he was a poor student, and forever in trouble. He was placed in a foster home for one year, during which time he became a model student in school and a mannerly young man. The mother resisted all efforts of social workers to help her change her lifestyle. In accordance with Utah state law, which in essence says a child whose problems have been corrected must be returned to the parents, Willie was returned to his mother. In less than six months Willie was his old self again. The foster parents, who had come to love Willie like their own, were heartbroken when they found out what had happened.

While most of we parents have not let the atmosphere in our home become as bad as what Willie had to live with, it is often the case that some undesirable condition or situation has been allowed to develop in our homes which disrupt Mother Nature's plans for proper development. Sometimes as parents, we unknowingly contribute to the development of conditions in our homes which can effectively thwart honest attempts to properly raise our children. We may let certain family habits develop that can undermine our parental ability to effectively deal with child behavior problems.

Working with problem children, I have identified what I feel are five characteristics found in families with no serious behavior problems in their children. These characteristics are accountability, responsibility, sensitivity, actions rather than words, and family unity. On the other side of the same coin, I find children who create problems for their parents generally have a poor sense of accountability for their actions, have few, if any, responsibilities in their families, have parents who infrequently express their true feelings of appreciation or disappointment to their children, have parents who often do not do what they say they will do, and do not feel a part of the family. These are the major goals Carol and I focus on so we can be successful in remodeling the many problem children we take into our home.

### Accountability

One evening Carol and I were returning from the circus with our car loaded with the family. All the children were excited because we sat on the front row and the animals in the grand procession passed within two or three feet of us. (This was something I did not appreciate when the elephants passed by.) The children were busy chattering as we drove along, when suddenly Shawn's helium-filled balloon that was tied to his wrist, popped. While playing around, Kit had accidentally popped Shawn's balloon. He did not mean for it to happen, but it did.

"O.K. Kit," I said. "You now have to give Shawn your balloon." This he tearfully did.

Now it would have been easy for me to have said "That's O.K. I'll get Shawn another balloon," but what would Kit have learned from the experience? He would have learned that he was not accountable for his actions. His tendency to be careless and rambunctious would have increased, because there would be no reason to be careful.

Experiences like these are what try parents' souls. Watching a four-year-old boy obey his father and tearfully give up his balloon without complaining, was almost more than I could take. I thought of nothing else all the way home. Early the next morning I took Kit aside and told him how proud I was of him for doing what needed to be done. We talked for a while about what had happened and why it was the right thing for him to give his balloon to Shawn. We talked about the fact that Kit did not mean to do it, but his actions still resulted in Shawn losing his balloon.

While my son and I spent an unpleasant night, my consolation came from knowing the more painful experiences Kit could have later in life if he did not learn early to be accountable for his actions. Almost without exception, the one thing most problem children have in common is a lack of feeling accountable for what they do. Most of the problem foster children that come to our home have come from environments where they did not have to consistently experience the consequences of their actions. People around them made allowances for their actions so they did not have to reap the unpleasantness of what they did.

> "Terry really did not mean to hurt the neighbor boy."
> "It wasn't Wendy's fault she did not turn her assignment in. She was upset all week."
> "I can't help myself when I get angry."
> "He should not have made me mad, then I would not have hit him."
> "The police are picking on my son."
> "My teacher gave me a bad grade because she hates me."
> "I'll overlook what you did. I know you really did not mean it."
> "If I try to reprimand him this time, people will be watching."

Mother Nature has intentionally programed our life with pleasant and unpleasant experiences. It is a natural part of life that each of us during our lifetime overstep our bounds and interfere with the rights of others. In this manner we identify what our boundaries are. When we are young, the improper things we do to others are minor incidents. Mother Nature's plan includes those being offended to react so the child causing a problem experiences something unpleasant. In this way we naturally learn to be accountable for what we do. However, when parents, teachers, and friends make allowances for such children, they do not learn to be accountable for the little things they do wrong, and little wrong actions lead to bigger wrong actions. And why not? They have not learned that they are wrong.

In other places in this book I have told about a young infant whose mother always rushed to catch her young son before he crawled off the edge of the bed or table. She always caught him from falling off the couch. One day while changing his diaper on the patio table she left him to answer the phone. In her absence, he crawled off the end of the table onto the cement patio; he now has brain damage. Unfortunately, he had not been allowed to learn to be accountable for his actions. Bumping his head or rolling off a low couch onto a rug could have been experiences that would have taught him to use caution in what he did.

Teaching accountability is one of the first lessons Carol and I work on when problem foster children join our family. "It is not my fault," "I can't help it," "Don't blame me" "I did not mean to do it" are all comments which fall on deaf ears in our home. If one child pulls a harmful practical joke on another, he or she is made accountable—even when they did not intend anything unpleasant to happen. Accountability is one of the first rules Mother Nature arranges for a child to learn in life. Hopefully we parents help rather than hinder her efforts. Accountability is possibly the most important lesson in life for success and happiness.

### Responsibility

> "I can't wait until I'm an adult and can do anything I want."
>
> "I hate being told what to do. I can't wait to get away from my parents."

Most parents hear these comments from their children at one time or another. And often we smile when our children say such things, because we know from experience that the freedom they long for does not come about as they expect it will. We, as parents, learned that freedom only comes through responsibility. We wanted children; now we are responsible for them. If we want a home of our own we must earn money and convince some bank we are responsible enough to borrow the rest of the money we need. If parents want to take three months and do what they want, they must accept the responsibility of providing the money necessary to do that or face the consequences.

Freedom of speech and action only come with accepting the responsibilities that go with such freedoms. An important aspect of our training to become adults is to learn to accept responsibilities. Society is a group of people who have learned to trade responsibilities. Policemen are willing to accept responsibility for controlling crime if we provide them money to buy food they do not have the time or desire to grow. The farmer is willing to grow the food if others will make cars, TVs, and toys. Each person accepting certain responsibilities not only gives himself some freedom, but freedom of choice for others also.

Children should be taught to accept responsibilities. Families are stronger when each person accepts certain responsibilities. Children need things to do. They need to learn the lessons of responsibility. One fourteen-year-old foster boy we took in would not keep his room clean. To correct the problem my wife cleaned his room for him but quit fixing his meals. "I only have so much time," she told him, "and if I clean your room I do not have time to fix your meals." It wasn't long until he learned the value of accepting the responsibility of cleaning his room.

In most homes there are a variety of responsibilities that can be given to children of all ages. Four- and five-year-olds can empty wastebaskets. Three- and four-year-olds can pick up toys and clothing strung around the house. Ten-year-olds can clean out cars, wash dishes, and clean windows. A good suggestion is for parents to post weekly duty rosters which outline the daily duties and responsibilities of each child. Be sure to set up pay offs for the children meeting their responsibilities. Giving weekly allowances for chores completed and letting children earn extra privileges (staying up later, going to friends' homes, getting to see an extra movie) are good consequences which can teach a child that accepting responsibility pays off.

There is an interesting byproduct of giving children responsibility. It reduces behavior problems. Psychological studies show that bickering, fighting, and many other disruptive behaviors are dramatically reduced when children have an hour or two of responsibilities each night in the home.

Responsibilities can also be used to directly reduce problem behaviors. One child constantly left his clothes, bike, and toys laying around. After constant nagging did not resolve the problem, his parents announced the family would have a sergeant-of-arms whose job was to make sure all the children kept their things picked up and put away. They put their slothful son in charge, and it worked. Given the responsibility to oversee others helped him improve his own conduct.

It is important that parents realize a child is training to become an adult. As he or she gets older they need to gradually learn to shoulder total responsibility for themselves. It is our duty to provide a gradual transition, from them depending on us, to really not needing us. We should not fight the teenager's desire for freedom, but gradually build up the responsibility needed for the child to cope with his or her freedoms.

### Sensitivity

One of the major mistakes parents make in childrearing is failure to express their feelings. Few things can upset the parent–child bond more than the parent failing to take a few seconds from each busy day and expressing sincere appreciation to their child for something they have done well or expressing mild displeasure when they do something wrong. (Usually we express more displeasure than appreciation, however.) These expressions of sensitivity to the child are road signs the child needs to navigate through daily crossroads where the choices are proper and improper actions.

The successful boss or job supervisor is the one who makes comments several times each day about what you are doing. Instead of waiting till the end of the year to tell you how poorly your yearly record is or to tell you how good you were, the successful boss gives sensitive feedback much more immediately and frequently. Lack of good quick feedback is the main culprit for failing businesses. The same is true for failing parents.

There are two unfortunate things that happen when parents fail to show daily appreciation. On the one hand, the child quits trying to get that feedback, gives up on waiting for parental attention, and seeks out others who will pay attention. On the other hand, the situation may cause the child to more clearly want the attention of the parent so he or she goes out and exhibits such bad behavior that the parent must take the time to express some feelings. Far too many teenagers get in trouble with the law just to get attention from their parents.

Ask your son to get you the paper, then thank him for doing it. Thank your child for cleaning up her room. Thank the older daughter for taking her younger sister with her to the store. And every once in a while back up those words of appreciation with good deeds yourself. Because that ten-year-old has done certain things right, let her stay up an hour later some night. Because he cleaned his room several times this week without being told, express appreciation with words followed by some treat. Carol and I make sure we take a few "seconds" each day with the problem teenagers we take in and express our appreciation for something they have done. In some instances we simply walk over to the teenager watching television and smilingly ruffle their hair or pat them on the shoulder to let them know we care. Over the years we have seen these small daily signs of sensitivity crack the exteriors of seemingly hardened teenagers in the same way Christian religions say the sound of Joshua's horn was able to break down the walls of Jericho in one of the stories in the Bible. Parents will simply be amazed at the changes that occur in their problem child after a few weeks or months of showing little daily signs of sensitivity and appreciation. In fact try it on your mate. You will like the results.

### Words with Action

One of the first things that shows up when working with problem children is they do not believe much of what they are told. A mother yells at her four-year-old not to play in his breakfast cereal, but he continues to do so. The twelve-year-old is told to come right home after school, but he does not. The mother tells the daughter how much she means to her, but never goes to the school plays the daughter is in. This problem of talking more than acting is one all parents have to some degree. If someone was able to sit parents down and replay on video all the times in the past week each of us has substituted words for actions, the parents would be unpleasantly surprised. Fortunately for most parents we follow through enough times that our children do not give up on us. Our children learn that at least some of the times we parents do what we say, so they continue to pay attention to what we say.

Without exception, every foster child we have taken in whose problems include not doing what their parents want has tested us during the first week to see if we do what we say. (Keep in mind some of the children we work with are child beating and suicidal cases whose problems and needs are different.) We have never had a child who did not do what they were told or acted impolitely during the first two days of being with us. They start out cooperative and easy to deal with. Invariably within the next five days things happen. They do something to find out if we do what we say. In some cases they fail to do their house chores (which they have already done at least two days). They may not get themselves up in time for school, or fail to clean their room. In some instances they start an argument to see what happens.

> "Do they follow through on promises they make to me?"
>
> "Are they just threatening, or do they mean it when they tell me I'll be disciplined if I do not stop this?"
>
> "Can I count on what they say or can I ignore their words?"

These are the kinds of questions problem children invariably have in their minds when they come. And it is the result of previous experiences with adults whose actions do not match their words.

Each of us knows someone who does the same thing to us. This person talks a lot but does little. He may tell me he can make money on a certain deal, but never does. He may say he will pay back borrowed money, but never does. Remember how frustrating it is to deal with people whose words you cannot believe. We have a tendency to treat people who do this to us the same way children with this problem treat parents. We either learn to let their comments go in one ear and out the other, or we learn to avoid dealing with these people. When our child does not seem to pay attention to what we say, perhaps that tells us something about ourselves as parents.

The solution to the problem of children who do not do what they are told is relatively straightforward. As parents, do not make promises you do not intend to keep. Do not make threats you do not intend to carry out. Although oftentimes we feel it is okay not to keep our word to our child, the consequences for such actions eventually seem to catch up with us.

## Family Unity

Most have heard the saying "No man is an island." Few realize how true this statement is and how important it is for proper child development. The fifth major cause of teenage deaths in this country is suicide. The number of violent crimes (robbing and killing even cooperative victims) committed by teenagers is more than doubling every five years. And one of the conditions in the home highly correlated with these figures is lack of family unity.

Each of us has that eternal seed of mankind within us. We are part of something much bigger than ourselves. With society's present emphasis on individuality and independence, we often fail to recognize the importance of making sure our children are able to satisfy their internal promptings to fulfill their identity through bonding with others. We all need to feel part of that bigger picture of life.

When families fail to provide that feeling, children seek out gangs and clubs. As they grow older they try to identify with social causes such as "banning the bomb," "stopping use of nuclear power," "the right for life." In many instances, they will sacrifice their lives for gangs and causes as seen in newspaper accounts of young people taking hostages and even threatening to blow themselves up with the hostages.

Feeling part of something bigger than oneself provides a security and increased sense of self-worth that is missing in the individual drawn toward suicide and acts of violence.

There are a variety of ways children can help sense a feeling of family unity. One of the main ways is to emphasize the family rather than the individuals in the family. Plan a family activity.

Discuss any problems or disagreements that have occurred within the family during the previous week. Emphasize the way each family member's duties around the home help strengthen each other. Let the children provide feedback to the parents as to whether they are too strict or permissive, require too much or too little, spend too much or too little time with the family. (Remember do not take all comments and criticisms at face value.) Guide and counsel the children through group discussion.

The key is to plan family meetings and activities that benefit the children. If your children hate such meetings and do not want to participate in family activities, it should tell the parent that such things are not rewarding to the child. Let the children help select family activities and let the family meetings be of value to all family members. Parents should govern family meetings with persuasion more than force.

## MAKING PARENTING FUN

Besides the five conditions just mentioned, there are a few less important but valuable things parents can do to help make parenting a more pleasant and joyful experience. All of these things require little additional time or effort from parents; yet the benefits a parent reaps from them can be quite large.

### Keep a Book of Remembrance

A common quip most people have heard is "If you want to get rid of unwanted company, start showing home movies." It is true that home movies are of much more interest to the family than they are to others. It is also true that there are few things that can excite children, including teenagers, more than seeing themselves in pictures and movies. Foster children who have become adults and move away enjoy looking at our old home movies they are in when they come to visit.

Couples of all ages find strength for their family by looking at old photos, diaries, and movies. Being able to look back at the good times often makes it easier for us to deal with current troubles. Journals and photo albums often help us get a better perspective of ourselves. If you keep a personal daily journal you will find that no other book will mean as much to you when you are older.

## Do Not Expect Too Much

A young executive friend of mine often talks about his mother and mother-in-law. When his mother comes over to visit he feels uncomfortable. His mother always has to be doing something—washing the dishes, vacuuming, and always, always talking about the future and what else he can become. His mother-in-law is a farmer's wife. When she visits she also pitches in. But unlike his own mother she enjoys doing things with her daughter and son-in-law. She acts contented as they all just sit around and chat.

"My mother is definitely not happy," he recounted to me one day. "Although her children are all happily married she cannot seem to enjoy us for what we are. It is as if she will not be happy unless we excel even more. Yet she has a doctor, lawyer, and schoolteacher for sons and sons-in-law. My mother-in-law seems to be satisfied with her children as they are. She looks perfectly content and happy at what we all have become."

This situation is one we parents often find ourselves in. Our son is not the star on his little league baseball team. Our daughter is not the best speller in her class. Parents should make efforts to help their child achieve, but still be able to appreciate and enjoy the child if he or she is not number one. Too often we fail to enjoy what our child is doing because we expect too much. We have the tendency to do the same thing with our jobs. Older parents often find their children have grown up and they have missed sharing certain experiences (a child's excitement at learning to ride a bike or making the team) because they were either working or they were expecting more than what the child did.

This idea of not expecting too much holds for ourselves as individuals also. We spend so much time working to get the promotion that we do not enjoy what we have. People can spend a lifetime planning to be financially sound so they can do what they want, only to find that they are now too old to do it. We also expect to always make the right decisions about our jobs and families. Remember Chapter Two discussed the point that parents have the right to make mistakes. It is part of life, so do not be too hard on yourself when you make them.

## Add Spice to Your Family Life

On TV you see commercials for perfumes, colognes, and the like, suggesting a person should have a mysterious side to them. That is really not a bad idea when talking about the family. For years psychologists have advised marital partners with problems to add spice to their marriage by not being totally predictable. If fans were certain their team would always win, very few would go to the games. A major reason ball games draw such crowds is the expectation of seeing things you did not expect. Look what Mohammed Ali did for boxing. He had a great gift for drawing crowds because you were never sure what he was going to do next. Look at the effect uncertainty has on gamblers at Las Vegas or Friday night poker games. Most games are based on uncertainty. Husbands and wives can add a little mystery to their romance by not being totally predictable. Husbands can send their wife a card or flower for no reason at all. They can do a dozen different nice things unexpectedly for their wives. Wives can change their hairdo, fix an extra special meal, bring something nice home from their job, or unexpectedly whisper a seductive offer to their husband during some banquet.

It is important to remember that pleasant surprises are always welcome while unpleasant ones can be disastrous. The apprehension of not knowing when your mate is going to fly into a rage can only hurt a relationship. Being surprised by not getting to go to an already promised dance for no reason at all, or being yelled at for no apparent reason, are two effective ways of weakening parent–child bonds. On the other hand unexpected happenings in life where someone has something to gain and nothing to lose can have amazingly positive effects on a family.

How would you like your children to give you a hug when you arrive home from work? Just stop, buy a pack of gum, and give a piece to each of your children who hug you, and be sure to tell them how much you enjoyed the hug. Intermittently bringing even little things home has a large effect on children getting excited when either mom or dad come home from work. It also creates a pleasant atmosphere for the rest of the evening. Psychologists have spent a great deal of research time on this idea of surprises and have found that parents who do unexpected positive things (bring home candy, tell their children how much they love them, make a batch of popcorn to watch TV with) generally have attentive and affectionate children.

## BEING A GOOD PARENT ON A SMALL TIME BUDGET

There is a strong misconception going around that parents must set aside a lot of their time to do nothing but interact with their children if they want to be successful parents. Recall from Chapter Two that Ann was devoting nearly eight hours a day with her son, yet that time did not strengthen the bond between them. She was ready to give him up for adoption. Before the reader gets the idea that I am against parents spending time with their children, let me say that parents *need* to spend time with their children. Nothing can improve a parent–child bond more than time spent together. It is important to remember, however, that too much time together can be detrimental.

I believe this idea is supported by the fact that Mother Nature places the most fruitful childbearing years during the time couples are struggling with so many other problems. Women are most suitable for bearing children at the beginning of marriage when husband and wife not only have to learn to live with each other, but also when finances are a big problem. Women are more unsuitable to have children after they are forty-five years old when they and their mate have learned to live with each other. And after forty-five couples are typically much more financially capable to be able to spend more time with a child.

Mother Nature intended us to be good parents on a small time budget. In fact it may be the only way we can be good parents. All too often we see the parent with nothing else to do spoiling the child, giving the child everything asked for, and constantly doting over him. It happens so often that jokes about such happenings are a part of our society. When ice cream is always available we tend to lose our appreciation of it. When a child has hundreds of toys, he is often at a loss to find one which satisfies his interest. A child with few toys tends to be more creative in finding new things to do with that toy. Perhaps this is true for parents also. Perhaps we lose some of our value in our child's eye when we are always there more or less chasing them. Parents always around their children are the parents more likely to be chasing after their toddlers in stores. They are also more likely to be out trying to find their children in the neighborhood. Children with mother always around are more prone to accidents than children whose parents are not always there. Children without parents around all the time have to learn to depend on themselves more, and have to learn through minor experiences that there are things in the world that can hurt, if one is not careful.

Obviously a child needs a parent or guardian around a certain portion of the time. So how much time is that? Well, the answer is *no one really knows.* We do know the successful parent can spend less than twenty minutes intentional interaction time per day on each child and still be a good parent. What are some traits successful parents have in common that allows them to be effective on a small time budget? Below are listed some ideas from adults in families where both parents hold down full-time jobs.

### Involve Children in Nonjob Activities

Working mothers should involve their children with them in things such as fixing dinner, cleaning the house, and going shopping. In this way two birds are killed with one stone. Required tasks are completed and time is spent with the children. Many parents hesitate in starting such practices because they find in many cases it initially takes more time to complete the task than if they did it themselves. That is OK, for over weeks and months you will find they get better and can shoulder more of the load themselves. Think back. Some of the fondest memories you have of your childhood happened while working with mother or dad.

### Check on Friends

Most successful parents take the time to check out their children's friends. When you realize most of the things your child will learn while you are away from home comes from experiences with playmates, then checking on the playmates and their families is not a bad idea. Many behavior problems parents have to deal with can be avoided if parents help their children in selecting friends. Some people argue parents should not interfere with a child's choice in friends. In all my experience with wayward foster teenagers, I find one of my most effective aids is to reorient the teenager in terms of friends and activities. Curtailing their interactions with other problem teenagers and arranging for other more suitable activities (for example, softball playing for an aggressive teenage girl) to express their feelings can be very helpful.

### Use Aids in the Community

Most successful parents with little time to spare use available help in the community. When their job takes up time they could use with their children they may use some of their money to hire responsible people to be with their children when they cannot. Using this principle, many wealthy and busy people pay for their children to attend private schools that have faculty to provide many of the experiences these parents feel their children will benefit from. More everyday parents may use nursery schools for preschoolers. They may find adult-supervised after-school activities involving sports or crafts work in which their children can learn from adults other than themselves. They may have neighbors to watch their children until getting home from work. They get to know these adults they select to substitute for them, so their children receive the kind of care that is compatible with their convictions. There are summer camps, YMCA–YWCA programs, adopt-a-grandparent programs, private schools, foster care programs, scouting, and all sorts of other sources parents can draw from to help successfully raise their children. Chapter Twelve talks about these sources to help.

### Develop Independence

Most successful parents arrange for family experiences which increase the independence of their children. These activities generally entail developing responsibility for one's own actions. For example, one set of parents whose three children ranged in age from six to twelve did not use a babysitter. They taught their children to take care of each other. They would alternate putting the nine-year-old or twelve-year-old in charge. It was made clear that all the children *must* obey whoever was in charge. If the person in charge told another child to stand on their head in the corner, that child must do it immediately. When the parents arrived home, however, if any of the children felt they were asked to do something unfairly they were to tell the parents. And if the one in charge used their authority unjustly, he or she was immediately disciplined. The parents would always leave the number of a close neighbor by the phone, who they could call for immediate help if needed (and the neighbor was notified by the parents before leaving). These children were learning to be more independent and responsible for their actions. My wife and I liked that approach so much when we heard of it that we have used it successfully for over ten years, even with hard-to-handle foster children.

## DIVORCED AND SINGLE PARENTS CAN BE EFFECTIVE PARENTS

The idea that a divorced or single parent has a more difficult child-rearing situation than parents with "partners" goes without saying. Most people have a poor understanding as to what effect divorce or death of a partner will have on their lives. The standard of living will almost always decline, so financial worries and hardships become almost unbearable for many. The loneliness, isolation from society, and changing reactions of friends, is something you have to experience to believe. A very high percentage of divorced parents say they would not have filed for divorce if they had realized what would result.

Yet death and divorce are two aspects of society that do happen, so let's dwell for a few moments on issues that are particularly important to adults who preside in single-parent families. First, how do you handle the problem of your children only having one parent? Children are certainly aware things have changed, and have many questions. The best way to start off as a single-parent family is to sit down and lay your cards on the table. In some instances single parents try to avoid the problem and act as if nothing has happened. They try not to think about it, do not want to talk about it, and avoid it as much as possible by postponing tasks that need to be done (for example, going through the belongings of a lost husband). People who experience losing a mate naturally build up emotions inside them which must be released some time; like the battery in a light, it will not discharge as long as someone avoids letting it out. Like gas in the stomach, it will continue until it is deactivated somehow. Unfortunately we have no pills which will neutralize the problem completely. You and your children should squarely address the problem. Have a good long cry if need be; but do not try to ignore it.

There is an interesting point to be made here. Generally speaking, the single parent who has obligations and responsibilities get over the problem faster than the parent with few or no competing obligations. A working wife who loses her husband and now has to worry about meeting the bills, will usually cope with the situation better than a wife who is financially secure, stays at home, and even has a maid to do her housework. The point Mother Nature makes from this is *get involved.* The more life does not allow you to dwell on your problem, the better you are at gathering up your marbles and getting back in the game. Expect to feel some pain for a while; that is natural. Do not be ashamed of your feelings; but do not let them take over either.

Children will also feel sorry for themselves about what has happened. You, as the parent, should try to nip this problem as soon as possible. While you can sympathize with their problem, be careful that you do not justify their tendencies of feeling sorry for themselves. Most of the foster children we receive have been dealt a poor hand. For example, one boy was used in a shoplifting ring by his mother when he was seven. At age nine he stood before a judge and heard the mother he loved dearly say she did not want him any more; then she walked away from him. He went through half a dozen caseworkers and foster families over the next few years. At age fourteen he was removed from a family that adopted him four years back because he lied to his adopted father, and the father felt he could not cope in the community with a son who did not tell the truth. "That will be a bad reflection on me and I do not feel capable of changing him at this late date," commented the father who gave up the boy with some reservations.

What do you say to such a boy who has all the right in the world to cry in his room at night when he thinks no one hears? If anyone had a right to be bitter, he certainly did. How do you give him a good feeling about himself when those around him kept giving him away because he lied and stole no more than most kids his age? When he joined our family he was treated like everyone else. He was given house chores, he was given no special treatment. When he did confide in me with his feelings, I would act somewhat sympathetic. Having trouble keeping emotions inside myself, I would say everybody has problems, and some much worse than his. I would point out he was a handsome and healthy young man with a full life ahead of him. What was important was that he was healthy and alive; and he was definitely going to be with us for as long as he wanted to be. Sympathy is an excellent medicine used in small doses. Too much of it causes the problem to get larger.

After children adjust to their new family style they tend to become more demanding. Like a horse checking out a new pasture, the child often unconsciously starts testing the parent to see where the new fences are. In divorce situations they often pit the two parents against each other to get more of what they want. It is important that parents just be themselves, use the natural strategies discussed in this chapter, and not try to overspend in terms of money or time.

## TURNING CHILD ENEMIES INTO ALLIES

Most books on childrearing do not address the issue of dealing with a child who has become a bad apple. There are a growing number of children who not only do not mind their parents, but intentionally go out of their way to make their parents uncomfortable. Some do whatever they feel like in front of other people, not caring that their parents will be embarrassed. Others intentionally act out in front of company so their parents are put on the spot.

Some children have reached the point that they no longer care about their parents, who want to know if it is possible to do anything in such situations. The answer is yes. While such situations are far from easy to solve, there are strategies that can produce positive results. Foster parents are continually confronted with such problems. A large number of children placed in specialized foster care programs are there because they and their parents can no longer deal with each other. And many foster parents successfully remodel the child so he or she can be returned home. Chapters Fourteen and Fifteen include a great deal of information for parents who need to transform a child from an enemy into an ally.

*Questions from Parents*

**Q:** My sister and her husband seem to implement accountability and responsibility with their children, but their kids are unruly. Why?

**A:** Suppose you knew someone who would smile and wave *every other* time you saw him or her. And on the alternate occasions you met, that same person sneered at you. Would these smiles and waves have a positive effect on you? Probably not. Many parents likewise send contradictory signals in implementing the five conditions I presented. The *more consistent* a parent is in using these conditions, the more positive effect they will have on the children (and the whole family for that matter). More is said about this idea of consistency in later chapters.

**Q:** Which of those five family conditions of accountability, responsibility, and so on, is most important?

**A:** Those five conditions are like the motor, transmission, frame, wheels, and fuel for a car. All are needed to make it work. Accountability will not be effective if sensitivity or family unity is lacking. One condition complements the other. It is important to realize that *no* psychological principles (no matter how sophisticated they may sound) will have a greater positive effect on children than the five mentioned in this chapter.

**Q:** Do omissions of any of the five conditions produce different problems with children?

**A:** Yes. Children not taught accountability are more prone to antisocial acts of stealing and mischief. Children who fail to sense family unity are more prone to acts of violence and suicide. Suicide is the fifth leading cause of death in teenagers. And violent acts (armed robbery, assault of the elderly, and killing of cooperative victims) by teenagers more than double every five years.

**Q:** I have tried to make my children more responsible by giving them house duties, but my children fight my attempts. What is wrong?

**A:** Nothing is wrong. If you have previously been doing what they should do, their reaction of fighting your efforts to give them responsibilities is a natural reaction of people to resist anything which requires more out of them. Do not get upset about their reaction. Just make sure you do not let their resistance pay off by your giving up. Be persistent; their resistance to what you are trying to do will fade with time. And your relationship with your children will strengthen from what you have done. Future chapters give ideas on strategies you can use to get them to accept responsibilities.

# 8

# How to Stop Them: Three Ways to Get Rid of Undesirable Dimensions in Children

One of the most common questions asked by parents is "How do I stop my child from acting certain ways?" The most common reply psychologists give to that question is "I really cannot answer that question without knowing much more about your child." Although this answer frustrates many parents, it is true. First of all, every child is different, and seemingly subtle little differences between two similar children can make a great difference in how the problem should be handled. Second, a psychologist, more than a butcher, plumber, mechanic, or lawyer, must be particularly careful not to give the wrong advice. And third, there are a number of problems in children which parents need professional help to handle effectively. Many of these, such as homosexuality, speech impairment, bedwetting, fears, smoking, and drinking, are discussed in Chapter Thirteen with advice to seek professional help.

The majority of day-to-day behavior problems children have, however, can be handled by parents. Kicking, biting, tantrums, crying, destructiveness, lying, cheating, and a host of other things children have invented to annoy parents, can be handled if one becomes familiar with a few basic strategies. This and the following chapter explains and illustrates the six most effective strategies used by psychologists to handle day-to-day problems children create for parents.

## USING THE INCOMPATIBLE RESPONSE APPROACH TO YOUR ADVANTAGE

One of the most common approaches used by parents to get rid of undesirable activities in their children is to place the children in incompatible response situations. One of the reasons parents use it is the same reason children use it on parents—it takes little time to set the strategy up. As mentioned in Chapter Five where examples of children using it were presented, it basically entails putting an individual in a situation where only one or two courses of action are possible.

### Stopping a Marriage

An obstetrician in a large Western city used the incompatible response strategy to stop his son from doing something he felt the boy would later regret. John was in his third year of college and had been accepted to medical school for the following year. He had also met a girl, and they had decided to get married. "Stay single until you are out of medical school and I will continue to pay 100 percent of your education costs," his father told him. "Marry before that time and I will not help you at all financially."

That might sound like a harsh and meddling parent; and perhaps he was. Knowing the father, however, I realize his main concern was whether his son would finish medical school. The chances of a married student completing medical school are much less than a nonmarried student. Both finances and social pressures put on by having a mate seem to be the reasons. The father had known too many young men and women who had to drop out because of marriage.

After several weeks of thinking of little else, John made his decision—he did not get married. Currently he is a practicing obstetrician in California, married, and the father of three children. Today he is glad his father put him in that situation. "I had no way of knowing at the time how demanding medical school would be," he commented to me. "At the time I did not feel my father was thinking of my best interest, but now I am sure I would not have made it if I was married."

**Stopping School Sluffs**

Three young men, sophomores in high school, were skipping school. Frank and Mike were twin brothers. Like Andy they were from what is called single-parent families. Both fathers had left their wives several years before. Both mothers lived on welfare, and the twins' mother did not even have a car.

At the request of the principal, I began working with the three boys. I started by asking them to go with me down to the university gym to play basketball and lift weights. Being athletically inclined they accepted. For over two months I took them to college ball-games, out to eat hamburgers and cokes, swimming, and all sorts of places. I found they even enjoyed just going downtown when I had to run errands. Not having fathers they enjoyed doing many things I initially felt would bore them. My intent was to make myself pleasing in their eyes. I wanted them to enjoy the time we spent together.

After becoming quite close I again invited them to a ballgame for the following weekend. "But listen," I said, "I hear you guys have been skipping school. Any of you three miss school this week and none of you get to go. I then gave a quick three-minute speech on bad points of skipping school. Three months earlier none of the three would have listened to what I had to say. I had put them in an incompatible response situation, and I was hoping going to the ballgame with me was worth not skipping school. It was . . . and we went.

The next time I put them in that type of situation they tested to see if I would keep my word. I went while they did not. We became quite close over the years. I am happy to report they finished high school—something the principal said would not happen when I first met the boys.

### How to Tell If This Strategy Will Work

One of the nice things about the incompatible response strategy, in contrast to some of the other strategies, is that it can work on people of all ages, and on most types of problems. The key to its success is making sure that the choice you present is perceived by the child as having greater benefit than the actions you consider undesirable. I experienced a sad situation where a young college girl became involved with a young man in a drug cult. Her parents put her in an incompatible response situation. "Leave him or never come home again," were the choices they gave her. She chose the young man. Two years later she died of an overdose. In this situation the girl perceived staying with the fellow as a better choice. The parents felt coming home would be the better choice by far. Sometimes you have to try to look at the situation through the eyes of your child. Not so much to understand their side and agree with them, but to understand their position so your approach has a better chance of working.

### Things to Watch Out for

Several things can be done to maximize the effectiveness of this strategy. First pick something that the child surely likes. A mother was worried about her son's fear of water and asked for my help. While teaching him to swim I also worked on his fear of diving. I rented a face mask to let him see clearly what was under the surface of the water. He came to enjoy swimming around underwater in the public pool. Wanting also to teach him not to fear diving boards, I purchased a good-looking snorkel and mask. After showing them to him, I said "These are yours to keep if you jump off the ten-foot diving board ten times today." He showed a strong hesitation. First he tried to talk me into receiving them for jumping off the low board. Then he continued to play in the pool, although I could tell he was still being tempted. After a few minutes he ran down to the high board and jumped off ten times in a row. Pulling himself out of the water for the tenth time, and looking somewhat like a drowned rat, he pulled a smile of satisfaction on his face and ran for the snorkel and mask.

If the boy had immediately said "no" to my offer I would have known that the snorkel and mask were not worth it to him. The way he vascillated at my offer indicated the fear of going off the board and the desire for the snorkel and mask were close to being equal in value. Had I thrown in swim fins, the choice would have been easier—and I was prepared to do it.

In situations like this, having the prize there and visible produces a much stronger incentive than telling the child you will go buy one for him. Just like the adage about a bird in the hand; a prize in view is worth two promises.

Be a person of your word. The boy tried to get the prize by doing something less. That is a common thing. If the parent can be manipulated to give the prize even when the child does not do what the parents want, then the child will learn to manipulate you into getting your offer besides doing what he planned to originally. If I had allowed the boys to sluff school and still go to the games, they would have. Be sure you are ready to stick to your word when using this strategy.

**Implementing the Strategy**

There are several ways you can implement this strategy. One approach is to allow the child to experience unpleasant consequences which appear to be of his own making. "I won't eat stuff like that!" was the type of statement Roger would consistently make at his aunt's house. "That's fine," his uncle replied. "These are the kinds of foods we eat around here. But if you do not want to eat, you can go play." Making sure he could not get food other than at meals, Roger's aunt and uncle put him in an incompatible response situation. After missing two meals Roger became an active participant at mealtime.

Annie was a twenty-three-year-old girl with an unusual tendency of overdressing. With towels wrapped around her head, she would put on several layers of clothes. Three dresses, two overcoats, and eighteen pairs of nylons, two towels, a hat, and a large shopping purse stuffed to the brim, was a common outfit for Annie at the state hospital. Using an imcompatible response strategy, the hospital staff placed a scale outside the cafeteria door and began weighing

Annie before each meal. "You're a quarterpound too heavy," the attendant said. "What do you mean I'm too heavy?" Annie replied. "You cannot go in until you weigh less," said the attendant. "How am I supposed to weigh less?" she inquired. "I don't know," replied the attendant. "I was told to check your weight and not let you in if you weighed too much."

After telling off the attendant, Annie decided she did not want to miss lunch, so she removed a coat to gain entrance. Following this tactic the staff eventually got Annie dressing in a much more reasonable fashion. Interestingly, Annie's parents then began taking her for rides away from the hospital—now that she no longer looked like a three-hundred-pound Arabian sheik sitting in the back seat of the car.

Another alternative to use of the incompatible response strategy is to arrange good activities during times bad activities occurred in the past. When teenage boys and girls are out on scouting trips, they cannot be on street corners. Many a potentially delinquent child has been retrieved by finding them paying jobs. Again, however, the key to such working programs is that both good and bad activities cannot be combined. Many girls left babysitting may invite other girls or boyfriends over. Teenage boys earning money at grocery stores may fool around on their job. Make sure the child does not get paid for not acting responsibly.

## Things to Keep in Mind

The incompatible response approach can be employed on people of all ages. A young boy was taught to quit sucking his thumb by making sure no one in the family interacted with him whenever he was sucking. A young handicapped three-year-old girl was taught not to bite her hand by hooking up a radio headset which would only work as long as she continually squeezed a bulb switch in her hand. Usually, however, this type of strategy is used on older children in more complex situations. Behaviors such as biting and crying may be handled with this approach, but most parents use it for situations such as controlling what teenagers do with their time. One of the nice effects of this approach is that it helps children by giving them chances to make decisions about their actions.

## EXTINCTION—DON'T MAKE IT WORTH THE TROUBLE

In Chapter 1 the story of Ann wanting to give Troy up for adoption was an example of using extinction. Extinction is a strategy that will work on almost every type of behavioral problem—from infants throwing tantrums to teenagers constantly pestering the parent to borrow the car. There is a natural explanation for the effectiveness of extinction. Mother Nature has programed mankind to do things for reasons. And if you remove the reasons for someone's actions, those actions will stop.

I must admit this was one of the most difficult ideas for me to accept when working with people. In my early years in the profession there seemed to be many situations where people appeared to do things for no reason at all. I saw a young six-year-old bang his head on the floor time and time again for no apparent reason. Time and time again, I have heard or seen the extinction strategy work in even seemingly unusual situations.

### Extinguishing "Dirty" Talk

Luisa was a nine-year-old girl in a third grade class. During the middle of the year she began talking dirty to the little boys in her class in front of teachers. After several weeks of talking with Luisa, the teachers decided to approach their school psychologist.

"Ignore her remarks" was his suggestion. "Pretend you don't hear them and go on with what you were doing."

Somewhat puzzled the teachers took his advice and in a short time the dirty talk stopped. Being a graduate student at the time, and doing some research at that particular grade school, I asked the school psychologist how he came to such a quick conclusion.

"Ever been up to the state mental hospital?" he asked.

"Yes, I have done some research up there," I replied.

"Then you know," he said, "that sexual talk like that being said by the young girl is common. And the reason it is common up there is because it gets the hospital attendants' attention much quicker than talk about the Kentucky Derby. Luisa's talk gets the teacher's attention.

"There are instances where such talk is not aimed at the teacher's attention. Before coming to this school I was a psychologist at the youth center at the state mental hospital. Sexual talk is quite frequent up there. Unfortunately extinction doesn't work well on the teenagers at the center. Up there the boys listen to girls who start those kinds of conversations. At this grade school those little boys do not understand what Luisa is saying, but the teachers do."

### Getting Rid of Disruptive Classroom Behavior

Pete was an eight-year-old boy whose favorite saying was "I won't do that!" He had recently moved into the school district and created quite a commotion in class every time he was called on to participate. The teacher called Pete's mother and explained the problem. The mother offered no help, so Pete was referred to the school resource teacher, Mrs. Bennion, whose job it was to work on a one-to-one situation with problem children.

"I won't do it! And you can't make me!" challenged Pete. Mrs. Bennion had placed some special blocks with letters on them before him. The task consisted of rolling the blocks like dice, then seeing if the child could make a word out of any combination of the blocks. Mrs. Bennion had sat down next to Pete on the "little people's" chairs which surrounded one round table in the small resource classroom. After instructing Pete as to the object of the game, and hearing his reply, she started reading a magazine, seemingly ignoring Pete.

"I won't do it, and you can't make me," he replied again while trying to get her attention. For a few moments he sat and just looked around. He appeared somewhat puzzled as to what would happen next. Mrs. Bennion continued to read.

After a few minutes he reached for the blocks, rolled them, but did not try to make a word. "This ain't no fun, and I like recess," he said softly as if he wanted a reply. No reply came. Again he picked up the blocks and rolled them, but this time he tried to sound out a word. Mrs. Bennion put the book down and started working with him as if nothing had happened. The next day Pete started off as he had the day before, even a little bit more adamant, but settled down within fifteen minutes as Mrs. Bennion continued her strategy. Within two weeks he had quit saying "I won't do it." Combining the strategies of ignoring unruly behavior and giving him attention when he did his assignments, Pete's classroom challenges became a thing of the past.

### How to Tell if Extinction Will Work

I am continually surprised to see how many problems in children can be eliminated simply by ignoring them. Throwing tantrums, asking for things while shopping, repeatedly asking for things even after a parent has said no, grabbiness, telling "tall" stories, whining, saying "I won't do that," and interrupting conversations are a few of the common things children do which can be effectively handled with the strategy of extinction. All of these are actions which are typically maintained in children by attention from parents.

Actions like crying, pouting, sadness, and withdrawing from people may also be handled by extinction. There are other things that may cause these particular actions in children, however. A baby may be crying because its diaper is soiled; a child may pout as a somewhat natural reaction to some disappointment; a child may be sad because of something someone has said to them; and sometimes a child withdraws from other people because they have had an unfortunate experience. When parents are faced with a child's actions that may be due to more than attention, there are things a parent can learn to recognize that indicate whether their children are doing such things as crying or pouting for attention. First, a parent can distract the child to some other activity. Bring a rattle to the infant; or take an older child (two, through six years old) and start some interesting task (for example, coloring or playing with a toy). If the child stops crying then you can be pretty sure your child is one who cries to get attention, and you will be ready for him/her from then on.

A second approach is to ignore the behavior and see if it gets worse. In Chapter One, Figure 1 illustrated the point that if the extinction strategy is working it will cause the actions to become more severe for a while before it starts to get better. If the child begins to exaggerate and prolong his actions (for example, cries louder and longer, pouts more openly, starts looking even sadder, or overacts in withdrawing from people) you have another good indication that extinction will work on your child. Third, keep track and see how often your child does it. If it is happening more than you would normally expect, that is also a good way to spot when a child is manipulating you to get attention.

### Something to Watch Out for

If a parent decides to use the strategy of extinction, there is something to watch out for. Psychologists sometimes refer to it as *bootleg attention.* Keep in mind you are not the only one who can give attention. Often parents will use the strategy of extinction only to find the child keeps up what he was doing because others give him attention also. Mothers cannot extinguish a child's manipulating cries if father still gives into them. The family needs to work together on the problem. Many years ago we took a ten-year-old girl into our home who earlier in her life had been placed in a mental institution. She displayed some behaviors typical of mentally retarded children (for example, shuffled her feet slowly when she walked, tucked her chin in her neck, softly slurred her speech). For two months we worked on her speech using an extinction strategy saying "I'm sorry Maria, we can't hear you," and ignoring her. When we failed to put our ear next to her mouth to listen as others had done, the volume and clarity of her speech increased to normal. When my wife went in the hospital for a gall bladder operation, my mother came to run the household. Being busy with my work and at the hospital, I failed to notice what Maria did to my good-intentioned mother. Seeing my mother putting her ear close to Maria's mouth one evening, I later explained the circumstances. After mother failed to respond to Maria's whispering, Maria began talking normally to her also.

### Implementing the Strategy

Implementing the strategy of extinction generally requires patience and forethought. Like any good General going to war, pick the time and place so you have an advantage over your opponent. When possible, don't start this when you have company, when you are at a shopping mall, or in other such situations where distractions and bootleg attention is possible. Pick times when you are home alone with the child, or when everyone else is supporting what you are doing.

One of the most effective techniques for extinguishing unwanted actions involves *reverse training* . Generally speaking, parents do not give in to the child every time he makes a demand for attention. We, as parents, are not usually consistent. Because parents are not consistent, children learn sometimes it works and sometimes it doesn't. The result of being inconsistent is that the tendencies for the child to exhibit those undesirable actions becomes stronger. Just like the person in Las Vegas who plays the slot machine doesn't win every time he pulls the lever, the child learns to try again and again. Now, when a parent decides to ignore the child's annoying actions, the child will persist, not realizing the parent is no longer going to respond to his desires. The principle is the same for someone learning a stamp machine is broken versus realizing a slot machine is broken. Stamp machines generally pay off every time. Few people put in money a second time if they do not receive stamps on the first try. On the other hand, a person would feed a slot machine many times before they would realize it was broken and not going to pay off.

The secret to extinguishing a child's annoying habit quickly is to attend to him every time he yells, pouts, or whatever, for a while. After you have acted like a consistent stamp machine for five to ten times, then you consistently ignore the child's demands. By reversing a child to constant attention, then extinction, the effort it takes to get rid of the child's annoying actions is less than one third what a parent would normally need to give.

### Some Things to Keep in Mind

Several things should be kept in mind about the strategy of extinction. Although it takes more time to stop a child's actions than several of the other strategies, its effect is more long-lasting because extinction directly inhibits the child's desire to commit the act. Extinction is a particularly effective technique on young children. It can even be used on babies. Mothers who switch their child from breast feeding to bottle feeding may employ a form of extinction.

## PHYSICAL RESTRAINT—THE HOLDING PATTERN FOR NEW DIRECTION

There was a Jewish couple who tried for years to have children. After almost twenty years, Hershel arrived. Hershel's father owned a chain of drug stores, and the family was deeply involved in the proper social circles. While Hershel's parents would have been happy to have any child, their Jewish beliefs gave them extra joy in receiving a son.

As Hershel (or Harry as he later preferred) grew, his parents showered him with love and attention. His wants became their desires. As Harry's actions began to create problems his parents could not bring themselves to discipline him harshly so they decided to use physical restraint. Whenever they were worried he might create a problem, they would lock him in his room.

One day Harry's mother was giving an elegant lawn party for state dignitaries. She instructed the gardener to keep Hershel by his side and away from the backyard events. In an attempt to comply with her requests, the gardener took Hershel to the far side of the garage and convinced him to help plant pansies and other small flowering plants.

After some time Hershel became thirsty. With no warning Hershel quickly jumped up, dirt clinging to his hands and knees, and rounded the corner of the garage where a five-gallon crystal punch bowl sitting on a long white linen-clad table was in full view. Making a beeline for the table, this four-year-old climbed from a chair onto the table and proceeded on hands and knees to the punch. About this time one of the guests directed Hershel's mother's attention to the table which was about one hundred feet from them. With a facial look that would bring a smile to Alfred Hitchcock's face, the mother started for the table.

Reaching the punch bowl well ahead of his mother, Hershel

noticed something in the punch—maraschino cherries. As you probably know, maraschino cherries do not float. Using his dirty hand, Hershel proceeded to salvage the cherries from the bottom of the bowl. He was only partially finished with his task when his mother and a maid arrived.

While this situation would not be considered a successful use of physical restraint strategy, it is so seldom that one is privileged to witness such a complete but harmless fiasco, that I wanted to share it with you. In some cases it is reassuring to experience events like this (particularly when it is someone else's child), and realize such things happen to other parents too.

A successful use of physical restraint is illustrated by how a businesswoman in town handled Hershel. Like most wealthy women, Hershel's mother liked to shop. And when she shopped, she spent. It was nothing for her to spend $300 for a dress, or go through $2,000 in an afternoon. So, as you might expect, shop owners loved to see her come into their stores. They did not enjoy Hershel quite so much. He had an unending desire to run up and down the aisles swinging his arms to intentionally knock clothes and hangers on the floor. On one occasion he even climbed up on an unguarded cash register and stomped on the keys while sitting on top.

One businesswoman used a rather effective physical restraint technique. When Hershel and his mother came through the door, this woman would signal one of her salesgirls, and both the salesgirl and the owner would greet the two. While the owner waited on the mother, the salesgirl would use candy and other handy enticements to get Hershel in the back room. Once back there Hershel would be physically held, if necessary, to keep him there. After mother had completed her buying, Hershel would reappear as he and mother were escorted to the door.

## Types of Physical Restraint

Physical restraint is one of the most common strategies used with younger children. Parent after parent holds their young child in their arms as they shop. Shopping carts in grocery stores usually have seats for children located in such a way that it would be difficult for the child to get down by himself. Parents often put fences around backyards and public playgrounds to allow the children some freedom and opportunity, yet protect them from roaming dogs, or busy streets. Grandparents and relatives often employ physical restraint by putting knickknacks on shelves out of the reach of young grandchildren. Parents often take their teenagers with them on trips—not because they want their kids with them, but because they want to make it physically impossible for them to throw unchaperoned parties while they are gone.

There is one form of physical restraint which I have come to appreciate—the leash and halter on children. For years this idea made me uncomfortable, but the more popular alternative is often worse. The next time you go shopping notice how parents restrain children. They hold them in a number of innocuous positions. Some hold the child upright, but squeezed close to the body. Some hold them by the hand and are often lifting the young one upstairs by one arm. Some hold the child around the waist and carry it like a sack of flour.

The leash gives the child much greater freedom to explore our world. It allows the child more physical and psychological experiences. All things considered, it is a welcome alternative to what most of us do with our children.

### Making This Strategy Work

There really is not much that needs to be said on how to use physical restraint. There are some things to consider, however, when using it. First, physical restraint has few, if any, long-lasting effects. You may stop certain actions for the moment, but unless other approaches are used in conjunction with it, the child will do what he intended when the restraint is gone. Children raised in a fenced backyard do not learn to be careful when playing. Children do not learn to be careful or considerate by the removal of knickknacks before they arrive, or by parents locking up their keepsakes. In many cases physical restraint seems to challenge the youngster to show they can get out. They climb up on couches to reach shelves to show it can be done.

Physical restraint is effective in controlling inappropriate actions that can arise in situations that occur infrequently. Parents of a family visiting relatives in a large and unknown city may not allow their daughter to go out with a fast-talking young man. A father may not allow his son to go shooting wild rabbits with older teenagers because of what could happen. A key to effectively restraining unwanted actions that can occur often is to provide alternative activities where the pleasures of such events can be experienced under proper supervision or with prior training for the youth.

*Questions from Parents*

**Q:** I have tried the strategy of telling my three-year-old son to be quiet and I will give him some gum but it has not worked. He still runs around after the gum. Is he too young to understand, so the incompatible response approach cannot work with him?

**A:** The incompatible response approach will not work if the child can do both. And that is what it sounds like is happening in your case. He gets the gum, and then he can be rowdy with the gum. To solve your problem, you either need to withhold the gum until the time you want him to be quiet is up; or consistently take the gum back from him when he starts being rowdy. The second approach is perhaps a little better than the first because waiting for a payoff is a difficult task for a three-year-old. You should realize the second approach may not work the first or second time you do it. He most likely will have to learn from experience that he does in fact lose the gum if he does not do what you say, because in the past he has learned to get around you. Not giving the payoff until after the desired behavior is accomplished works better with older children who have less difficulty with controlling themselves.

**Q:** I tried the incompatible response approach on my teenage daughter using a reward which I know was of more value to her than what she was doing. How come it did not work?

**A:** Making sure the payoff for doing what you want them to is more valuable than what they were doing, is an important ingredient to the success of an incompatible response strategy. It is possible, however, that your daughter knows from past experience that she can do both. For example, a professor friend wanted his wife to lose weight and offered her a trip to the Orient if she lost thirty pounds. He told me she tried but failed to lose the weight. "Did you go on the trip?" I asked. "Yes, it was already planned, so we went anyway," he replied. His wife kept eating and still received the trip. Be sure you are not allowing your daughter to do the same. (By the way I caution husbands and wives from using the approach on each other. It can have disastrous effects.)

**Q:** I have tried what you call extinction on my child, but it does not seem to work. I consistently ignore my six-year-old's tantrums but they still continue. Why? Does extinction always work?

**A:** Extinction will *always* work on children. If a parent is consistent in ignoring tantrums yet they continue to occur, it generally means that the other parent or children in the family still respond to those actions. Cut off the payoff and the tantrums will stop. A second situation where extinction does not seem to work is when parents have been quite inconsistent—sometimes giving in and sometimes holding out. In this case, extinction takes much longer (possibly weeks) to work. You might try not removing payoffs for tantrums but also administering some punishment (spankings, time outs—see next chapter). The addition of punishment will hasten the elimination of tantrums.

**Q:** Aren't there some things children do that extinction will not work on?

**A:** If there are, psychologists do not know of them. It is true that some animals have instincts (for example, certain types of dogs instinctively kill rabbits and chickens) which are not susceptible to extinction. Humans, on the other hand are not as strongly controlled by Mother Nature. Almost anything we do is changeable, so these strategies work on us.

**Q:** Physical restraint sounds like a poor method for changing the child. Should parents use it?

**A:** Physical restraint *is* a poor method for changing behavior. It really does very little to change problem behavior. Its value comes in restraining the child in necessary situations (for example, from running into the street, from picking up glass figurines in stores) until other strategies have been employed to teach the child to control his or her actions.

**Q:** Doesn't restraining a child by placing him in his room have harmful psychological consequences? My children really act out and get upset when I try such things.

**A:** The acting out tantrum behaviors a child exhibits is not a direct indication of internal psychological turmoil. It is more an indication of the parents' sensitivities. Children with deaf parents cry little and physically move around a great deal when throwing a tantrum. Does that tell you anything? Children learn to do what works. I observed a four-year-old boy in a nursery school screaming and rolling around on the floor. After a few minutes he stopped, noticed no one was paying any attention to his actions, got up, went over to a wagon, and began playing.

# 9
# How to Stop Them: Three More Ways

## SATIATION—MAKING THEM SICK AND TIRED OF IT

### Smoking

When I was a teenager I recall an incident with a close friend who decided he was going to try smoking. Somehow his father got "wind" of Rick's activities. Soon thereafter his father purchased four of the cheapest and greenest cigars available on the market. He took his son out in the garage and told him he did not want Rick to try smoking behind his back. "Here's some cigars. You and I will just sit here and smoke a couple each. Let's just talk and enjoy." It wasn't long until Rick was greener than the cigars. Although Rick never tried smoking again, it is important to point out that satiation is generally an unsuccessful strategy when the child has a pretty fair history of smoking. It is interesting to note, however, that a relatively new rapid-smoking technique, based on the strategy of satiation is one of the most effective techniques for getting chronic smokers to stop. More is said about this in Chapter 13.

## Biting, Pinching, and Kicking

There are several unpleasant activities children do which the strategy of satiation has been quite effective in eliminating. Biting, pinching, and kicking are three prime examples. They are behaviors which typically occur infrequently. All of us, for example, has kicked at a patch of snow, a stone on the sidewalk, or a can on the side of a road we were traveling. They are also behaviors which usually lose their pleasantness when they occur repeatedly for a short length of time.

Chad was a five-year-old boy, the youngest in a family of seven. Being the smallest in a relatively large family, he found it difficult to get his share of attention. Somehow he stumbled on to the tactic of kicking other people when he wanted to get someone to listen to him. He also learned it was effective when he was mad at other kids at school. Upon spotting Chad kick a classmate, his teacher took him outside the school to the front steps.

"I want you to kick this step," she demanded, "and you will continue to kick it until I tell you to stop." It didn't take long until Chad's desire to kick left him.

One of the old school approaches of writing five hundred times on the blackboard "I will not throw spitwads in class" is a form of satiation.

## Making This Strategy Work

There are three things parents should consider when using this strategy. First, you must be capable of making them repeat the act. This is one reason satiation works better on younger children. Second, behaviors that are biologically cyclic, I mean behaviors relating to recurring biological drives like eating and sexual behavior are not greatly affected by satiation. The problem of overeating in children is not effectively handled with the strategy of satiation. I am also familiar with a situation where a young man was on a mission for his church. Having confessed to his superiors that he had been looking through a skin magazine, one of his superiors decided to try satiating him on magazine pictures portraying sexual indecencies. It did not work.

Third, satiation is most effective on activities in which the act itself is done because it is gratifying, rather than being pleasurable because other people attend to the child for what he has done. If a child kicks another child because kicking is a satisfying feeling in and of itself, satiation will generally eliminate future occurrences. If, on the other hand, a child is kicking because it is a means of getting attention from others, satiation may still work, but it will be somewhat less effective.

## STIMULUS CHANGE—A STRATEGY FOR THE CREATIVE PARENT

Of all the means available for eliminating undesirable actions children commit, the one I enjoy working with most is what I call stimulus change. I can best explain it through an example. All parents have found themselves kneeling next to a crying child. He may have tripped and skinned his knee; she may have fallen and scraped her hand. After a few moments of consolation the crying continued. "Look at that big bird," my wife called out in just such a situation as she pointed into the sky. My two-year-old son stopped crying and looked up. What she did was re-direct what he was concentrating on, and it immediately stopped the annoying cry. How often have we found ourselves in a good mood, then someone we thoroughly hate comes into view. That quick change in the things (psychologists call them stimuli) we were concentrating on changes our whole attitude. Now we are burning inside instead of being happy. Most kindergarten teachers are masters at the stimulus-change . A quickly grabbed toy or picture often changes a shy and frightened child into a contented and curious individual.

### Stopping a Marriage

A rather successful businessman in Washington was approached by his twenty-year-old daughter. "I've been dating a young man at college lately, and I want to bring him home to meet the family at the end of the semester. We are thinking of getting married."

"That's fine," replied the father who was already aware of the young man. "But I have to go to Europe on business then and I have made arrangements to take the whole family. Let's bring him over after we get back." The girl had a past history of falling in love and her father was not impressed with the young man. Having been to Europe previously, he took his family to a place they had been before—a place where she had fallen in love before. While there, the girl had a wonderful time and the father subtly, or possibly not so subtly, worked on changing his daughter's mind. After a few arranged dates, the girl's interest in marriage began to fade.

### Stopping Arguments

One summer afternoon I was busy in our fruit orchard with seven of our children. Two of the teenage foster girls staying with us were throwing not too subtle comments back and forth at each other. They had not been friendly for several days and things seemed to be getting worse. I decided to try the strategy of stimulus change.

We were hooking up a sprinkler system. I had the two girls working together on one pipe fitting. I intentionally turned the water on before they were ready and they were sprayed with water. I then ran over and chewed them out, saying they were not doing it right or they would not have been sprayed. I told them they would now have to finish by themselves, while the rest of us went in the house. It took them another hour working together to finish and they were so busy being mad at me that they resolved their differences. Later I apologized for being so mad and blamed my behavior on not feeling well.

### Making This Strategy Work

This strategy is used in a variety of interpersonal situations. Coaches try to stir their players. Bosses try to light fires under slow-moving executives. Army officers try to get that little extra. One woman used it in an unusual way to get her husband to take her out to dinner. "When I ask to go out to dinner, he usually says he doesn't want to go. So when I really want to go out, I pick a fight with him. In no time at all we make up and then I suggest that we get out of the house for a while."

Stimulus change can be effectively employed on kids of all ages for all kinds of situations. It can be used to stop bickering, crying, fighting, pouting, and sadness. It can be used to motivate children to try harder. I particularly enjoyed this strategy because its uses are limited only by the parents' creativity and ingenuity. It also changes situations quickly in most cases.

## PUNISHMENT—AN EXAMPLE

One could hardly discuss how to get rid of undesirable actions without mentioning punishment. Punishment on the one hand has been given credit for saving more wayward children than any other type of discipline. On the other hand, punishment has been made responsible for setting more children on a wayward course than any other training tactic. While punishment and all its ramifications are discussed in detail in the next chapter, let me illustrate some of my own uses of it.

Angie was an Indian girl, fourteen years old, when she came to stay in our home. At the age of five she had been adopted by a middle-class family which already included three children, two boys and a girl. At this tender age she was already resentful and defiant about life in general. The Jensen's threw a "welcome to the family" party for Angie, and in one of her frequent angry moments she broke every present she was given. Over the years her parents found that was a sign of the times to come.

By the time Angie was fourteen, the Jensen's asked the Department of Social Services for help. Angie was in junior high. She had a grade point of .1 (F–). She was absent from school more than she was in class and loved to torment teachers. She would hit her mother if she tried to stop Angie from leaving the house. Angie ran with a rough crowd, was into drugs, and had been in the local police detention center several times.

Social Services asked my wife and me if we would take this girl into our home and try to help. At that time we had other teenage girls in our home that most foster homes could not handle. Some were incest problems, some were suicidal, some were the recipients of child abuse by their parents.

We took Angie in, and like all previous foster kids she seemed easy to talk to and gave the impression of having no problems. Within three days it started. At the end of her first day at public school she wasn't at the appointed pick-up place. She told the other kids to inform me she had met some new friends and was going to the basketball game. She said she would be home around seven. I immediately went to the school, found her, told her basketball season was over four weeks ago, and reminded her of our earlier talks in which she was asked to please clear any requests for extracurricular activities ahead of time.

We went home and had another heart-to-heart talk in which she said she was sorry and that she had not understood before. Two days later she came home from school with my wife and then sneaked off to another girl's home. When I arrived home at six that evening she was still gone. I called some of the junior high students I knew, and found her within an hour. After returning home we had another talk. "This is the last one you get free," I said. "From now on you are going to pay for going against my instructions." I reminded her that my wife and I were there to help, and she said she was sorry and hoped we could all work together.

The next day she started planning to run away with two other girls. She threatened the other two girls into stealing money and jewelry for the trip or she would "punch their lights out." They planned to skip school during first period on the next Thursday. Having heard through my grapevine about the planned runaway, I checked around and found they planned to take a bus to Idaho. I called Social Services and told them what Angie was planning. They felt we should put her in the detention home. "No," I remarked. "She has been there before and it did not help. This is the first time she has been in a foster home. Let's not let her run from it. If she does I am afraid we will never be able to reach her." I suggested they let me try something.

The morning of the runaway attempt I took her in my home office and asked her if everything was going all right. She said everything was fine. We talked for a while, then I pretended to head for work at the university. I drove to one of my graduate student's apartments and traded my car for his little yellow Volkswagen. I and two other men posted ourselves so we could see every exit from the school. A few minutes later my wife arrived and dropped the kids off. Angie ran straight to her waiting friends, then went in the school. The bell rang and all the kids went to class. Because we had told the school counselor earlier what was happening, he called my wife and said, "They did not go to their first period class. They are hiding in one of the restrooms." "Fine, just leave them there," replied my wife.

Halfway through first period they came sneaking out of the school, heading for the nearest bus stop. I pulled up and got out of the car. Angie's eyes were as big as silver dollars and I slowly said, "OK, tough girl, get in the car!" When we arrived home I got out my board of education, had her bend over the couch, and connected with three swats. Acting like the meanest thing this side of Hell I said, "Those swats were to get your attention. Now I am going to tell you how this little game of yours is going to be played! You have played everyone who has tried to help you, including your parents, social worker, and the police, for fools. You expect everyone to play by your rules. Well, I have news for you. I make all the rules for you here. You are going to be kept upstairs in your room in pajamas and not allowed in any other part of the house, except the bathroom, until you "earn" the privilege of rejoining the rest of the family. You do not even get to go to school." (That comment really surprised her because all her life people had pushed her to school, and now I told her she could not go.) "For the next five days you will scrub walls, floors, and whatever else I tell you. And then if you have done well, you may return to school. A teacher will bring your assignments each day and you will do them in your room."

She began yelling that I could not do that to her, and she wanted to talk to Ed at Social Services. I let her call Ed; she explained what happened, and said she wanted to go home. Ed said, "OK you can go whenever Dr. Robinson says you can." Looking hurt and alone she went to her room.

Over the next two days she worked as hard as anyone I have seen her age. I was proud of her and how she seemed to be putting her shoulder to the wheel. Keeping a firm tone, I told her how much I appreciated her efforts to cooperate. I also told her she could now come out of her room and rejoin the family. Each evening she worked on her schoolwork, and after the five-day period Angie was allowed to go to school. Over the next two years she never sluffed a class, and went from an F-minus grade average to a C-plus average. During the first term my wife and I spent many hours sitting and helping her with schoolwork. I'll never forget that look in her eyes when that first report card showing a 2.3 average came. She was as proud as a new pup. Before, she felt she was not as smart as other kids. After that she studied mostly on her own.

Many nights while she stayed with us, she came into my office while I was writing and we would talk. Often she would strut and complain that we were too strict and made her do too many chores. "I got up whenever I wanted at home," she would remind me. I would remind her of how much good I saw inside her, and how much I enjoyed seeing it coming out. Angie loved to tease. She also liked sports. We had her join a girls' softball team and went to her game. Finally it was decided that she could return home and Angie was told. Several days later she asked if she could call her mom. My wife said OK. After talking to her mother for twenty minutes, Angie said, "Carol, my mother wants to speak to you." Mrs. Jensen told my wife that Angie asked if she could stay with us and not go home. My wife said she and I would discuss it when I came home that night.

Waiting for me to get home Angie seemed nervous and said to Carol, "Maybe we better not ask him. I have told Doc so many times I hate it here that I'm sure he is going to tease me about it."

And she was right. When I heard, I smiled and began to kid with her. Then I put my arms around her and told her how happy that made me and how much I appreciated having her around. We went for a long walk and talked of fun times—how she pushed me fully clothed in our swimming pool and how I intentionally sprayed her and another girl with the sprinkling system in the orchard. She remarked that the spanking I gave her two years back really hurt. I asked how come she did not cry when I spanked her. "Because I did not want you to know how much it hurt," was her reply. We talked of how much she had changed and I told her I felt that it was time for her to rejoin her other family and try to make a go of it with them.

In June of 1979 her parents came to take her home. She has written, called, and has come back to visit us many times since. She, like the rest of us, is far from perfect, but she is as fine a daughter as any parents could want. There may be those who feel spanking Angie, locking her in her room when she first came, and grounding her from watching TV (she loved TV) several times while she lived with us, was unnecessary. However, someone would have a difficult time convincing me, and Angie for that matter, that a milder approach could have pulled her off the course she was on when she arrived at our home.

*Questions from Parents*

**Q:** My daughter has a habit of giggling. Could satiation work on this behavior?

**A:** Yes, it can. Keep in mind I said it *can,* not that it will. How you employ this strategy will determine its effectiveness. Be sure you require your daughter to keep it up until she is quite sick and tired of doing it.

**Q:** What if I use a satiation strategy and it works only for a little while. Can I try the same strategy again on the same problem behavior?

**A:** Yes, you can. Satiation may be employed more than once. Have the child repeat the behavior longer the second time.

**Q:** I have a hyperactive child who constantly pesters us with questions. What is a good strategy to use on him?

**A:** Strange as it may seem, satiation is one of the more effective ways of stopping a child's pestering. Most hyperactive children have a low tolerance for doing the same thing over and over. Hyperactive children who pester actually do it in spurts—they do it for a while, stop for a while, then do it again. It just seems as if it is continuous. Making a hyperactive child repeat his questions and comments many times in a row generally causes a drastic reduction in pestering. The treatment may have to repeated every once in a while, however. Be sure to support this strategy by providing tasks the hyperactive child likes to do which helps them learn to do things by themselves. Putting puzzles together, embroidering, and other such tasks are often enjoyed by hyperactive children, and can be good for them.

**Q:** I have tried the strategy you call stimulus change and have not been too successful. Why?

**A:** One of the main reasons this strategy fails is because parents are not effective enough in switching the child's attention. Many times it takes good acting. For example, players must really believe their coach is upset. A parent must really look interested when she says "Hey, look up there!"

**Q:** I tried punishing my young daughter for sucking her thumb. I would pull her thumb out and slap her hand. It did not seem to work. What will?

**A:** Try a different form of punishment. There are bad tasting solutions you can buy which can be "painted" on the thumb. When the child goes to suck he or she receives an unpleasant experience. This approach can be quite effective. It works best on younger children. It also is more effective if you subtly place the solution on the thumb. The quicker the child realizes it is the solution that is aversive, the sooner he or she tries to circumvent your plans by washing the solution off. Strange as it may seem, psychologists have found that many children will quit sucking their thumbs if parents repeatedly praise and reward children for not having their thumb in their mouth. This strategy often takes a while to have an effect, but often is successful.

# 10
# Punishment

None of the chapters in this book created the amount of apprehension this chapter did as I wrote it. The use of punishment is an issue to which few people are ambivalent. Either you strongly believe in it or you are strongly against its use. And I knew whichever position I took I ran the risk of offending a large number of readers. I also realized the largest body of readers and child-rearing experts at this point in time favor a nonpunishment approach to childrearing.

> "Punishment is a primitive approach to childrearing."
> "An intelligent and mature individual can find a better way to handle children than use of physical force."
> "Punishment of children turns those children into child beaters and wife beaters."
> "There are many nonpunishment tactics such as *time out* that can be used instead to control inappropriate behaviors in problem children."

All of these are rather intimidating statements against the use of punishment. It is unfortunate that such statements have influenced so many people, however, because all those statements are *false.*

Now I am sure that what has been said so far about punishment has raised the ire of many of you readers, particularly the last sentence. And I am writing such statements with some reluctance—not because what I say is false, but because it is not what many like to hear. However, punishment is the victim of some rather bad publicity, and that publicity has led to many "experts" advocating some rather incorrect principles of discipline.

"What makes you think you are right and the other experts are wrong?" "How could so many people come to the wrong conclusion?" "Couldn't you be wrong?" Those are three good questions, questions that I have been asked several times when giving talks to PTAs, foster parent groups, and other such parental organizations. And they certainly deserve an answer.

To understand how easy it is for any expert in childrearing to be wrong on some issue, one needs to consider some of the problems psychologists have keeping abreast of issues. Literally thousands of psychological research articles and hundreds of books are published each year. Since it is impossible for each psychologist to read firsthand everything that is written, we strongly rely on "second sources" or condensed reviews other people have written of the original works. It is like reading *Reader's Digest* to keep abreast of new magazine articles coming out which the average person does not have the time to read, so they read condensed versions in the *Reader's Digest.* Many psychologists rely heavily on getting their information from second sources.

Not all psychological investigations are equally well controlled. Some investigators are quite meticulous when studying the effects of punishment while others are not. As a result, not all studies done on punishment come up with the same conclusions. Some studies suggest punishment is not effective. There are other studies, however, that show punishment is effective in controlling problem behaviors. Because not all studies come up with the same conclusions, it is possible for us psychologists to support our personal bias of punishment's role in life by selectively citing research which supports what we believe.

With these points in mind I'll state why I believe punishment is effective. First, almost *every* psychologist who is an expert on punishment and is intimately familiar with the original works (not second sources) proclaims punishment is effective. A number of references have been included at the end of this chapter in case the readers would like to read them for themselves. Secondly, during the many years my wife and I have taken foster children with behavior problems into our home, I have seen punishment effectively change their actions time and time again.

I realize these previous statements make many people uncomfortable. These statements were not made to offend anyone, but to provide information the reader may use in deciding for him- or herself how to discipline their children. As I said previously, there are many child-rearing experts who disapprove of the use of punishment, so you are not alone if you feel uncomfortable with what has been mentioned.

## A SENSITIVE ISSUE

Two years ago the Utah State Division of Social Services gave my wife and me an award at the yearly banquet for our years of service in the state's specialized foster care program. I was invited to speak at that banquet on any topic I felt would be of benefit to foster parents. After seeing a memo discouraging the use of punishment to foster parents from directors of the state program, I decided on my topic—*six effective ways to deal with undesirable behaviors.*

At the banquet I talked about the six techniques mentioned in the previous chapter. I intentionally saved the technique of punishment for last. Prior to giving the talk I had told several of the social workers from the social service office about what I was going to say.

"Oh boy," one of them replied. "We will see fireworks that night. Miss ______, one of the assistant directors of the state's Division of Social Services, keeps sending out advice that the use of punishment is harmful, and she is going to be at the banquet."

As I talked at the banquet I kept my eye on the assistant director. After discussing the five techniques of extinction, physical restraint, satiation, incompatible responding, and stimulus change, I turned my remarks toward punishment.

"Now, let's turn our attention toward punishment techniques

which many behavioral scientists consider the most effective means of controlling undesirable behavior." Watching her eyes widen I continued, "I doubt there is an issue in childrearing which is more misunderstood even by professionals in child care, than punishment. To help clear up some of these misunderstandings I have brought with me tonight five college textbooks on learning written by behavioral scientists who have rather thoroughly reviewed the research done on punishment. In 1966 Azrin and Holz compared the alternative ways one can use to eliminate or reduce undesired behaviors and concluded: 'As a reductive procedure, punishment appears to be at least as effective as most other procedures for eliminating responses.'

"In 1968 Boe and Church reviewed the 684 research articles written on punishment from 1900 to 1968 and concluded that punishment is an effective method of controlling behavior. In 1978 Schwartz reviewed the literature on punishment and summarized by saying: 'Does punishment work? In the light of all the research discussed here, it is surprising that question is asked at all.'

"In 1977 Walters and Grusec wrote a book entitled *Punishment* and reviewed all the work on punishment done by learning and developmental psychologists. Their findings were the same as for Azrin and Holz, Boe and Church, and Schwartz."

I went on to explain that behavioral scientists, who are experts on punishment procedures, consider punishment an effective means for dealing with problem behavior. By this time the assistant director was having heart palpitations and difficulty waiting for the end of my lecture.

After covering some of the important points to keep in mind when using punishment I concluded my talk. Within a minute or two after the banquet ended she reached the table where I was sitting. After introducing herself to me she said, "Are you familiar with Dr. ______'s book on child care? She says punishment should *never* be used. And Dr. ______'s book on discipline points out that punishment is a very poor and ineffective method of teaching."

"I am familiar with both of those books," I replied. "And I feel both books provide some important information on childrearing for parents."

"Then why did you argue punishment was an effective method

for controlling undesirable behavior when they are both against it? Why are both of them against punishment if it is supposedly an effective procedure?"

"I cannot answer your question as to why either of those authors are against the use of punishment because, as you may recall, neither of those authors cite any research to support their contentions. One just adamantly denounces it, while the other refers to how he raised his children. I base my position on punishment on two things, (1) the general concensus of all punishment research is that it is effective, and (2) in all my years of taking children of all ages and backgrounds into my home, I have found the use of punishment to be effective in molding these children with problems into successfully oriented individuals."

"Well, I do not see why we cannot properly help these children without having to resort to spanking," she replied.

"Now wait a moment," I interjected. "I did not say spanking was something parents *must* do to their children. Nor does the research literature claim it must be done. The literature simply shows that punishment, of which spanking is only one form, *can be* an *effective* method—not the *only* method. The point I was trying to make in the talk is that punishment is not the ogre that many child-rearing specialists are claiming that it is. Punishment is, in fact, a very natural part of life which can play an invaluable role in molding our characters to become successful members of society."

By this time a large group of foster parents had gathered around. "Dr. Robinson, I cannot tell you how much I appreciated what you said about punishment," one foster parent commented while we were standing there. "You know, I have become confused and have felt guilty about using punishment, yet there have been a number of situations in which it seemed to be necessary."

That man's remarks were the concensus of the foster parents who stayed to talk to me. About thirty of us chatted for close to an hour and exchanged suggestions with each other as person after person brought up situations where punishment could be used effectively. When one person brought up the idea being passed around today that punishment leads to physical abuse, I gave them a possible alternative explanation. "I have a feeling that the nonpunishment philosophy is responsible for a large portion of child abuse," I said.

"Parents are told that punishment is not effective and should not be used. As parents repeatedly refrain from reprimanding their child, the natural feelings inside them continue to fester and grow until eventually the pressure bursts and the parents overpunish, so the punishment given far outweighs the value of the offense."

Parents often find themselves with contradictory information. On the one hand they are told punishment doesn't work, and on the other hand they recall instances, perhaps in their own lives, where they saw or experienced a situation where punishment did stop undesirable behaviors. A parent goes to spank a misbehaving child and the child quickly sits down and says, "OK, OK, I won't do it again. Just don't spank me." A mother going shopping downtown avoids parking in a no parking zone because she had been punished in the past by having her car towed away. Such instances cause dissonance in the minds of parents who later begin overreacting with punishment as the solutions proposed by society do not seem to be realistic.

## A SCIENTIFIC LOOK AT PUNISHMENT

Due to the fact that there are such large discrepancies between child-rearing experts as to whether punishment should be used, it might be beneficial to take a closer look at punishment and see how it fits in Mother Nature's plan of life. What role, if any, does unpleasant experience play in nature?

Back at least as far as the Greeks, man, in his search to understand himself, has realized that life is an interrelationship of three different kinds of experiences. It was said that life was composed of positive, negative, and neutral experiences. Positive experiences were felt to be those events in life which brought joy and pleasure to an individual. This pleasure could come in (1) a materialistic form such as food or perfumes, (2) an entertaining event such as a theatrical play, or (3) an internal feeling of satisfaction such as the pride one experiences in watching their child grow and develop. Negative experiences were considered to be mirror images of positive experiences, but unpleasant in value. Unpleasant odors such as sulphur gas, uncomfortable events such as sitting through a boring oration, and thoughts of impending disasters such as the thoughts of the Christians before being fed to the lions during the Roman Empire, are all examples of possible negative experiences. Neutral experiences were those relatively few experiences in life for which we do not seem to care one way or another.

As intellectuals studied the importance of these different kinds of experiences on personal development, it was concluded that the positive and negative dimension of experiences was an important consideration. So important, in fact, that the scholars proposed the *Hedonistic Principle.* The Hedonistic Principle says that man is guided by the value of experiences he encounters. He is drawn towards pleasure and enjoyment while he learns to avoid things which accompany negative experiences. In fact they argued negative experiences were necessary for man to develop a proper perspective in life. A man learns as much from experiencing pain as he does from experiencing pleasure.

In studying man the scholars identified another important principle of life—the principle of *Associationism.* They noticed that things which are associated tend to produce a mental bond such that the thought of one item brings forth the thought of an associated item. For example, if I asked you to say the first thing that comes to your mind when I say "fork," you will very likely say "spoon." Fork and spoon are paired together (or associated as psychologists prefer to say) so much in our everyday life that a mental bond is formed between them. Associationism was the principle behind why women wear perfume and men wear cologne. They pair themselves with positive things, and through association, they are perceived to take on some of that value. "You run with a bad crowd and it will rub off on you" is a statement heard in childrearing which is based on the idea of associationism.

From the time of the Greeks up to the 1900s, scholars had pretty much agreed that the principles of *hedonism and associationism* were true and self-evident. After all, you did not see man or any other species of animal in Mother Nature's scheme which did the opposite. Man does not search out and eat the foods he dislikes. A man or woman does not choose a mate they find offensive. Animals do not seek out other animals which feed upon them. Mice do not search for cats, and rabbits do not run to wolves. And if there were any species with these inclinations, they died out long ago. By the start of the twentieth century, however, people became aware that scholars could be just as opinionated and wrong as anyone else. Gregor Mendel, for example, was a monk who dabbled in the sciences. In 1866 he experimented with cross-polinating sweetpeas and discovered the secret of how genetic codes pass information from one generation to the next. He wrote up his findings and sent them to the noted genetic scholars of the time. Unfortunately, Mendel's findings did not coincide with the ideas of the scholars, so they laughed at Mendel's work. They kiddingly wrote back and said they liked his idea; and why didn't he go study the ragweed. Mendel took their advice and spent the rest of his life studying ragweed, a plant whose genetic makeup is so complex he was unable to break its code. It was thirty-four years later before geneticists through experimentation rather than philosophizing came to find in 1900 that what Mendel found in 1866 was the key to understanding how biological information is passed from one generation to the next.

Because of such miscalculations by "educated" men, people began demanding proof to back up beliefs. They were not satisfied with opinions only, for unsupported opinions could be wrong. Experimental analysis of man's behavior was demanded, so psychologists began devising experimental strategies which could more effectively answer psychological questions. Edward Thorndike (1847–1949) published one of the first experiments on the effects of punishment in 1898. Thorndike set out to experimentally study the principle of hedonism (the pleasure principal) which was under attack at that time by people who felt somehow the idea that man sought after pleasure was beneath man's dignity. These people had no data to support this idea, but it just did not seem right.

Within twenty years after Thorndike's beginnings, psychology as a science was well on its way to experimentally studying the importance of positive and negative experiences on man. Two words *reinforcement* and *punishment* came into being to represent positive and negative experiences.

Two problems arose also, however. First, how do we define what we mean by reinforcement and punishment. We cannot really study something until we settle on and agree as to what exactly we are talking about. Some psychologists had begun limiting the term punishment to physical pain, while other psychologists claimed degrading remarks about a child by the parent could also be considered negative by the child. Eventually psychologists agreed on the definitions:

> *Reinforcement* is the application or removal of some stimulus which "increases" the frequency of a behavior.
> *Punishment* is the application or removal of a stimulus which "decreases" the frequency of a behavior.

Now these definitions might sound somewhat confusing. And you might wonder why they did not just say reinforcement is giving something pleasurable when a child behaves the way parents want, and punishment is giving something unpleasant when the child does something wrong. Well, the answer to that question requires a bit of explanation, and that explanation is given in the next chapter so it won't confuse the issue of punishment being discussed here. Suffice it to say psychologists have found rather ingenious techniques they can employ to use the *same* object or experience to either punish or reward behavior.

Getting back to the way experts defined punishment, they came to realize that certainly more things than spankings could be done to punish children. They found that there literally is a host of things that could be used as punishment. Punishers could include:

*Punishers*

| | | |
|---|---|---|
| Spanking | Removal of privileges | Missing a meal |
| A frown | Being grounded | Verbal scolding |
| Withdrawal of attention | Having to sit on a chair | Having to go to bed |
| Time outs | Taking away a toy | |

According to behavioral scientists all of these "could" (not always can) be used to decrease inappropriate behavior in children. Therefore, all of these are potential punishers. It is important to notice that many of these actions which can be punishers involve no physical action on the child. Experts in punishment research have *never* distinguished spanking as the only form of punishment like many child-rearing books suggest.

After defining punishment, the second problem researchers had to deal with was the question of ethics in studying punishment. Do psychologists have the right to intentionally arrange conditions in an experiment so a child experiences something unpleasant? This question is similar to asking "Can we take adults and force or coerce them to smoke cigarette after cigarette to see if smoking causes cancer?" In the case of cancer the conclusion was reached that it would be unethical to do that to humans, so two alternative scientific approaches were used. First, we carried out what is called Ex Post Facto (after the fact) research. We studied people who already smoked and compared cancer rates in smokers to nonsmokers. Second, we introduced animals into smoking research and did things to animals that were considered unethical to do to humans. While little direct experimentation was done on humans, the Ex Post Facto research on humans and the experimentation on animals left little doubt that smoking does cause cancer.

Now, psychologists were not quite so worried about the irreversibility of the effects of punishment on people as they were about smoking. Yet they have had a tendency to shy away from direct punishment experiments on humans and have opted to attack the problem more frequently with Ex Post Facto and animal research. So, for the past fifty to seventy years a fair amount of research has been done to study the effects positive and negative experiences have on one's life.

Before we discuss what has been found out specifically about punishment, let's discuss for a moment the issue of whether aversive (unpleasant) experiences in one's life is unnatural as some people are currently contending. There are a number of people who presently argue that parenting should focus only on arranging positive experiences for a child. As one recent public spokesperson said, "Parents who punish their children in any way are reacting on a rather primitive and unnatural level with the child. There are higher planes from which we should deal."

As previously mentioned, the importance of both pleasant and aversive experiences in one's life has been acknowledged down through the ages. Since the 1900s a large amount of research on the human mind has found that contrasting both positive and negative experiences is fundamental in brain functioning. Among the many findings, Olds and Milner in 1954 found that the brain includes a variety of centers (more properly called nuclei) that when stimulated produce pleasurable sensations. A rat will press a bar hundreds of times to receive one-half second of stimulation in these various areas. Other centers in the brain have been located which produced pain when stimulated. Such pleasure and pain centers are found to be an integral part of nature's plan, for almost every animal with a relatively well developed brain (including humans) has these centers. And the more well developed the brain, the more these centers appear to be integrated into the brain's functions. The human brain is not designed with only positive centers, it has a host of aversive centers also. All of Mother Nature's more developed creatures are internally wired to deal with contrasting pleasurable and unpleasant experiences. *Unpleasant experiences are a natural and valuable part of life.* One of the most universal findings in research on learning is that animals, including man, learn from both positive and negative experiences. Learning is not restricted just to positive or rewarding situations. Punishment no more causes trauma and maladjustment in children than rewarding experiences causes a child to become spoiled and maladjusted.

## FALLACIES ABOUT PUNISHMENT

With the previous points in mind, let's take a look at some of the commonly heard statements about punishment which are fallacies.

### Fallacy No. 1: Punishment Causes Trauma

One of the most often heard fallacies about punishment is that it produces trauma. It has been argued that if you use strong physical forms of punishment, such as spankings, it creates such an emotional stress in the child that it throws the child's psychological equilibrium off to the extent he can no longer cope with the world in a normal way. The person becomes permanently anxious, withdrawn, fearful, and easily upset. Over time the individual is said to become maladjusted and emotionally distraught as the trauma develops in the person. It is further argued that the stronger the painful event, the greater the trauma.

Actually strong painful events do not cause trauma. If that were true all adults would display traumatic behavior. Throughout life each of us has experienced some rather painful experiences. Many of us touched hot stoves when we were young, but we do not go through life afraid of stoves. Many young boys play hard, contact sports such as football and boxing. In such competition they experience many painful situations, yet they do not automatically become fearful, withdrawn, and cowardly.

It is most certainly true that painful experiences do arouse an individual. The mind is prewired to pay particular attention to incoming signals signifying a painful experience—be it physically or mentally induced. Pain and unpleasantness are signals of impending danger for a person. The danger may be an inflamed appendix or the realization that our newborn child died during the night. Both are painful situations, yet people do not automatically become permanently emotionally maladjusted from such experiences. While such experiences may produce deep pain for a while, most people can adequately deal with such crises, and psychologically readjust to a normal life. The psychological arousal which pain generally creates is a healthy aspect of life. This arousal is not an indication that emotional maladjustment must follow.

The main cause of traumatic fear and emotional stress in children is *inconsistency,* not just painful experiences. If we, as parents, are inconsistent when we deal with our children, we can produce trauma in them. Father laughs at little Freddy's swearing in front of people and says, "Isn't that cute," then later he spanks Freddy for saying the same thing when they are alone. Laurie's mother tells her to use her initiative and try new things. Later, Laurie tries to fix the stopped-up vacuum cleaner only to have her mother yell, "You idiot! Now you have really broken it. Why can't you just do what you are told?" In cases like these, the children are given two completely different signals—*Do this, but don't do this.* Nothing is harder on a child than to receive conflicting signals and be unable to discern why such conflicting signals are being given. Producing uncertainty is the key to producing inner psychological conflict from which emotional trauma arises. This is one of the keys to effective brainwashing—create emotional stress in the person by creating inconsistency and uncertainty in his/her mind. Show him water runs up hill, black is white, and white is black. Tell him to turn left then yell, "I said right, not left!" Such tactics are much more effective in causing trauma and emotional stress than brutal, painful experiences by themselves.

People can generally handle pain and disappointment—if it is consistent. We no longer fear the stove that gave us the painful burn when we were young. The stove is consistent; it only burns when it is hot. It does not sneak up on us. It only burns when hot if we touch it. Punishment may be used effectively to change behavior. The secret is to be consistent in what you do to avoid emotional stress.

### Fallacy No. 2: Punishment Causes Aggression

"Do not punish children because it makes them hostile and aggressive." This statement is actually a partial truth. It is true that if a child is punished (for example he is spanked, she is grounded from dating for a month) he/she will initially attempt to retaliate with physical or verbal actions. This is a very natural reaction which Mother Nature has instilled in each of us. If something painful happens to any of us, our mind warns us and stimulates us to react. If we drop a gallon of milk on our foot while rummaging through the refrigerator, our mind lets us know that part of the body is hurt. The more pain we feel, the more damage has been done to the foot. The physical pain in this case lets us know the foot needs help and special care. We react to this situation by not demanding so much from our foot. We use crutches or quit walking until the damage heals. These actions are taken to reduce the pain and help the healing process.

If a child experiences pain from punishment, the natural tendency will be to terminate the pain. This may be accomplished in two ways. First, do what the parent and society wants so they will not punish, or second, attack the parent so the parent will quit punishing. Both of these are natural reactions people of all ages have. Being aggressive back to the parent is natural, but *it will only occur to the degree that it is successful in getting the parent to stop.* If a ten-year-old boy can push and wiggle so mother cannot effectively spank him, he will do so. If he is not effective in avoiding the punishment, he will be more prone to try the other approach—do what she wants him to next time.

Most children learn to adjust to what mother and dad want them to do at a tender young age when physically retaliating against the parents is almost impossible. Children who use the tactics listed in Chapters Three and Four use screaming and crying to control parents when they are young. If the child has not learned proper restraint, or has been effective in influencing the parents' tendency to punish, they are prone to use stronger physical and verbal methods on their parents as they grow older.

### Fallacy No. 3: Punishment Is Unnatural and Ineffective

From the points made earlier in the chapter, it should be apparent that experiencing painful situations is a natural part of life. The mind is genetically endowed to deal effectively with such experiences. Parents who try to eliminate punishment from a child's life are building a distorted preception of life for that child. Our world is full of punishment. Children get burned when touching hot stoves. Children walking into streets can get hit by cars. A boy at school may be hit when he takes a toy from another child. A child may be teased at school for getting the low score on a test. A man may be fired for talking back to his boss.

Trying to eliminate punishment in the home may cause more painful problems for children later on because they did not learn how to cope with minor painful experiences early in life. Dianne was a fifteen-year-old girl who had such a problem. Dianne was the only child in a relatively well-to-do family. In the winter of

1970, Dianne's boyfriend told her he no longer wanted to go steady and took his ring back. A few hours later her mother found her in the bathroom where she was attempting suicide by slashing her wrists with a razor blade. Six months later Dianne made a second unsuccessful attempt.

In talking to her mother, it became apparent that her parents had gone out of their way to make their child's life as painless as possible. If she did not want to do something, she did not have to. When Dianne was a young child her mother stepped in to stop squabbles with other children. Her mother did volunteer work at the schools to keep an eye on Dianne. They never spanked their daughter, but disciplined her by keeping a close watch on her. They had stepped in almost every time Mother Nature confronted her with some sort of disappointing situation. She had not learned to take disappointment. Mother Nature programs progressively stronger disappointments in our growing years to prepare us for the stronger and more serious disappointments of adulthood. Without those minor disappointment experiences, Dianne's chances of properly coping with the real world were taken from her.

During one meeting, I told her mother how the parents of a certain family had planned disappointments for their children. I told how the children were required to fast from eating a meal once a month to help teach them self-control. "Oh I think intentionally doing something like that is just being cruel to the children," she commented. "I would not be cruel to my child like that." Unfortunately the mother did not see how much more pain she caused for her daughter by not allowing her to learn how to handle mild disappointments when she was young. The heartache and pain Dianne went through when her boyfriend rejected her far exceeded those disappointments her parents had saved her from when she was young. Ten years and two divorces later, Dianne and her three children are now living with her parents in Denver, Colorado.

Experiencing painful situations is a natural part of life. Such experiences can be effective learning experiences which can help each of us grow and develop properly. Often we parents may try to circumvent tribulations for our children only to end up creating insurmountable problems for them later in life.

## Fallacy No. 4:
## The More Punishment, the Better

Unfortunately there are parents who feel the more punishment a person experiences, the stronger that person becomes. These parents use punishment as the main vehicle for communication with their children. It is important to remember that punishment should be considered a seasoning (like salt and pepper) rather than the main course (like steak) of a disciplinary diet. An overdependence on punishment can have undesired effects on the child the same way overuse of salt and pepper can spoil a steak.

Overuse of punishment on children can produce what is called *learned helplessness.* Learned helplessness is a condition found in children where the individual shows little, if any, initiative. Such children have low opinions of themselves, lack the desire to try to accomplish things, and believe they will fail at even simple tasks. Seeing the "give-up" attitude in depressed and low-achieving individuals, Dr. Martin Seligman attempted to produce this phenomenon in dogs. He successfully produced this state by consistently shocking them whenever they tried to do anything. Eventually the dogs would just lay down and continually get shocked, even when all they had to do to avoid the painful shock was stand up and walk two feet away. As a result of overpunishment, children may be reluctant to do even the simplest types of schoolwork—schoolwork they are quite capable of doing. They have learned that trying does not help.

Another point to keep in mind is that punishment tells the child *what not to do, not what to do.* If a child does something wrong and is punished, that punishment gives little feedback as to what should be done. It just tells what was incorrectly done. There is a common game where someone picks an object in a room and a second person tries to guess what was chosen. If the person guessing is simply told "No, that's not it" every time a guess is made, he is still very much in the dark as to finding the object. If, however, that person is given positive feedback such as "You are getting closer," the object can be found much more quickly. Positive feedback provides much more information than does negative feedback. Negative feedback is informative, but not to the degree positive feedback is. Such is also true of punishment in comparison to positive or rewarding consequences.

How can I tell if I use too much punishment? The answer to that question is not too difficult. A good rule of thumb is to use *nine* parts reward and praise for every *one* part punishment. Thank a child for doing what you want, praise him/her for positive social behaviors nine times more than reproofing him/her for inappropriate behaviors. Too often we parents find ourselves ignoring children when they are doing positive things and devote most of our interaction time with our children to punishing them. To check yourself, monitor your daily responses to your child for a day or two. If your ratio is 5:5 (5 positive to every 5 negative) you have some adjustments to make. If your ratio is close to 2:8 (two positive to eight negative), chances are your child finds little enjoyment in interacting with you. He/she most likely does not follow your instructions closely and probably spends most of the time with his friends or neighbors. Change the ratio and you can do much to change the child.

### Fallacy No. 5: Children Hate Parents Who Punish

Generally speaking, parents who discipline their children with punishment (in conjunction with the ratios outlined previously) are rated much more highly by their children than parents who use little if any punishment, or parents who overuse punishment. Most children perceive aversive experiences such as punishment as a natural part of life. Parents can produce negative feelings in their children if the parents dramatically overuse punishment. This is a rather rare phenomenon in our society, however, as Chapter Fourteen explains.

## TACTICS FOR EFFECTIVE PUNISHMENT

Punishment is not automatically an effective procedure to use to eliminate unwanted habits and actions. Its effectiveness, or ineffectiveness, depends on how it is employed. There are things which can be done to maximize the effects of punishment. Five of the more important things to consider are explained below.

## Punishment Is Relative

One of the most important points to remember when using punishment is that *punishment is relative.* What is considered punishment by one person, may not be punishment to another. It is true that there are certain experiences that almost everyone finds unpleasant. People do not like slamming their fingers in car doors; spankings are unpleasant for most; and everyone agrees that being shocked is unpleasant. However, when it comes to unpleasant experiences parents may use as punishment, there are differences from child to child as to what is effectively unpleasant. One family with six children had two boys ten months apart. When the oldest boy was six years old, spankings were most effective in stopping undesirable actions. Spankings for the other son were effective, but not half as effective as making him sit on a chair (what psychologists call *time out*) for fifteen minutes. Having to sit while other children were playing was almost more than Benny could stand; and he would rather be spanked than have to sit still by himself.

Sandy was an attractive sixteen-year-old girl whose foster parents punished her by not allowing her boyfriend over for a week or two. Limiting her television viewing had no effect on controlling her temper. Christine was a rather boyish fourteen-year-old who couldn't seem to get enough TV. Boys meant little or nothing to her. The foster parents used TV restrictions to discipline Christine.

"How come you ground me from television when I do something wrong. Why don't you restrict me from boys like you do Sandy?" Christine complained.

"When was the last time you dated?"

"I haven't," she replied.

Smiling, her foster dad said, "Somehow I don't think you understand the principle behind punishment . . . or do you?"

Christine knew the principle quite well and wanted her dad to shift to a less unpleasant punisher.

Keep in mind that the same punisher may have different effects on two different children. With some thought, most parents can identify what each of their children strongly dislikes. Restricting television, being grounded from activities and social events, and other social restrictions may be as effective as spankings in getting rid of undesirable actions.

### Punishment Should Be Intense

One of the more difficult to accept attributes of punishment has to do with intensity. One of the most well documented principles is that punishment should be intense to be effective. Mild or moderate punishment generally has little if any effect, and in many cases actually increases the undesired acts.

What is considered intense? That varies from child to child. For a young child, a scowl from mother may be considered an intense punisher. Such a child feels unhappy when mother is unhappy. For other children, strong spankings are required to stop their actions. Most of the foster children brought into our home are insensitive to the more subtle forms of punishment. They could care less if my wife or I are unhappy. Most of them have had talk after talk with the police, parents, and social workers. They are relatively free of any guilt feelings for things they have done. In fact, most of them are quite insensitive to the feelings of others, including other children their age.

The story is told about a farmer who sold a mule to his neighbor and said, "Show love and concern for this animal and he will do more work for you than any two mules."

The next day the neighbor went out to work the mule, and the mule just stood there. No matter how much coaxing and care the neighbor gave, the mule would not budge.

After complaining to the farmer, both men returned to the mule whereupon the farmer grabbed a club and hit the mule on the side of the head.

"Hey, I thought you told me to give him consideration and love!"

"Well, first you have to get his attention," the farmer replied.

There is more fact than fiction in this story when it is applied to children with behavioral problems. One of the main values of punishment is to get the child's attention and let him/her know that such behaviors are not acceptable to you or society. Any teacher can testify to the fact that no matter how important or valuable a prepared lesson or task is, it is useless if the student does not listen. Getting the child to stop and think is one of the values of an intense punisher.

This issue of intensity of punishment is one of the more important points to influence psychologists' attitude about punishment. Around 1900, Dr. Edward Thorndike was one of the first to experiment on punishment. Originally he said it was effective. Later he employed some rather mild punishers and then changed his mind—arguing punishment was of little, if any, value. Later, punishment research in the 1930s, 1940s, and 1950s confirmed his findings. It wasn't until the late 1960s and 1970s that psychologists varied intensity of punishment and established quite convincingly that mild and medium punishers are not generally effective, but that intense punishment is very effective.

A final point to keep in mind about punishment intensity is that physical punishment such as spankings are not necessarily the most intense. Anyone who has sat through a divorce knows the tongue can be mightier than the hand. Separating husbands and wives can inflict pain on their mate that no physical beating can match. Chapter Eleven discusses alternative forms of effective punishment that society considers quite acceptable.

## Punishment Should Be Immediate

The more immediately punishment is administered, the greater its effect. Earlier in this chapter, the principle of *association* was mentioned. One of the most basic laws of man's behavior is that events paired closely in time become related in one's mind. It is true, for both rewarding and punishing consequences of one's actions are more effective the closer they occur to the actions themselves. If you are going to punish a child, do it as quickly as possible after the offense. Do not say, "Wait until your father comes home." *Do it and get it over with.*

Shouldn't I think before I act? Definitely. Both parents should sit down and consider most of the undesirable acts their child may commit and put them into certain categories. Agree ahead of time that certain types of actions receive certain consequences. While this might sound difficult, it is quite easily done. Then when the act is done, the punishment given is appropriate to the offense.

A second point to remember about punishment is, *do not prolong it.* Oftentimes parents say something like, "I have to spank you, but I want you to realize what you did, and that I love you." How would you react if a fellow came up to you and said, "Your neighbor hired me to beat you up. But before I do, I want to tell you how much I really like you and hate doing this." Are you going to listen to the positive things he says? Obviously not. You will more likely say, "Please, please don't hit me! I'm sorry! Tell him I did not mean to offend him! I've got money! Do you want money?"

When confronted with a parent who wants to talk, the child will reply with such comments as: "Please don't spank me! I won't do it again! I'll be good!" Sound familiar?

Your discussion with the child merely prolongs the agony and waters down the behavioral effect of the punishment by delaying it. Administer the punishment, let its effects sink in, then discuss the episode a few hours later.

### Do Not Allow Escape

As previously mentioned, it is natural for children to react to punishment. Their first tendency is to focus on the person administering the punishment and do whatever might get that parent to remove the punisher. In some cases the child will try to get away by running. Some young children wiggle and squirm to get out of the grasp of the parent. Other children cry or yell such things as "I hate you" or "You are just being mean to me."

When children do try to avoid being punished, they say things that are not necessarily true, but the things they say are usually sensitive issues for the parent. To stepparents they may say "You're just doing this because I'm not really your daughter/son," or "You don't love me as much as your real children." Children who know their parents can be played against each other may say "Dad never is this mean to me" or "I love Mommy better than you. You are just mean to me." If parents might not know for sure that the child did the act, the child may try to avoid being punished by saying, "I did not do it; Johnny did."

If the child is successful in influencing the parents' attempts at punishment, he/she will try the same tactics the next time. In such cases, the application of punishment has little beneficial effect on the child, and the parent generally gives up, concluding punishment does not work.

If the parent makes sure the child is unable to avoid or escape from the punishment given, the verbal complaints against punishment generally fade, and the child focuses his efforts on not repeating the punished act. Most discipline failures experienced by parents are due to children being able to avoid or disrupt the parents' efforts to punish.

### Provide Alternatives

It is important to remember that children find enjoyment in doing the things you may dislike. There is a reason for doing the things they do. Children are rewarded for stealing; they end up with items they did not previously have. Throwing spitwads in class can be funny. Screaming at mother can result in getting her attention. Many of the acts we consider inappropriate are functional for our children. If they were not, the children wouldn't do them in the first place.

With this in mind, parents can effectively deal with most inappropriate behaviors by punishing *and* providing acceptable alternatives for the inappropriate behaviors. Many problem behaviors children express are behaviors which are acceptable in other situations. And many other totally unacceptable behaviors can be eliminated if the goals for which the children are striving when emitting these inappropriate acts are made possible by emitting acceptable behaviors. Striving for mother's attention is a behavior which is acceptable at certain times, yet unacceptable at other times. Stealing money to buy clothes is a totally unacceptable behavior which can be controlled to some extent by providing alternative means for obtaining clothes.

Rusty was a hyperactive, sandy-haired second-grader who was always hanging around the teacher's desk. Besides reprimanding him for being out of his seat, the teacher arranged special times after class that Rusty could come in and "help" the teacher as she cleaned up before going home. When the teacher took my suggestion of after-class time, Rusty's hanging-around actions were easy to control. By providing him with times when such actions were permissible, Rusty's "hanging-around-the-teacher" behavior during class was more easily eliminated. One inventive mother arranged certain times every few days when her young children could throw rocks, play with some "special" flour and sugar on the basement floor, and make mud pies under supervision. Any time she found her children doing something inappropriate, which could be done properly, she arranged times for it. One sharp fifth-grade teacher almost totally eliminated paper throwing, yelling, and other noisy in-class acts by arranging a special five-minute time each day when such things could be done *if* everyone had been good up to that time.

Elliot was a fifth-grader caught stealing from lockers at the community swimming pool. He said he had been stealing to buy clothes his parents could not afford to get him. They were immigrants to this country and unskilled. They were quite poverty stricken because they did not believe in accepting welfare. One of the local businessmen gave Elliot a part-time job. In this way, Elliot's stealing was eliminated by providing him with a socially acceptable way of getting clothes similar to what his classmates wore. Many parents eliminate tantrum behavior in their children by punishing such behavior, *and* making sure more socially acceptable ways for getting parents to listen are rewarded.

Providing suitable times or more suitable behaviors is a welcome complement which greatly increases the effectiveness of punishment. Undesirable actions are much more easily controlled when alternatives are provided by insightful parents.

*Questions from Parents*

**Q:** With so many alternatives to spanking, why is spanking such a popular punishment?

**A:** Perhaps it is most popular with parents because it is the most well known form of punishment. From a scientific point of view, spanking is a good choice because its effect can be maximized better than other forms of punishment. For example, it is easier to vary the intensity of spanking than such things as taking away privileges. You can more easily tell the severity of the spanking than removing privileges. The effect of spanking is also much quicker than the effect of removing privileges. If taking away privileges could have as quick an impact as spanking, and as intense an effect, then taking away privileges could be just as effective as spankings.

**Q:** I have previously heard the term *time out,* and you mention it in the chapter. I am not exactly sure what it means. What does it mean and why do so many experts advocate its use over spanking?

**A:** The term *time out* can be related to the term used in a basketball or football game where a coach or player stops the game that is going on. A parent employs a time out when he or she removes the child from whatever he is doing for some length of time. For example a mother may make her three-year-old daughter sit on a chair for twenty minutes or so because the child was too rowdy while playing in the house. In such a situation sitting on the chair would be considered a "time out." Later on the child is allowed to return to the previous activity. Experts advocate the use of time out because it is a form of punishment which is more socially acceptable because it does not entail any physical expression on the child. Teachers can use it with less chance of upsetting parents than spanking. Aunts and uncles prefer it for the same reason.

**Q:** I have heard that people who are child beaters were beaten by their parents. Is this true? And if it is, how does this relate to your advocating punishment?

**A:** It is true that there have been studies done which show there is a high correlation between parents who are child beaters and having been beaten as a child themselves. There is also a higher correlation between sick people in doctors' offices than sick people in lawyer's or architect's offices. This does not mean that doctors cause sickness. Presently, there are a number of psychologists studying the reasons for child beating and hopefully we will understand the problem better in the next few years. As to the second part of your question it is important to remember that *childbeating is not punishment.* Child-beating is a physical abuse, and is unacceptable in any way, shape, or form! People against the use of punishment often argue "How can you use physical force on a child—without teaching him to use it?" In 1970 we carried out a research project on children age four to ten. With parental permission we gave each child four options if some other child hit or displayed some other form of physical aggression on the child. We would tell the offended child "OK, you can do back to him exactly what he did to you, have us spank him, have him sit on a chair for thirty minutes, or forget it. In almost every case the child chose a form of punishment for the act which was less painful than what he received from the child he now could have punished. In talking with the children, it became apparent that punishment helps instil compassion for others. People who have had unpleasant experiences in life generally do not wish such experiences on others they care for.

## PUNISHMENT REFERENCES

Schwartz, B. *Psychology of Learning and Behavior,* New York: W. W. Norton Co, 1978.

On page 233 of one of the more popular texts used in Psychology of Learning courses Schwartz says "Is punishment effective? In light of all the evidence discussed in the preceding pages, it seems odd that one should ask this question at all. If the experiments we have been discussing show anything at all, surely it must be that punishment works."

Honig, W. K. *Operant Behavior: Areas of Research and Application,* New York: Appleton-Century-Crofts, 1966.

In Chapter Nine of this highly acclaimed basic research learning reference text, the point is concluded on page 433 that punishment is more effective than the other popular psychological strategies in reducing undesirable behavior.

Hulse, S. H., Egeth, H., & Desse, J. *The Psychology of Learning,* New York: McGraw-Hill, 1980.

This book is most likely the number one selling text on learning used in college and universities. When talking about the practical use of punishment, the authors state ". . . it is useful to recognize that the use of suppression produced by punishment can be an important technique to incorporate in clinical settings." (p. 158).

Walters, G. C., & Grusec, J. E. *Punishment,* San Francisco: W. H. Freeman, 1977.

Walters and Grusec reviewed all the research on using punishment on animals and humans. In their concluding remarks at the end of the book they state ". . . a good case can be made that punishment is a more effective technique for behavioral change than is reinforcement. And this leads us to an inescapable conclusion: Punishment will always be a necessary tool for behavioral change."

## BIBLICAL REFERENCES

| | |
|---|---|
| Proverbs 23:13, 14 | "Withhold not correction from the child; for *if* thou beatest him with the rod, he shall not die. Thou shalt beat him with the rod, and shalt deliver his soul from hell." |
| Proverbs 13:24. | "He that spareth his rod hateth his son: but he that loveth him chasteneth him betimes." |
| Proverbs 29:15 | "The rod and reproof give wisdom: but a child left to *himself* bringeth his mother to shame." |

# 11 Four Ways to Get Them to Do What You Want

Have you ever taught a timid mentally retarded ten-year-old how to handle the constant teasing she receives from classmates? Have you trained a rat to leap four times its height to a platform above, to walk a tightrope, and run an elevator? Have you taught a pigeon to play tic-tac-toe against humans—and win? Can you teach pigeons to work on assembly lines where they spot and remove defective electronic parts? Can you transform eighteen hyperactive, underachieving third graders into over-achievers in three weeks? Could you transform a fourteen-year-old, rebellious, ninth-grade dropout into a class-attending, above-average student who helps around the house? Can you teach a fish to read?

All of the aforementioned things I, or a psychological colleague, have accomplished. Later in this chapter I will explain in some detail how I went about getting the subject, be it human or animal, to do what I wanted done. While teaching a mentally retarded child to successfully deal with life, and teaching a pigeon to work for hours on an assembly line, require a substantial amount of professional expertise, they are not feats that cannot be accomplished to some degree by any parent, once a few basic principles are understood. The intent of this chapter is to furnish concerned parents with some rather simple but effective techniques they may use to successfully get their children to do what they want. It should be kept in mind that it would require many books to fully explain all that will briefly be covered in this chapter. The reader is getting a very quick and brief exposure to some important psychological concepts. Space does not permit me to address all the ramifications and questions which may come to the reader. Some of the more common questions parents have posed to me are included at the end of the chapter.

Keep in mind that the strategies discussed in this chapter are quite powerful. People are often fooled by the simplicity of what is to be covered. I can testify to you that someone may be able to explain more sophisticated and intellectual sounding strategies for dealing with children, but none are more effective than those presented here. I believe Mother Nature's plan is much simpler and straightforward than we psychologists like to admit. Too often we like to withdraw to our laboratories and build grand theories to explain some rather simple natural relationships.

## PROVIDING CONSEQUENCES IS THE KEY

There are two main abilities parents would like to have. First they would like to be able to get their children to do a number of things. These things often include helping around the house, being courteous, being kind, being creative, and being industrious. More specific actions may include being home on time from a date, cleaning up bedrooms, mowing lawns, and doing school assignments. The second thing parents would like is to be able to get their children to not do certain things. These things often include infant's crying, teenagers disobeying family rules, discourtesy, and impulsiveness. More specific actions may include swearing, fighting with brothers and sisters, complaining, and arguing.

One of the most powerful psychological laws is the fact that *man's actions are determined by the consequences (or results) of those actions.* A consequence of one's actions is defined as the "result of" or "what happens because of" the behavior. An American child learns to say "Please pass the butter" because such a request results in obtaining a particular object he wanted. When that child moves to Germany he will learn to say something different to obtain the same object because "Please pass the butter" does not result in his getting the butter. Parents turn up thermostats because the *consequence* for doing so is the room gets warmer. The consequence for turning on an air conditioner is a cooler surrounding. Young children often help parents when the consequence is expressions of gratitude. Older children often help parents because they get a feeling of satisfaction from helping another human being. Feeling warmer, feeling cooler, receiving the butter, getting parental affection, and feeling satisfaction can all be consequences for doing different things. They are the reasons we do things.

Consequences can also cause us not to do things. If we touch a hot stove, the consequence influences us in the direction of not doing that particular act again. Making unpleasant remarks to our friends results in them avoiding us, so we do not make unpleasant remarks. When the consequences of what we say and do are unpleasant to us, we learn not to say and do such things.

The main key then to getting a child to either *do something* or to *not do something* is in providing the proper consequence or reason for that act. If a parent wants a child to *do* something, make sure that what the child does results in a consequence he likes. If a parent wants a child *not to do* a certain act, make sure that act results in a consequence he considers unpleasant.

What has just been said is the secret to getting a child *to do* or *not to do* what you want. Sounds simple, doesn't it? Well, it is. And it works.

Now, I am sure a number of you parents are saying "Hey, I have tried that approach and sometimes it does not work." Let me quickly reply that I have heard that comment many times. And every time we look closely with the parents at the situation we have found a good reason why it is not working. We often find what we like to call *hidden defeaters* in these situations where consequation does not seem to work. *Hidden defeaters* are things we parents do which defeat the effectiveness of the consequences we may be using. Let me take a moment and mention some of the more common hidden defeaters.

## HIDDEN DEFEATERS

### Failure to See Value

Parents often experience a situation which baffled psychologists for decades. "I rewarded my child but he still would not learn to do what I wanted." "I spanked my child hard, but he still kept doing it." These types of statements suggest the simple idea of rewarding what you want done and punishing what you do not want done, does not work. It is interesting to note that parents were not the only ones drawing these conclusions. In many instances, psychologists looking at specific situations drew the same conclusions. There were times when rewards and punishers did not seem to work as the behavioral law of consequation predicted that they should. For over one hundred years psychologists were confronted with situations which appeared unexplainable by consequation; and it has only been in the past twenty years that psychologists themselves have found the answer. The answer lay in the fact that we psychologists and parents often perceive the situation differently than the child. What we perceive as a reward or punishment to the child is often not how the child perceives it. Their value system is often different from ours.

To illustrate what I mean, let's take a look at a seeming contradiction that psychologists were unable to explain until recently—*masochism*. Masochism is basically situations where children (and adults for that matter) inflict pain upon themselves for no apparent reason. Some children, if left unrestrained, will continually hit themselves in the face with their fists causing broken facial bones and bleeding. Some unrestrained children will beat their heads on cement floors repeatedly. Such children will often cause permanent damage to themselves. If there was ever a situation which seemed to illustrate reward as punishment does not work—masochistic situations surely did. And for years many psychologists argued that the idea of consequation must be too simple to be true because masochistic children were living proof such an idea was wrong. How could anyone believe that it was pleasurable for the child to inflict such pain on himself?

The answer to the apparent contradiction came when certain

psychologists began scrutinizing the actions of masochistic children. After several years of close observation a somewhat startling conclusion was drawn. It appeared to the psychologists that these children were in fact doing it because of something pleasant they received from doing it. And that pleasant something was *attention*. The psychologists concluded the children hit, bit, and clawed themselves to receive attention from those people around them. They inflicted painful injuries on themselves just to get people to come and hold them so they could not hurt themselves.

Sound fantastic? That is what other psychologists felt too, because in most cases the children seemed to fight the people trying to stop their self-injurious acts. The attention obtained from those restraining the children did not appear to be enjoyed by the children. So how could it be that the attention was causing the children to abuse themselves?

The psychologists studying masochism proposed three ways to test their theory that attention was indeed rewarding, and causing the self-injurious behaviors. First, they hypothesized that if they were right, a masochistic child placed by himself with no one around would eventually quit hurting himself if no one responded to his seemingly painful acts. To test the hypothesis, they placed a head-banging five-year-old boy in a padded room without his usual strait jacket on. Sure enough, after banging his head many, many times he quit, and even days and weeks later was no longer doing it.

Second, they hypothesized that the masochistic child had learned to adapt to most of the pain of hurting himself over months and years of such actions. Knowing another principle of consequation which says although you may adapt to some painful events, a different type of pain will most likely cause you to stop what you are doing, the psychologists decided to see if they could stop head banging in a masochistic child by milding shocking him. Placing the boy in a padded room unrestrained, they watched as he immediately began to bang his head. A half-second-long shock of much less intensity of that experienced when putting a finger in an electrical outlet was given immediately to the boy when he banged his head the first time. Acting somewhat startled the boy stopped, looked all around, then sat for a few seconds. He then banged his head a second time—and was shocked again. He stopped quickly and sat motionless for about thirty seconds. After trying to bang his head one more time, and getting shocked, he did not try it again. Later the therapy for the boy revolved around giving him all kinds of attention for doing acceptable, nonhead-banging activities. It worked.

Third, now having some idea of what was causing masochism, psychologists set out to see if they could produce it. Using rats, pigeons, and dogs they found they could develop masochism in animals by providing pleasant experiences for the animals if they would inflict pain on themselves. Pigeons could be trained to peck a disc which would cause them to receive an intense shock just to get a few grains of food. Mildly hungry rats could be trained to bite their tails off for a few sips of water. It quickly became apparent to us that painful self-injury could be produced in animals by giving them a little bit of food just like children can injure themselves to get a little bit of attention. While we parents and psychologists have a difficult time perceiving a little bit of attention or a small amount of food as being worth putting one's self through injurious acts, animals and children can apparently perceive the value of the experiences differently.

To put this back into everyday terms, let's look at a problem one couple had with their young son. "When we put him to bed he cries," the father notes. "I tell him to stop or I will come in and spank him. Many times he does not stop, so I spank him. It is a pretty hard spanking, but in a few moments he often starts crying again." The father recounted this story as I was explaining to him and his wife this simple principle of consequation. He felt his story pointed out what I was saying was not true for his son.

I asked him if it might be that it was more painful in the child's mind to be alone in a dark room than to have a parent close by in the room and being spanked. This is the case in many instances. Teenagers may get in trouble with the law to get the parents' attention. While we parents view getting in trouble with the law as being quite unpleasant, a child may often endure such socially unpleasant experiences (and the yelling parents usually give them for such actions) because sharing time with parents, even while they are mad, is better than no time at all.

**Inconsistency**

On occasions, parents decide to reward a child when they do what the parents want. Often such acts by the parents do not seem to have the desired effect. The child does not seem to respond to being rewarded. It is important in such cases to remember that life did not just begin for that child. That child has been around us for quite some time. And during those earlier times together we parents were most likely inconsistent with how we dealt with the child. Sometimes we provided pleasant consequences when they did what we wanted, and sometimes we ignored what they did.

The human mind acts like a small computer. It keeps track day after day of how people react to what we do for them. If people appreciate what we do, our mind makes a record of that. If we are reproved when doing something for someone, a record is kept in our mind of that also. In most cases we are unable to recall these events at will, yet their effect is there in our mind to influence our future attitudes and actions.

When we parents show our appreciation for our child's actions, we must remember our actions will be recorded in that child's mind along with how we have dealt with him in the past. If rewarding a child when he does what we want has little immediate effect on the child's later actions, that is a good indication that the child did not associate the reward as resulting from what he did. His unconscious mind tells him past activities have not produced such rewards. When inconsistent consequences have been experienced in the past, it takes a number of consistent applications in a row before the child's mind begins to tell him "these actions I just completed will be rewarded."

In the laboratory we began our training of pigeons to play tic-tac-toe by first trying to get them to peck a small, round, illuminated disc with an "X" on it. Pigeons do not automatically peck the disc. They must be *shaped* to peck the disc by initially rewarding a pigeon for any head movement made in the direction of the disc. The next time the pigeon is rewarded for making a closer movement toward the key. As you require the pigeon to get closer and closer for each successive reward, you can eventually get the bird to peck the disc. An experienced trainer can train a naïve pigeon with no previous experience to peck the disc in ten minutes or less. Often times we have relatively untrained college students come into our university laboratories to learn how to train the pigeons. These inexperienced trainers often take a week to shape a bird. The main reason they take so long is they are not as consistent in rewarding the bird's movements toward the disc. Sometimes they inadvertently give the food when the animal is standing, or actually moving away from the disc. When this happens the bird gets confused as to what it is supposed to be doing. The same thing often happens in the case of a child whose parents begin to reward him when he does something right. The relationship between the act and the reward is unclear until it happens consistently several times in a row. We parents may often conclude rewards or punishments are ineffective after we administer them because we have not been consistent with their use in the past.

### Immediacy

A third way we parents often defeat ourselves in getting our children to do what we want is by *delaying* the administration of the consequence. The quicker the consequence follows the act, the greater the effect. In the laboratory we reward the bird's action within one-half second after it emits the behavior we want. If we delay giving the reward even three seconds, the bird is almost impossible to train. In the last chapter of this book, I explain how I turned eighteen hyperactive, disruptive, under-achieving third graders into hard-working students within three weeks. I based my program on providing positive consequences (for example, playing pinball machines, playing popular electronic games, riding horses) when each child completed so many assignments. Another person tried basically the same program on his students at a different school and failed. There was one main difference between his program and mine. In my program each child was allowed to go play the games immediately after they completed an assignment. In his program, each completed assignment resulted in a check being placed on a chart and every Friday the children completing assignments go to play the games. What he failed to realize is having a third grader wait a week is much too long a time. Parents often defeat the effect of consequation by not rewarding or punishing the act immediately. Let your child know immediately if she has done something right, or if she has done something wrong. Do not wait until later that evening to thank the child for what he or she has done. Delaying the consequence greatly reduces its effectiveness.

**Lack of Capacity**

On one occasion two foster parents approached me about a foster child they had. He was in seventh grade and was a very poor student. "First we tried rewarding him if his grades were good," they said to me, "but the rewards did not improve his grades. Next we grounded him for a week at a time. Each Friday he had to bring notes home from his teachers. If they indicated he had not been studying in school, he was grounded until the next Friday. Efforts of having him sit at a study table every night for two hours did not help either."

A closer look at the situation revealed the problem. Although he was in seventh grade his math competency level was that of a third grader. Those math assignments were like a foreign language to him. It would not have mattered if they had promised that boy a new motorcycle or threatened to beat him black and blue. Neither consequence would have an effect because he simply did not have the skills to do what was being asked of him.

I had a similar problem with a fourteen-year-old foster boy who joined our family. Each child in our family had six tasks to do each day. These included such things as making their bed, cleaning their room, setting the dinner table, emptying wastebaskets, washing the cars, and so on. While all the other children had little trouble completing their jobs, he averaged less than three jobs completed every day.

About three weeks after he came to our home I took him and another son, Kit, to the shoe store to get Kit a new pair of tennis shoes. While at the store the foster boy looked at all the shoes, spied an expensive, good-looking pair and said, "Please buy me these shoes." I replied "No" and reminded him we had come to get Kit shoes, not him. I thought for a moment about his desire for the thirty-five dollar tennis shoes and said, "I'll tell you what. I will buy those shoes for you and we will take them home. If you go one week without missing one of your daily chores, I'll then give you the shoes."

He thought over my proposition for a moment. Then with head bowed, he said "I guess not." It became apparent from how he acted in that situation that he did not have the capacity or self-control to complete six easy tasks for seven days. He knew he did not have the ability to do it, and did not want to go through the disappointment of failing. What I was asking of him was more than he could do. It would not have mattered how much I promised him, he could not succeed in doing what I asked. I realized I must lower my demand to possibly doing all his jobs for one day (for a smaller payoff). Once he had developed the capacity to do that, I could expand it to two days, then three and so on. Like shaping a pigeon to peck the disk, I needed to slowly mold his ability. It worked! Many times we parents conclude that consequences do not affect our child's actions when the problem is the inability of the child to do what we ask.

While no amount of reward or punishment can get a child to do what is beyond his capacity, there is a way to expand his capacity. Let me illustrate by first explaining how we train a rat in the laboratory to leap a distance three times its height, something rats will not automatically do no matter how much you reward them. First we place 2″ x 4″ blocks of wood on top of each other in a stepwise fashion as shown in the diagram on page 175. We initially reward the rat for walking up the steps from Level "A" to Level "B". This is something the rat easily does. Then we begin removing the blocks one at a time on every third or fourth attempt by the rat until the requirement of leaping from Level "A" to Level "B" is completed without any blocks present.

This same strategy is used to teach skiers how to do flips on the ski slopes. First they learn to do the flips on trampolines, a much easier task than on the ski slope. Later they attempt the flips on the slopes. Using this strategy, more skiers are doing more complicated stunts than were even tried twenty years ago.

Putting the issue of capacity back in perspective for parents, the point being made here is that sometimes we ask so much of

our child that no amount of reward or punishment can have an effect. We can improve our possibility of success with our children if we gradually build up our demands on our children. By placing on a horse just a bridle first, then a bridle and saddle blanket, then a saddle, and last, a small rider, you have a great chance of the horse doing what you want without bucking your demands.

## FOUR WAYS TO MOTIVATE

I hope the first part of the chapter has given you confidence in the idea that a person's actions can be influenced by the consequences of those actions. While the idea of consequation may seem rather simple, proper application of consequences (or payoffs as some people call them) can make a parent very effective in motivating children to do what the parent desires. Psychologists have come to realize that Mother Nature's system for motivating human action includes four basic options. First, parents can motivate a child to do something by *giving* them something they *like* after they do what we want. Some children will take out the trash for a candy bar; others will do it for a smile and "thanks" from mom. Second, parents can motivate a child to do something by *taking away* something they *dislike* when the act is completed. Some children will take out the trash to remove the bad mood mother is in. Third, a parent can motivate a child *not to do* something by *giving* the child something he or she *dislikes* immediately after the child does the unwanted act. Some children will refrain from messing up the living room because they were given a spanking the last time they did it, while some children will refrain from messing up the living room because they were scolded the last time they did it. Fourth, a parent can motivate a child not to do something by *taking away* something the child *likes* immediately after the child does the unwanted act. A daughter does not stay out late because the last time she did her parents took away privileges she had by grounding her for one week. A young boy does not swear because last time he did his playing privileges were taken away and he sat on a chair for thirty minutes.

If one looks closely at the four ways parents have to get children to *do* or *not do* certain acts, similarities and differences between the four options begin to appear. The following figure clarifies the similarities and differences. Parents can get children to *do* something

| | GIVE | TAKE AWAY |
|---|---|---|
| LIKE | DO | NOT DO |
| SOMETHING THEY | | |
| DISLIKE | NOT DO | DO |

either by *giving* something the child *likes* (for example, candy bar) or *taking away* something the child *dislikes* (for example, take away the nagging). Parents can get a child to *not do* something either by *giving* something the child *dislikes* (for example, spanking) or *taking away* something the child *likes* (for example, taking away the right to use the family car).

## Do—Give What They Like

Most parents realize they can get children to do things by giving them a positive or satisfying payoff. Unfortunately, this option has received an undeserved bad reputation, and there are two main reasons for this reputation. First, this option for getting children to do what you want has been labeled bribery. If a parent rewards the child for doing what is wanted, others claim the child is being bribed. Getting a child to do something for a positive payoff of some kind *is not* bribery. If that is true, then your boss bribes you to work. A young man proposing matrimony with a ring is bribing his potential mate. A young mother bribes her sick youngster by giving hugs of assurance as he takes the needed medicine. Almost every act each of us commits daily is for a positive payoff. We smile and wave at our youngster as she starts for school because we know she will pay us back with a smile and a wave. We take a shower because the resultant feeling of being clean is rewarding. Yet few of us would see bribery as part of such every day occurrences.

Technically speaking, bribery is the use of any of the four options where the intent of the parents paying off is to receive personal benefit of the payoff. If a mother gives a noisy child a cookie so the child will quiet down and give mother peace and quiet, then mother has bribed the child. The child was paid off to benefit the mother. If, on the other hand, the mother gives the noisy child a cookie to quiet him down in an effort to teach the child consideration and self-restraint, then the child has not been bribed. In this case the payoff benefits the child directly (and the mother indirectly). If a mother coaxes the child with reasoning to be quiet so she can get some rest, the child is still being bribed. A father threatening to discipline a child if the child disrupts his watching of TV is bribing the child to do something which benefits the father, not the child.

Bribery is not synonomous with the term reward. Rewarding behavior with positive payoffs is a natural and integral part of everyday life. The intent to benefit one's self through paying off others, not the act of paying off, is bribery.

The second main reason parents shy away from rewarding their children is because they have heard that such acts teach the child to want material rewards. Some people claim children can get hooked on the idea that they should not do what is asked of them unless they get something for their trouble. Most parents have employment for which they expect to be paid financially for their labors. Yet most of us daily help other people without expecting any more than a smile and a word of thanks. If gaining material rewards hinders one's attitudes about sacrificing for others, then people with poor-paying jobs or people on welfare should be more prone to help other needy people because they are less hooked on materialism. But such is not the case.

Giving young children candy or toys when they do what you want does not automatically distort their ability to do things for others without getting some material benefit. In fact, rewarding children with material things is an important first step in teaching the child to eventually do for others for nothing more than internal satisfaction. This point may become clearer by giving an example.

Every once in a while psychologists are confronted with an autistic child. Autistic children are children who have, in essence, withdrawn from the world around them to a large degree. Most autistic children sit by themselves away from playmates and do such things as rock back and forth, continually wave their hands and arms, and spin toys. Generally speaking, they actively fight anyone who tries to hug them or show other signs of affection. These children do not respond to questions or commands from others. Psychologists who are successful in treating such children generally start from the basics of Mother Nature's hierarchy of rewards by rewarding any positive actions of these children with food. Because these children will not respond to affection, they start with food, a more basic reward, and work with the child just before mealtime when the child is hungry. When hungry, such children will return to reality and can be taught to speak, answer questions, and do things like dress themselves, to receive food. With each positive action the psychologist not only gives a bit of food, but also slips in a hug and comment such as "That is very good, Annie." After weeks of such training, hugs and verbal comments alone can act as payoffs, where initially the child fought such actions. Later such children can be trained to talk and play because it is internally satisfying.

Such training is a long, hard process, which points up the fact that Mother Nature has ranked payoffs in a hierarchy from the basic rewards of food, to material objects, to social rewards like hugs and affection, to activities, to doing things for social acceptance, and finally to doing things because it just makes you feel good inside. Somewhat like austistic children, most of the foster children Carol and I receive are at the level of wanting material things, such as money, for payoffs and we frequently use such payoffs. But we, like the psychologists working with autistic children, pair verbal comments and signs of affection with money, and eventually pay off most positive behaviors with words of appreciation. The philosophy we work under is "first get the positive behaviors going using the most effective reward they respond to (usually it is money), then develop in the child the right reason (or reward if you want to call it such) for doing those positive behaviors." This second stage of getting the child to do at least a few positive actions without receiving material payoffs is an important step which many parents fail to do.

## Do—Take Away What They Dislike

Getting someone to do what you want by taking away something they dislike is a tactic few parents use. For children, however, it is a well-used strategy. Albert screams and cries at the store until mother gets him some gum. Cynthia pouts and complains until dad concedes and lets her take the car. In both situations the child creates an unpleasant situation for the parent. When the parents *do* what the child wants (gives the ice cream, the car) the children *take away* the unpleasant conditions (crying, pouting) the parents dislike.

Parents can use this strategy, too. A two-year-old may seem to ignore her mother's request to pick up the toys. If the mother stands silently with a disappointed look on her face, it may take but a few seconds before the child picks up the toys so mother will take away the unpleasant situation of being silent, and will return to being a smiling mother. A teenager may find his mother unwilling to iron his clothes because he just drops them anywhere in the house. His mother removes his unpleasant situation of having wrinkled clothes by returning to ironing when he *does* what she wants—pick up his clothes. In both cases the mother gets the child to *do* what she wants by taking away an unpleasant situation for the child.

Parents often use this strategy on each other. The mother becomes quiet and withdrawn because father did not take out the trash. Sensing an unpleasant atmosphere, the father *does* his house chore so his wife will take away the unpleasant condition.

### Not Do—Give Something They Dislike

If a child does something the parent dislikes, the parent may successfully get the child to *not do* it again by giving the child something he dislikes. Spankings, scoldings, lectures, and writing on the board five hundred times "I will not throw spitwads" are examples of things children dislike. When parents give such experiences to their children, we call that punishment. A parent's use of punishment can be an effective deterrent of bad behavior in children, particularly when it is used under the conditions outlined in the previous chapter.

### Not Do—Take Away Something They Like

Spanking or scolding a child are not the only ways to get a child to *not do* something. There is an alternative approach which is much more socially acceptable because it does not entail using any form of physical force upon the child. This alternative approach involves *taking away* something a child *likes* when he or she does something wrong. If a girl does not do her house chores her parents may take away her privilege of watching television. A teacher may take away the child's privilege of going to recess because he acted up in class. A ten-year-old may lose his privilege of riding his bike for a week because father found it left out in the rain. A child may be required to sit on a chair and not play with his friends for thirty minutes because he hit a playmate. All of these examples illustrate a form of punishment called negative punishment. It is called negative punishment because the parent removes (a minus or negative sign symbolizes removal or take away in our language) something the child likes and previously had access to before he/she did something wrong. This strategy can be quite effective in getting children to *not do* certain things parents do not want done.

## HOW WELL DO THESE FOUR WAYS WORK?

The four types of consequences just discussed are the most effective ways psychologists have to change a behavior in humans or other animals. Most people have visited animal parks and have seen and been amazed when seals play tunes on horns, two or three whales leap out of the water and do synchronized flips, pigeons play ping-pong, chickens play baseball, monkeys ride small motorcycles, and elephants stand on their back legs. In psychological research laboratories, monkeys have been taught to use the American Sign Language of the deaf and to do math such as addition and subtraction. Animals rocketed into space by the government have been trained to do special tasks while in space. In all of the aforementioned situations one or more of the four ways discussed here were used to get the animals to do the rather difficult and sometimes sophisticated tasks. Having worked in and directed several university psychology laboratories across the country, and having worked on a number of governmentally funded psychological research projects, I can testify to you that *no* other psychological approaches are as effective or more widely used than the four methods for getting animals to *do* or to *not do* desired tasks mentioned here.

What about humans? Psychologists have existed for over one hundred years. The psychological laboratory set up in Germany by Wilhelm Wundt in 1879 is considered as the birth of psychology as a profession. During the first fifty years of the profession psychologists were so awed by the seeming complexity and intricacy of man that we overlooked the possibility that understanding Mother Nature's system for human development could be relatively simple and straightforward. Over the past fifty years, many psychologists have devoted a great deal of time studying the simple ideas of association and hedonism (the pleasure principle) philosophers have believed in for centuries. We have come to realize that the four ways mentioned in this chapter are the foundation of changing human behavior in Mother Nature's system. Man works to gain pleasure (be it the pleasure of money or self-satisfaction) and works to avoid pain (be it spankings or internal feelings of disappointments). The four ways discussed in this chapter are the main strategies thousands of psychologists use to effectively deal with problem behavior in children.

These four ways work! They can work for you as a parent. Forgive me if I seem to repeat this idea several times in the book, but so many parents have come to feel that little can be done. It is important to realize parents can manipulate their children.

Over the past few chapters a number of examples have been briefly presented where a particular problem behavior has been changed. Let's look in more detail at a particular child we took in and how a number of behaviors were developed and removed.

Maria was born in Puerto Rico in 1962. Her mother and father separated when she was three. A year later Maria's mother sent her to live with her father. Months later he pawned her off on a grandmother. Over the next few years the only person who really cared for Maria was an aunt. During her early years Maria was placed in a school for the mentally retarded in Puerto Rico. At age ten Maria's father decided to go to California and took Maria with him because he could get better welfare assistance with a child.

On the way to California Maria became ill so her father took her to the emergency room of a hospital in Provo, Utah. While examining the young girl the nurse noticed welts on her back. When calling Social Services, the nurse was told not to release Maria before they arrived. Feeling something was wrong, the father abandoned Maria to avoid possible prosecution for child abuse. Speaking few words of English, Maria was placed in a temporary group home until an unsuccessful search for relatives was completed. Within a few weeks she was placed in our home.

Maria was a dark-haired, medium-sized girl who wore her hair in two pig tails. She gave several behavioral indications of being retarded. She shuffled her feet when she walked, tucked her chin back to her head looking down most of the time, and spoke slow and soft while slurring most of her words. Her motor coordination was poor also.

Maria's physical hygiene habits left a lot to be desired. She did not bathe without being prompted, resisted attempts at having her hair combed, and slept with her soiled socks on. While around other children we heard her most commonly used English phrase, "I don't like you" which she blurted out boisterously if another child tried to bother her or coax her to play. For the first two months she was with my wife Carol, constantly shadowing her, always grasping her hand and behaving as if she was not sure what was going to happen next.

When school started we encountered a problem. Maria would get up, eat breakfast, then go back to bed. She was never ready when the school bus came. Knowing she loved food we used breakfast as a payoff. In the mornings Carol would wake her up and serve breakfast only after Maria completed showering, dressing, and cleaning up her room. We wanted her to *do* the aforementioned things and we *gave* her breakfast when she did what was wanted. It took about two weeks to get this habit established.

A second problem arose at school. Children would tease her. One day two boys began teasing her. She would yell "I don't like you." Then they began shoving her to get her to cry. That did not work so they hit her, shoved her down a few times, and tore her dress. Still she would not cry. (For the first year in our home she would only cry when alone in her bedroom at night.) After that incident I considered several alternatives to solve the problem. One would have been to go to school and get the teachers to scold the boys and help Maria, but what then would Maria do when no one was around to help her? Realizing that children usually tease because of the reaction of the person being teased, I decided to help her by changing her response to teasing. I decided to teach her to just smile and say nothing when being teased. I wanted to teach her to *do* something and I had two options. One, *give* her something when she did what I wanted or *take away* something when she did what I wanted. I chose the first option and set up a program around the dinner table (with the help of the family). We developed a game where a member of the family would say something obviously untrue about Maria such as "You have ears as big as an elephant." When Maria just sat and smiled at such comments the family praised her. She liked the game. Gradually over days and weeks we focused on more personal and potentially upsetting remarks such as "You dumb retard." Within a month no one could provoke Maria to do anything more than smile.

To get Maria to take her socks off, Carol used a second strategy. In the evening when all the children, dressed in pajamas, came to Carol and me for goodnight hugs, Carol would frown, act hurt, and make some comment to Maria about her socks. Within two weeks Maria was taking her socks off before coming for her hug. Carol used the strategy of *taking away* (taking away being sad and hurt) something when Maria *did* what was wanted (took off her socks).

As mentioned earlier Maria initially spoke very softly. We had to put our ear next to her mouth to hear what she said. The person who initially tested Maria at Social Services suggested this was due in part to her retardation. After living with her for a few weeks and observing Maria closely I came to realize many of the apparent behavior problems she had which suggested retardation were learned! She had learned to shuffle her feet, talk low, and act as if she was uncoordinated from the children she saw at the school for retarded children in Puerto Rico. Using the strategy of extinction plus *giving* something pleasant we went to work on her speech. When she spoke soft and low we quit leaning toward her and said "Sorry, can't hear you," and went on with what we were doing all the while ignoring her. When she spoke louder we made some comment such as "That's great. I can hear you," and then interacted with her. Within one week her talk was up to normal level. Notice we ignored bad behavior and rewarded proper behavior.

Realizing Mother Nature in everyday life presents both the positive giving consequences and the unpleasant *taking away* consequences, we made sure Maria's training included both. (Too often well-meaning parents forget the realities of everyday life and try to deal only positively with the child, making it more difficult to adjust to everyday life.) To get rid of her feet-shuffling behavior, I would yell at her when she did it. I was using the strategy of *giving* something she *disliked* so she would *not do* what was wrong (shuffle her feet). Her shuffling declined after a few weeks.

During the eight years Maria has been with us we have used all four strategies listed in this chapter. (We have also used all four on all our children.) Maria is presently graduating from high school with a B average. She was the best long-ball hitter in softball at her junior high. Over the years we eventually found her mother who has remarried and prefers to be left alone. Given the choice of returning to relatives (her aunt) in Puerto Rico and staying with us, Maria has chosen to adopt us and visit her aunt as often and as long as she wants. We have a fine daughter who gets up every school morning, forty-five minutes before anyone else, to wash her hair and help fix breakfast.

## SPECIAL ADVICE FOR EFFECTIVE USE

Most parents are going to be pleasantly surprised when they seriously try the approaches mentioned here. One should not expect to be one hundred percent successful at the beginning. Like most other skills you get better with practice. In closing this chapter let me throw in several suggestions which should make your efforts more effective.

*Diversify Your Approaches.* Do not deal with your child through only one of the four ways discussed for two reasons. First, all four approaches are frequently seen in everyday life. Bullies *give disliked* consequences to playmates; and bosses often do the same. Credit companies can nag, and so can mates. Do not build a false world of only pleasant consequences for your child. Second, when you alternate the taste of sweet and sour, each accentuates the effect of the other. (Taste lemon right after eating a piece of candy and see.) The same is true in life's experiences. Let sufficient punishments of inappropriate actions occur to maximize the value of rewarding consequences.

*Immediacy.* The sooner the payoff (be it reward or punishment) follows an action, the greater the effect. In animal training we program the payoff about one-half second after the response. To make police dogs jump barricades, one of the first steps is to pair the sound of a small hand clicker with food. Later when the dog jumps a hurdle, a "click" is made to immediately let the dog know he has done right. With children you can often call them by their full or middle name when they do something wrong to give them immediate feedback on the inappropriate behavior.

*Shape.* When trying to get a child to do something, require only a little at first, then gradually increase what is wanted. Teaching a child work, for example, requires one minute, then two, then five, and so on, until the child can do what you want.

*Prime the Pump.* It takes less energy to keep a car moving than to start it moving. The same is true for kids. Like planting a tree takes more water and nutrients initially, parents need to focus more effort (and possible stronger payoffs) to get the child started. Remember that the child will try to manipulate you and get more reward for what is done.

*Fade to More Internal Rewards.* Use candy, or opportunity for activities as payoffs for good behavior, but do not forget to fade to more internal rewards as months and years pass.

*Effective for All Ages.* The four approaches used in this chapter work for children of all ages. Choose the proper payoffs for different age children. Know what your child likes and dislikes, and select from these.

*Questions from Parents*

**Q:** When I give allowances to my kids for doing positive things, they soon begin asking for more money. What am I doing wrong?

**A:** You are not doing anything wrong. Once children realize that actions can get rewards, they will naturally try to get more reward for the same behavior, or do less for the same amount of reward. We all would naturally do the same thing to our boss if it would work. The key is not to give in to such pleadings, and the pleadings will fade.

Keep in mind your eventual goal is to get the child to do things such as clean up his room, keep toys picked up, and wash before meals, because he feels it is the right thing to do, not because it gets him money.

**Q:** Once you have a child cleaning up his room for money, how do you get him to do it without receiving an allowance?

**A:** As mentioned in the chapter, first give the money; then give money and praise both; then continue giving praise and fade out giving money by giving less and less or giving it only on intermittent occasions like slot machines; then give just praise; then praise only intermittently, until he is finally doing it without need of money or comment. This may take months, depending on the age of the child and the skill of the parent. Remember the child needs to learn to handle money so do not take it totally away. Even very young children need to be given money so they can learn to properly buy and save. Shift it to a second positive behavior you want your child to have, and go through the same process again. You can work on more than one behavior at a time. You may be in the phase of socially rewarding positive behavior number 1 while you are just starting to monetarily reward positive behavior number 2. This approach will work every time but requires the parent to develop some skill at doing it. So do not give up if at first you do not succeed. If your children are under ten years old you probably will have little difficulty getting it to work. If you are trying to remodel a teenager, this strategy is still effective, but you may need to seek some help from a psychologist trained in behavioral engineering.

**Q:** I read a book on childrearing which said parents should not worry about being inconsistent with their children. Is that true?

**A:** In the first place I know of no research reported in psychological journals which supports the idea that inconsistency in interacting with others strengthens a relationship. There is, however, a fair amount of published research showing just the opposite. Second, if I am familiar with the same book you are talking about, the book talks about inconsistency from a somewhat different vantage point. The point the book makes is that parents can get moody, and not always act the same way with their children. The author says parents should not feel bad about these types of situations where they are somewhat inconsistent. The idea that parents do not always feel or act the same day after day is true. Nor do they have to. *Consistency* does not mean *same.* The seasons (Spring, Summer, Fall, and Winter) consistently follow each other, but are not exactly the same. A parent does not always have to act the same way moment to moment to be consistent. A mother can be consistent in that she is moody in the mornings and happy in the afternoons. A father can be consistent in that he yells at his children when they ask him questions while he watches a football game, but answers those same questions from his children when he is just sitting in his favorite chair. Children can easily learn that dad is not sociable when watching football, but is at other times.

As long as children can detect that there are differences in the conditions when dad acts differently, then children are not adversely affected by differences in how we parents respond to them. If, however, dad is mad sometimes and not mad at other times with the child being unable to distinguish as to when he will be mad and when he will not, then the father's actions are inconsistent; and the child will be affected adversely.

**Q:** My husband reminds our son of things he did wrong in the past. He says he does it to help our son remember not to do it again. Does this approach work?

**A:** This is such an important question that I hesitate to answer for fear of not doing it justice in just a few words. Reminding a child of mistakes made in the past can be productive, but the *way* we parents normally do it causes more harm than good nine times out of ten. When a child does something wrong we say something like "Now you have just done it again! or "You dumbbell, that is the third time this week you did not do what you were supposed to." This kind of emotional feedback given at the time of a mistake often has a negative effect on the child. Generally speaking, such remarks cause the child to carry grudges. You do not forget his mistakes, so he will not forget yours. If you have not made a mistake lately, he waits until you do; and makes a big deal over your mistakes. A friend of mine who trains wild animals mentioned once that his mountain lions will accept reprimands from him if they do something wrong while he is training them. But after the reprimand, they expect him to forget the incident and not hold a grudge over the incident. If he holds a grudge, the animal senses it and begins to act differently. It then waits for him to make a mistake. Children tend to act the same way. Reminding a child of prior mistakes can have a positive effect if you do it in a positive way at some nonemotional time when the child is not worried about being reprimanded. Hours or days after the child errors and is reprimanded the father may take the child aside and with an apparent air of love say something like "Twice this last week you did . . . What do you think we should do to correct the problem?" Let your comments leave the child with the feeling that "Dad feels something must be done to stop these actions; and he feels it is for my own good." Be prepared for the fact that the child, even in this situation, will naturally try to get the parent to be too lenient.

There is a helpful suggestion for teachers and parents with a child who repeatedly does something wrong. Prior to the next occurrence, discuss the problem with the child and get him to agree with the discipline before it is given. "Harold, would you turn off the radio and go put it in your locker? If you bring it again I'll give it to the principal until the end of the term. OK?" Such a short positive exchange before the incident often makes the discipline easier for the child to accept.

**Q:** Sometimes my children work for rewards, but other times that same reward will not work. Why?

**A:** It is important to remember that all things are *relative*. A child may work for a piece of gum when he has none. If he already has gum, however, that same offer will not get him to do what you want. Many times parents fail to get children to do what they want for rewards selected by the parent because there are alternative rewards available for other actions. A child with a pack of gum may run around a doctor's office for the joy of running, rather than sit quietly for an additional piece of gum which holds little rewarding value for him at the time. Parents should evaluate each situation and make sure what is being offered is what the child wants.

# 12 Sources of Help for Parents

All too often parents view themselves as alone in their efforts to properly raise their children. We parents frequently try to shoulder too much of the burden of raising our kids when there are a host of places and people we can go to for help. Single mothers can be found who try to do everything themselves for their children. Children with two working parents too often see their parents failing to take advantage of help around them.

Parents can make childrearing a much more enjoyable experience if they stop to realize they do not have to do it all themselves. Parents do not have to teach their children everything themselves. Parents can enlist the help of schoolteachers, relatives, neighbors, private schools, and a host of other people and organizations, in providing their children with what they need. Children's lives are touched by many people. For example schoolteachers and schoolmates will have a tremendous influence on what a child becomes.

## HELP FROM WITHIN—USING THE FAMILY

The seemingly endless process of searching for solutions to everyday problems seems to be a major pastime for many parents. Past experiences, close friends, relatives, books on childrearing, and possibly even professional help may all be looked at and considered as the possible "source" of relief by the overburdened parent. Another approach, which I consider as one of my favorites, is through the direct observation of families with similar problems but who seem to know what they are doing.

This is not to say that some parents are endowed with the ability to run their families without flaws—but some families do not seem to be bothered with problems that raise major catastrophes in other households. Watching and observing their successes at times can help others who are struggling.

Several years ago, I had the opportunity to visit with a young American couple and their five children at their Army Air Base home in southern Germany. Jim, the father, was a helicopter pilot and a major in the Army. He had flown many missions over the jungles of Vietnam but was now assigned to a special European unit. His job included flying generals from Norway to Belgium to Italy and back again. He didn't enjoy leaving his family because his job often left them fatherless for extended periods of time.

At first, when I heard of Jim's situation, it sounded like the perfect place to find an overburdened mother in a foreign country, being run ragged by her own children—in this case five children. What I observed during my stay, however, was a family that made coordinated and concentrated efforts to help each other and work together. How did they do it? The oldest child was only eight and the youngest less than a year; this left heavy parental responsibilities and duties. What was their special formula?

Weighing these questions in my mind, I turned my attention to both parents to see how they handled various situations that arose. Joyce, the mother, was a small, soft-spoken lady, obviously not a belt-waving physical disciplinarian. She had come from a small town but was educated at a large university where she received a degree. She often remarked that school had taught her a lot but her true education came during her nine years of marriage and raising her five kids. Jim, a career army officer, was also a quiet, reserved type of person who enjoyed coming home at night, getting away from the war games, and spending time wrestling and tumbling with his kids.

After relating my observations of their well-behaved and happy family, I asked both Jim and Joyce "How do you do it? How is it possible for you to keep ahead of these five young ones?"

"Well," Joyce replied, smiling at Jim, "for one thing, we have learned to use each other."

She went on to elaborate that by the end of each day she was fairly drawn out. When Jim got home in the late afternoon it was then his turn to occupy the kids while she stole a few minutes for a nap, or went visiting, shopping, or whatever she wanted to do.

"The kids need *quality* time with their father because with his job they will never get the *quantity* of time they would like. So when Jim is home his time is concentrated on the kids," remarked Joyce.

"Another important factor in our family relationship is constant support," Jim added. "We have found our children, like most normal children, at times would like to work us against one another. Ask one parent, and if you get turned down, go work on the other. It's a good technique but we try to eliminate it as much as possible."

"Everything seems to run smoothly when you're working together but what happens when Jim is out of town? Does your emotional dam break by nightfall?" I inquired.

"That's the second important thing to know," answered Joyce. "First use each other, then use the kids. A good example is our eight-year-old daughter, Marsha. She is one of the top readers in the third grade, and one of the main reasons is that she comes home from school and reads out loud to her brothers and sisters. They love it because it's entertaining. I love it because I can get my other work done, and we both like it because Marsha is doing so well in reading and the younger kids are learning to attend and concentrate."

About this point in our conversation I began to feel that Jim and Joyce were the parents of the ultimate family, but then Jim explained about mistakes and discipline.

"It's not all a bed of roses; we have had lots of mistakes to overcome and some discipline has taken place." Jim continued by saying, "My wife and I try to make ourselves very special to our kids and lots of times disciplining will consist of just a stern look, a few words of disappointment in their action, or the withdrawal of ourselves until they feel that their mistake was wrong. Also there are those special occasions when an intense application of the manual method (spanking) does a very effective job."

## Help from Your Mate

Reviewing our conversation, some definite points were brought out and should now be expanded upon. First is the idea of each spouse using and helping each other. This demands a certain amount of communication and coordination between the two parents and can create friction if not accomplished properly. Can you imagine the problems which would come about if a young father walks home from a hard day at his job, completely exhausted, and all he can think about is taking a nap in front of the television? As he opens the front door his wife throws him her apron and says, "Here, it's your turn to control them, I'm going out with the girls. The supper's on the stove, don't wait up—bye." After the door slams the young father realizes what she has done and begins to boil. It's at this point the children can't understand why Dad only yells instead of plays with them.

Another example is the father who comes home, eats as fast as possible, then rushes out to bowl with his team or to the club with his friends. The wife ends up with the kids all alone both day and night.

If two people are going to benefit from each other, then acts of giving and taking must be coupled together with an enormous amount of understanding. This leads directly into another important idea to remember—constancy in the family. When two parents know, through communicating with each other, what the other expects and wants, then the child usually knows where his boundaries are. Let me illustrate this with a personal example. As I grew up and went through school my parents set down specific rules of how late we should be out, what type of parties we should attend or avoid, and even how we should drive the family cars. These rules, whether I followed them or not, were always made by both of them long before they were given to us kids. I knew exactly at all times where they stood on most issues (I knew where my boundaries were). Contrast this with a young man who grows up not knowing from one day to the next what is expected of him, for what he will be disciplined, or for what he can expect to be rewarded. Psychologists have long been able to take a normal test animal (a rat or monkey) and put it in an environment where everything is inconsistent, and change that curious little animal to one that is socially withdrawn and afraid to try anything. With no way for the animal to know or control the outcome, the experiment can be carried out to such an extent that the animal dies!

I am not trying to equate children with monkeys or rats (although more than a few parents have made that analogy), but keeping rules and regulations constant between parents and children is important.

Constancy requires a triangle of communication as it goes from one parent to the other then to the child. But there are many cases where one parent is missing in a family and the full burden falls on the shoulders of the parent who must stand alone. Through death, divorce, or jobs that keep one spouse away for extended periods of time, other methods must be found for the single parents to cope and raise their children efficiently for themselves and effectively for the kids.

In interviews with single parents who have problems and difficulties with their children, a frequent major problem is the feeling of being all alone and carrying the full responsibility of how their children turn out. Here it is important to point out several things. First, it is impossible for a single parent to become the sole breadwinner of the family and still give one hundred percent attention to the children at home. Second, like it or not, some extra dependencies are going to have to be placed on the children themselves such as doing the extra housework or babysitting. It may also be necessary to call on close relatives for advice and help in taking the kids. Church organizations, schoolteachers, and activities, and even national organizations such as Big Brothers of America can also offer additional help that can have tremendous influence on how a child's life is touched. Third, a single parent must realize that a great many successful and happy people come from single-parent families. With outside help the problems *can* be overcome.

## Help from Your Relatives

My wife and I have a friend in our neighborhood who has experienced many of these trials in the past couple of years. She has three blond-haired children, ages thirteen, twelve, and a baby just over a year old. The day her baby was born, her husband delivered the divorce papers and left her. He remarried a much younger woman a few days after the divorce was finalized. Although child support was being paid it was infrequent and often not enough to cover the necessary items for the children. Our friend took it upon herself to get a job and support the kids, but she soon found problems at home escalating. The older children felt resentment at having to curb their after-school activities with their friends and rush home to babysit the little one while Mom went to work. Soon bickering broke out and major disagreements occurred nightly while their mother was gone.

The answer to her problem came in the form of her own mother, who suggested she not lift the present condition and requirements of her children, but instead help them by increasing the chores. The wise grandmother knew from experience what she was talking about. The older children needed to feel they were also contributing to the family, so soon babysitting and other odd jobs were being found outside the home. The net result included cooperation in staying at home and babysitting, extra money for the kids to spend as they wished, and Mom now being able to cut down her working hours because she wasn't required to buy all of the luxuries her kids needed.

Relatives can be a great asset to parents in two ways. First, if they have children the same age and live close by both families can take turns taking care of the kids so one set of parents can, for short periods of time, escape. The second asset of relatives is found in the skills many have already learned and are willing to pass on. Psychologists are given substantial amounts of money over the years for helping youngsters get through difficult stages. Grandmothers have done the same job (many times better) for centuries for a lot less pay.

Speaking of grandparents and their value to the sanity of parents, there are organizations throughout the nation which help to match up youngsters with older people who have some love and help to give but have no one with which to share it. In many large cities today advertisements can be seen as to when and where to contact in order for parents and children to "adopt" a grandparent.

### Help from Your Kids

Added responsibility when children understand its importance can relieve much from the over-burdened parent(s). As in the first example of this chapter, Marsha was being used by her parents to help by reading and entertaining the other children. At times having kids help can cause parents to devote more time than if they had done the job themselves. This should be expected, but the learning value for the child and its skill development can pay off great dividends in the end. A father may find a large amount of time is spent in showing his son all about the correct and safe method of lawn mowing, but later it pays off as this son not only mows his own lawn but receives money for doing other lawns in the neighborhood.

"Using" the children this way works well unless parents begin to take advantage. Just as two people find themselves in an unsteady relationship when one does all the giving and the other all the receiving, so children can develop resentment when asked to do tasks for which they are unqualified.

While I was a graduate student, two other students and I rented an old two-story house in the "not-so-rich" district of town. The rent was cheap and it was big enough that it suited our purposes quite well. After a few months of living there we all had become well acquainted with Benny, a young eleven-year-old boy who lived next door. The day we moved in he showed up dressed in jeans, tennis shoes, and a worn-out, green, hand-me-down jacket. "I'll help you move in for fifty cents" were his first words. Although I was not immediately impressed with his attire, his hustling for money and hard-working attitude quickly won my attention. Almost every day he would be over at our house asking to clean, sweep, or whatever, for a quarter or fifty cents. On several occasions we also noticed him down at a corner car wash, helping students clean the inside and outside of their cars for an extra bit of cash. Throughout the neighborhood he was known for peddling newspapers, pop bottles, and anything else he could get that would bring him some type of return.

We admired Benny's initiative, and formed a special attachment with him. At least three afternoons a week, he could be found shadowing one of us through our rented house asking questions and commenting on the knickknacks we had. After he once explained he was a poor student in school, we zealous embryonic psychologists decided to remedy his problem by using some behavior modification techniques we had learned through our graduate training. Starting with math, we set up special times when he would sit at our kitchen table and do math. We gave him a lot of praise and some money for every so many math problems he would do correctly. Within a few weeks he was bringing home math tests with scores ranging from ninety percent to one hundred percent correct.

All of a sudden Benny no longer came over. Running into him on the street one day, I asked why he had not been coming over. "My father said I cannot come over any more," was his reply. "He said I spend too much time at your place, and he says you are doing my assignments for me."

The next day after school I went to see Benny's teacher. "I knew someone was paying attention to Benny when his grades rose," she said. "Every time I spend extra time with him he becomes one of my best students. With over thirty students in my class, however, I cannot keep giving him the amount of love and attention he needs. He then becomes one of my poorest students."

She went on to explain about Benny's family. His parents never came to parent–teacher conferences, and were seldom home in the evenings. On weekends the parents would give him two dollars, tell Benny to go buy food for lunch for all his four brothers and sisters, then not return until after six. Not being able to buy enough with two dollars, Benny would wash cars, run errands, collect bottles, and do whatever else was needed to come up with enough for lunch. The juvenile authorities were well aware of the situation, but were unsuccessful in legally solving the problem.

We never had a chance to help Benny again and I saw him only a few more times at the car wash before the school term ended. His parents had given him a large responsibility taking care of his brothers and sisters but they didn't leave him room to expand on his own life.

Parents should realize that several direct advantages come from using children in the correct way. For example, we all seem to learn better if we actually attempt something ourselves; this also includes children. I look to one of my friends who owns and operates a large farm as a good example. His eighteen-year-old son can plow an acreage of ground into a beautiful work of art. Upon inquiring how his son learned it, the answer was simple. The father only had one son and he had depended on him to plow since the boy was old enough to reach the brake pedals on the tractor. Thus, the advantage of letting the young child attempt some learning experience, whether it be setting the dinner table, making the beds, mowing the lawn, or babysitting, can blossom into a helpful asset to the parent. The child learns better and the parent can then depend more on the child in that area and free himself for other areas of interest.

## HELP FROM THE OUTSIDE

### Help from the School

Schools provide the greatest amount of outside supervision for children. Parents may capitalize on using the school as surrogate parents to teach their children many things. Besides the regularly planned schoolroom activities, school districts often provide a number of extracurricular experiences which parents may not have the time to provide. Things such as swimming programs, trips to art museums, musical experiences, and science trips are after-school and weekend options often made available through school districts. Junior and senior high schools usually sponsor various clubs that provide supervised experiences. Spanish clubs, auto maintenance clubs, ski clubs, intramural sports, and business clubs are only a few available in most schools to provide not only supervised activities, but to help build needed skills into our children.

We parents can often get a substantial amount of help from schools in raising our children. Parents should become acquainted with all that schools have to offer and tap a large potential source of child-rearing assistance.

## Help from the Schoolteacher

Schoolteachers spend a great deal of time with your children. How they interact with your children can significantly affect the raising of your child. Developing a close relationship with the teacher can be beneficial. Teachers often come to know a child better than the parent. A child may hide many attitudes and mannerisms from parents which reveal themselves to a teacher as he or she repeatedly observes the child in social interaction with classmates. A child may be careful what he says and does around his father, yet swear and be hard to handle in school. Parents often wonder how their children act when they are not around. Teachers are good sources for such information. Teachers can inform parents as to the kinds of friends their children have, whether they waste time in school, how courteous and considerate they are, and in general, give parents good feedback as to how their children are developing socially.

When parents take the extra time to get to know teachers, the teachers are generally very supportive in giving children any extra help parents feel they need. Teachers can help instill the values parents hold into their children. Advice from parents is more easily received by children who hear the same kinds of advice from their teachers. Get to know your children's teachers. Enlist their help in properly raising your children. Their help can make parenting much easier and more manageable.

## Help from Private Schools

Having friends and spending time with them usually is one of the most important dimensions in an adolescent's or teenager's life. Thus when something has this much value it requires some attention from the parents. When a child enters school and advances through the different stages, he associates with those whom he shares something in common. They grow together and influence each other. This is the exact idea of the upper-class banker who has his son attend the finest private school in the state, so he will associate with young men who are also from well-to-do families. Or the general in the Army who sends his "problem" son off to military school where he will learn discipline and associate with boys who are all well disciplined.

Often parents use private schools to provide an environment they feel can help them in properly raising their children. There has been a dramatic increase in enrollment for private schools throughout the country. Most parents are realizing the importance of the time their children spend in school and are electing to send their children to private schools. These private schools are usually chosen because parents feel such schools can more effectively help them in developing a stable and successful child than can public schools. Increased discipline, more rigorous academic programs, and more in-depth training in proper social skills are a few of the reasons parents use private schools.

Many "problem" children have been helped by being sent to private day schools that are not bound by the social and educational restrictions placed on the faculty of public schools. In some cases, problem children have become so difficult to handle, they need to be sent to private schools where the child is in a controlled situation twenty-four hours a day. The school mentioned in Chapter Seven is just such a school. To such places parents may send a teenager who becomes too difficult to handle. Such schools have programs designed to remodel the young boy or girl in such a way as to help him develop better social and academic skills and give him a greater appreciation for the rights and feelings of people around him. Fortunately, more parents are realizing the fact that children may become such a problem that outside help is needed. Many private schools have successful programs for helping families with problem children. Professional and financial responsibilities often limit a parent's ability to deal with a problem child. For such families private schools can help.

### Help from Foster Care Programs

Private schools are expensive. They are too expensive for many parents. Yet middle-income and lower-income families may include a child or two who have become unmanageable. Every state has programs in the Division of Family Services where parents can go for help. Most states have what are referred to as specialized foster care programs. Children who become unmanageable for their parents because of behavioral disorders (for example, lying, cheating, stealing, hyperactivity, aggressiveness) or character disorders can be helped by being put in foster homes where foster parents trained for such problems can handle them. The objective of these foster care programs is to place the unmanageable child in a more controlled environment, then work with the child and the parents. The child's inappropriate behaviors are worked on in the foster home for perhaps three to twelve months until the social workers at the Division of Family Services and the foster parents feel the child can properly handle himself. During this period the parents work with the social worker gleaning help and information so they are better prepared to handle the child when he returns to the family.

While most problem children (and many parents) shy away from foster parent programs, most children realize the value of the programs when they return to their family. Parents should wisely seek such programs when they have a child who becomes too difficult to handle. Such programs are quite successful when the problem between parent and child seems to be what people refer to as the "generation gap." Problem children receive a better appreciation for their own parents and family after an experience of living with a foster family for awhile. It generally helps put the world back in proper perspective for them.

### Help from Your Children's Peers

Most parents are familiar with the saying "Birds of a feather flock together." And it is certainly true that you are known by the company you keep. The people we associate with have an effect on us. If an honest child starts paling around with other teenagers who steal, he probably will come to do the same thing. If a girl seeks friends who like gymnastics, she will be strongly influenced to have the same likes. The company we keep can have a significant effect on us. Realizing this, parents can use this fact of nature to their advantage. Developing certain values and behaviors in your child is a great deal easier if the children your child interacts with have those values and behaviors.

Over the years the idea has become popular that parents are interfering when they attempt to arrange with whom their children associate. Most parents shy away from scrutinizing their child's friends for fear of being labeled a meddling parent. I have seen too many unfortunate situations, however, to let the idea of being labeled stop me from showing concern about my children's associates. One of the main keys to the success Carol and I have with foster children is becoming actively involved in deciding what teenagers they can associate with outside of school. Instead of mandating to them with who they can associate, we thoroughly screen the ones with which they want to go places and stay overnight. We then counsel our children and honestly explain any concerns we have. We allow them much more leeway with what they can do (for example, go shopping alone downtown, stay out late, go certain places) with teenagers who have the values we feel the children need.

Helping young children in choosing their friends is much easier than starting when the child is a teenager. Parents should start early. Do not be hesitant to step in with teenagers, however. A teenager's friends have too great an impact on their life for parents to fail to be concerned. Over eighty percent of the problem children in specialized foster care programs are teenagers. Teenagers get themselves into trouble quite easily, particularly in groups. Yet most teenagers make it unpleasant for parents who try to give them good counsel. Parental concern should not abandon them in their most important years. Keep in mind they are young adults closing in on their year of legal accountability. They should not be treated as six-year-olds. While they should have more freedom and responsibility, they should not be given free reign. Far too many teenagers are influenced by the wrong crowds. Actively work with your children in choosing the people their age who will have such an important effect on what they become. Let your child's friends help you be a better parent. If you feel uncomfortable about restricting with whom your child spends time, include the questionable playmate in your family activities. In this way you can provide at least some counsel and supervision.

*Questions from Parents*

**Q:** I am recently divorced and now find myself depending heavily on my parents to watch my two young sons while I'm at work. How can I tell if the burden is too much for my parents to handle?

**A:** Ask them. More importantly, you can reduce the burden of the children by letting your parents know you support a firm hand in dealing with your boys. Work on having your sons be more helpful in obeying your parents' wishes. Children who obey are much more welcome at other people's homes, and are less of a burden.

**Q:** Using your children to help the parents sounds like a good idea, but how old should my child be before I start letting him help with the chores?

**A:** Start at age two or three teaching him to pick up a particular toy or piece of clothing. As he grows older give him more to do. Studies show children with five chores to do a day are more prone to get all five done than do only one chore. The five help instill a stronger habit that is more difficult to forget to do.

**Q:** I would love to have my six-year-old help me in the kitchen as I prepare dinner, but she is so slow it is much easier to do it myself and be done with it. Is there any way to speed her up?

**A:** Yes, speed can be increased just like any other dimension of behavior. First comment to the child that the task can be done faster and give encouragement to do so. When you notice her doing it faster, praise her. Second, on some occasions use the more adversive approach of being gruff with her if she does not speed up. (Remember everyday life has both pleasant and unpleasant consequences.) This second approach can use some tact. With my children I often say "Hurry up and get that done or I'll pull your ears longer than a well rope." I do it in a tone and style which lets them know I obviously will not do such a thing, but that I want them working faster. This approach is based on the fact that you can swat an infant's bottom with a scowl on the parent's face and he will cry. Yet smiling while giving the same intensity of swat can make a young child laugh with you. The secret is how you arrange the situation.

**Q:** Where do you draw the line between having your kids help you and demanding too much from the child?

**A:** As mentioned in an earlier chapter, it is almost impossible to ask too much of a child in terms of helping the family. (Keep in mind it is possible to demand too much in excelling at something.) Almost everything the child can be asked to do will help that child later in life. Cleaning rooms and making beds are jobs which help a child be more independent. Mowing lawns or doing other requirements to earn spending money helps develop a work ethic. Doing services for parents such as shining shoes and bringing in the paper teaches the child to do things for others. An hour of daily duties around the house goes a long way toward building character in children. Many parents feel there are few duties around their home to be done. There are quite a few there if we think about it—washing dishes, setting tables, washing clothes, gathering dirty clothes, cleaning windows weekly, cleaning cars weekly, cleaning the garage, cleaning rooms, weeding flowers, and so on.

**Q:** I understand the reasoning behind helping to scrutinize with whom my child associates, but how can I be sure some "wayward" child may not be helped or influenced by the good aspects of my child? Should I still forbid my child to associate with him or her?

**A:** I hope the comments I made in the chapters about selecting a child's playmates were not too strong. While forcing a child to stay away from certain other bad children is something I have had to do with some out-of-control foster children, the parent should handle this issue in a more indirect manner with a typical child. Start when the child is young. Find out what the families of the children your child plays with are like. Do not let your child stay overnight with a child whose parents do not provide proper supervision. If your child dearly likes to be with a friend whose family life worries you, have the friend come over and play at your home. Remember, drugs, prostitution, lying, thievery, and rebelliousness to parental authority, are tendencies children most frequently pick up from their playmates and friends. Friends are extremely important to the proper development of a child. Help your child choose wisely. Love them enough to get involved; yet be wise enough not to totally dominate them.

# 13 Problems Requiring Professional Help

Self-help books are a popular commodity in our society today. In almost every bookstore there are shelves bulging with books about counseling your marriage, overcoming fears, and developing a positive self-image, to name a few.

While writing this book I often reflected upon its purpose. Of course the answers to all behavior problems will not be found within the pages of "Manipulating Parents." In fact, very few answers are found here. I recall a distraught parent coming to me saying, "I've tried everything and nothing seems to work." This type of comment raises an important question. At what point should parents seek help from a professional? What types of problems really require professional help?

To begin to answer this question, I would like to draw a simple analogy. Let's suppose that while you were carving a roast, the knife blade you were using slipped and cut your finger slightly. It would be foolish to consider going to a doctor for assistance because he would tell you what you already know, "Put some disinfectant on it and a bandaid around it and it will heal in due time."

In another instance, however, let us suppose you began having sudden sharp cramps, you are concerned about them, so you go and see the doctor. He examines you carefully, then diagnoses your problem as appendicitis. An operation will be needed to cure you. A delay in this case, or an attempt to help yourself, might cost you your life.

Now let us go back to our initial question. Just when should a parent go for professional help for a psychological problem?

Unfortunately, for several reasons, professional counseling is not as clearly defined as professional medical advice. In the first place, psychological counseling is often looked upon as a sign of individual weakness. When someone is depressed or has a chronic fear, society expects them to live with it or solve it themselves. Going to a psychologist is like admitting defeat. The old saying that "No one really gets better after seeing a psychologist, they only get worse," seems to be a prevalent misconception in our society today.

Just what can a psychologist really do? And when should parents turn to the psychologist for help? These are questions that I hope to be able to answer for you.

## RECOGNIZING A CHILD NEEDING PROFESSIONAL CARE

The first question most parents ask about professional help is "When is my child's behavior serious enough to require a professional's advice?" One of the best ways to answer this question is through examples.

Kathy, a pretty three-year-old girl, was severely mentally retarded. Not only was she mentally retarded, but she also chronically bit her hands until large sores appeared due to constantly being in her mouth. Kathy came from a large middle-class family whose parents were very conscientious and concerned. All their efforts to help Kathy had failed; consequently, they turned to me for advice and assistance.

Jim was a normal-looking child who could carry on a conversation with almost anyone. One unusual thing about Jim was that he could never sit still. He was always fidgeting and could not keep his attention on one project for longer than ten minutes. Jim was failing all his classes; his parents felt they could not control his continuous prowling through the house. Recently, Jim was caught in a fight with some older children in school. Jim's teacher thought Jim might be hyperactive. I was called in to see if I could help him.

The parents in both of these cases were good parents, just somewhat overwhelmed with a problem that seemed to be out of their control. They each felt that all of their efforts either made their child worse or had no effect. One of the first things I did was to help them understand that the situation was not hopeless and I was familiar with some of the treatments which had been successful in correcting some of the same kinds of behavior problems.

As in the case with Jim, there is something to be said about the confidence a calm psychologist can give to the distraught parent. Just reassuring Jim's parents that he had a good chance of improving with a properly designed treatment program was enough to encourage the parents to continue their efforts to help him. In the case of Jim, properly directing the parents' efforts was enough to help them cope with the problem.

Many parents have wondered just what kind of problems they should try to solve themselves and what type of problems require professional help. This question can be best answered by describing children's problems in two parts. First, the type of problem the child has and second, the degree of seriousness of the child's problem. To illustrate this idea, consider a simple behavior like thumbsucking. Most children suck their thumb (as well as other objects) during early childhood. If this problem is not serious, a parent can easily prevent thumbsucking by scolding the child when he sucks his thumb or by painting a bitter solution on the child's thumb. There are times, however, when thumbsucking can be a serious problem, as in the case of Kathy who we mentioned earlier. The thumbsucking actually spread to her hand and it was so severe that it resisted all efforts by the parents to stop it until Kathy was forced to wear splints on her arms that prevented her from bending her arms to suck her hands. This is an example of a problem that can vary in it's degree of seriousness. When one of these problems begin to hinder a child's normal development, a professional psychologist should be consulted.

On the other hand, such behaviors as homosexuality and drug

addiction are problems that require professional assistance no matter how serious the behavior is. Also, when a child seriously suggests killing himself, professional action should be sought immediately.

Keeping in mind that problems can vary in seriousness and type, let me suggest three categories that might be used to classify many problems children have. These are:

1. Problems rarely needing the professional.
2. Problems that sometimes need some professional help.
3. Problems that always need professional help.

## PROBLEMS RARELY NEEDING PROFESSIONAL HELP

Thumbsucking, bedwetting, childhood fears, smoking, and rebelliousness are some of the behaviors parents can almost always deal with themselves. Several of these unwanted behaviors have been discussed earlier and tactics to control such behaviors were mentioned. There are times, however, when these behaviors can become serious, get out of parental control, and require a psychologist's help. Let's take a few minutes and see how the professional psychologist tackles some of these behavior problems.

### Childhood Fears

Have you ever been afraid of the dark? I think most of us might recollect a time when we were afraid to go into a dark room for fear of being assaulted by some mysterious being who lurked about only at night. To most children, fear of the dark is only a temporary state as they mature into adulthood. Parental love and concern can be the best medicine for treating mild cases of childhood fears. In some cases, however, childhood fears can become incapacitating to the child. One incident that comes to mind is a very bright young boy who, according to his teacher, was failing in school and could not sleep at night because of a fear of dogs. This fear dominated his whole lifestyle. Just what would a psychologist do with a problem like this?

One common method used by psychologists is to put the child in an incompatible response situation. This procedure involves getting the child to imagine a very pleasurable scene, and as the child pictures this the psychologist slowly introduces the fear-provoking object (dogs) into the scene. Many psychologists refer to this process as systematic desensitization in relaxation therapy. Often this therapy will allow the child to imagine himself in the presence of fearful objects with no fear. Eventually, the child begins to accept the fear-provoking object in his controlled daydreams with the psychologist, then transfers this new confidence about dogs into real-life situations. In this particular case, the young boy was asked to close his eyes and imagine he had just been given a new pony for his birthday. He was to imagine that he was riding his pony and showing it to his envious friends. While the child was imagining this desirable event, a dog was gradually introduced into the story. Soon, the boy was petting the dog and playing with it without fear. At the end of the treatment his fear of dogs had virtually disappeared. His performance in school had improved and at last report he had no problem sleeping at night.

Of course, this is only a brief overview of one successful technique used by psychologists. There are many approaches that can be used to treat childhood fears and a professional will often try to fit the approach that will be most effective for each individual.

## Smoking

We have talked earlier about some of the ways to eliminate smoking behavior and methods we have discussed are very similar to the psychologist's approach. When a psychologist handles a smoking problem, he realizes that smoking is often a socially controlled behavior, especially with adolescents.

Some of the more common techniques used by psychologists are punishment, such as having the patient use a cigarette box that shocks the patient when he tries to get a cigarette. Another technique is a type of satiation. This involves having the subject rapidly inhale large quantities of cigarette smoke in several treatment sessions. This procedure satiates the smoker and makes smoking itself aversive enough to result in the patient's loss of desire to smoke.

Again, I have seen many parents successfully discourage a teenager's smoking problem, but if the condition persists, a psychologist might be contacted.

## PROBLEMS THAT SOMETIMES NEED PROFESSIONAL HELP

There are many types of problems where a psychologist might be useful in helping control the problem before it gets worse. Often the causes behind a child's unwanted behavior are unknown to the parent and a psychologist can assist the parent in identifying a cause and then perhaps prescribe a method to manage the behavior.

### Learning Disabilities

Learning disabilities represent a very wide range of problems that can be as mild as a slight remedial reading problem to as serious as an inability to distinguish a printed from a blank page. Learning disabilities are often manifested in the school setting. For example, the child may be falling behind in school and might complain about an inability to perform a mathematical operation such as adding.

Usually the teacher will refer the child to the school psychologist for treatment. When this happens the school psychologist will test the child, observe the child in the classroom, and decide if the child needs special help. Schools are generally equipped with a team of specialists trained particularly to help the learning-disabled child. Individuals such as a resource teacher, speech pathologist, and audiologist have specific training to help the child. The parents too may be involved in this process.

When parents notice a problem in their preschool child, a psychologist might be consulted for advice. Often, if a learning disability is caught early in a child's life and is treated properly, the child may not be hindered by it in his or her school years.

### Depression

One behavior that can cause parents some distress is depression. Depression poses several challenges. First, one of the major problems we must face when we discuss depression is what causes it. At present there is no clear-cut reason to explain why a person is depressed. Many psychologists have speculated that depression may stem from a traumatic event in a person's life such as the death of a loved one. Other psychologists have pointed out that a great majority of depressed people are "down" because they feel they have no control over their lives. This lack of control may be the result of setting one's standards too high. When this happens, the person can never feel good about what he does. Finally, some psychologists feel that depression may result from a combination of these reasons.

Another problem is the fact that a depressed person usually has no desire to change. His motivation to improve is gone and the psychologist must somehow create the motivation. In many behavioral disorders the psychologist need only redirect the energy causing the unwanted behavior into a more acceptable direction. With depression however, the psychologist must somehow create this energy within the person. It's always easier to keep a campfire burning, than to start one when the coals are cold and there is not a spark of fire anywhere.

With this in mind you should be able to recognize that even professionals are a little uncertain about how to manage this problem. Let's suppose, however, that a parent brought in her depressed child and asked for advice. What might be done?

First, an attempt should be made to locate the reasons behind his depression. This might involve an interview with the parent and child or having the child complete a few questionnaires. There are many tests that the psychologist has available to him that can assist him in locating the causes for a depressed condition. Often, these tests will be given along with an interview to get a better understanding of the child's problem. Second, based on my observations, I would suggest a treatment strategy. Of course, there are many strategies that one might use, but one popular strategy would be to reinforce the child for his positive behaviors and ignore the negative behaviors. For example, every time the child said something good about himself he might be praised and given some candy; when he talked negatively, he might be systematically ignored by the psychologist. Another treatment technique that is very successful, is to encourage the person to speak positively about himself. Speaking positively is a very rare behavior for the depressed individual. To increase the frequency of positive behavior a professional might take a behavior that occurs frequently and make that frequently occurring behavior (contingent) dependent on positive behavior. This treatment is called "Coverant Control Therapy." The successfulness of this approach is clearly seen in a patient treated by a psychologist named W. G. Johnson. The patient was a seventeen-year-old college freshman who was having severe depression. Johnson employed this treatment by making the boy recite a list of positive statements about himself before he could go to the bathroom. Each time he had to use the bathroom, he would recite several positive statements about himself. After two weeks of this type of treatment, the patient reported that he had overcome his depression. This is a commonly used procedure and has been effective with many depressive cases.

Again, the critical issue with depression that the psychologist must tackle, is to isolate the reason behind the disorder. Only then, can the techniques mentioned earlier be useful to the patient.

### Hyperactivity

Hyperactivity is another behavior of uncertain origin. Hyperactivity, however, is a behavioral disorder associated with a combination of symptoms such as restlessness, an inability to focus attention, poor school achievement, talking constantly, and so on. Hyperactivity also seems to occur more often in boys than in girls. Some experts have suggested that for every nine hyperactive boys there is one hyperactive girl.

Although I realize that almost every normal child occasionally possesses one of the qualities, the hyperactive child displays these symptoms to the degree that they can disrupt his schoolwork, and cause him to be cast out by his peers—not to mention the pressure it can cause in the home.

Many experts believe that hyperactivity is associated with some type of mild damage to the brain. Many hyperactive children, tested by neurologists, have shown signs of abnormal brain activity. This is not the case however, with all hyperactive children. For this reason doctors are uncertain about the origins behind the disorder.

One of the present attempts of psychiatrists and doctors to control the hyperactive child has been the use of drugs. Ritalin is one of the most common drugs used to control the disorder. Drugs have been marginally successful, but they are only effective as long as the child is constantly taking them. Additionally, the strength of the drug must be increased with prolonged usage to the point that an eight-year-old child might be taking a drug strong enough to kill a normal adult.

Another method psychologists use is what is called "Behavior Therapy." This therapy simply involves rewarding the child for appropriate behavior (positive reinforcement). Behavior therapy is often employed to control the hyperactive child in the classroom. Often, the teacher, under the direction of a psychologist, will set up a system where the child can earn points or tokens for good behavior. These tokens can then be exchanged for something the child wants, such as teacher attention, candy, toys, and so on. The teacher usually develops a "menu" or a list of desirables that are associated with a predetermined number of points from which the child can choose the reward for his good behavior. Behavior therapy has some obvious advantages over drug therapy in that behavior therapy requires no medication and the child is in control of his own behavior. Both approaches, however, are useful in treating the hyperactive child. Perhaps the greatest cure for hyperactive behavior is good old "Mother Nature." She generally allows the hyperactive child to gain control over his behavior as he gets older. Very few hyperactive children remain hyperactive in their adult years. Unfortunately, many experts have pointed out that older children with hyperactive histories tend to have learning disabilities which follow them into their older years. It is important to consult a psychologist while the child is still young, if hyperactivity is suspected.

## PROBLEMS NEEDING PROFESSIONAL HELP

When parents hear words like drug addict, rapist, alcoholic, homosexual, mentally retarded, and schizophrenic, they immediately think of the psychologist, and they should. These are basically the behaviors the "Neighbors can't deal with." As I think about some of the cases of serious problems I have had to treat, I can't help but feel that although psychological help should be sought, the parent should not abandon or give up on the child. I have seen some extremely serious problems in my office, and with proper counseling, have seen those children make remarkable recoveries. An effective parent can often greatly aid the psychologist in treatment. Perhaps even a parent–psychologist team might be very effective in some cases. But how does the psychologist approach these problems and what can he do to help a child faced with such a problem?

## Sexual Deviancy

As most of us realize, the world in which we live is far from ideal. The virtues of morality have given way to a society where sexuality is as openly displayed as the weather. In this kind of environment behaviors such as homosexuality, incest, prostitution, transsexuality, and other deviant behaviors are considered part of the normal routine of life. To give you an example of the open acceptance of sexual deviancy, a recent television show based it's theme around a love affair between an attractive mother and her young son.

Statistics seem to reflect this low morality in our society today. According to a national survey 64 percent of all the teenagers in this country between the ages of sixteen and nineteen have had at least one sexual experience prior to marriage. If this is not startling enough, a second national survey conducted among college students has indicated that as high as 82 percent of the men and 56 percent of the women had premarital sex at some time during their college life.

Homosexuality is also on the increase. One national survey estimates that approximately 4 percent of the population of the United States is homosexual. Transexualism, those who think of themselves as being the opposite sex of what they are is also increasing. In 1979 more than 3,000 operations were performed on individuals in which their sex was actually changed.

With this in mind it is easy to understand why so many children are enticed into sexually deviant behavior. Sexual deviancy is a serious behavioral problem and requires very careful attention. Many parents are not able to cope with a teenage son who declares he is a homosexual or a daughter who has been involved in a prostitution business with friends.

One of the major problems a psychologist faces with the sexual deviant is that his behavior is physically rewarding. It is often very difficult to find an alternative more rewarding than the deviant behavior; therefore, an attempt to channel the rewarding aspects of the behavior into a more acceptable direction, or to make the deviant act itself punishing, is another method often employed.

Some of the current techniques that are used to treat the sexually deviant are very similar to the methods we have discussed earlier in other chapters. The psychologist might employ a type of "shock" treatment wherein the patient is shown slides of sexually deviant behavior and if the deviant behavior causes the patient to become sexually aroused, the patient is shocked. The patient can avoid the shock by not becoming aroused when a slide displaying deviant behavior is shown. This treatment approach attempts to make sexual deviancy punishing to the patient.

Another technique is to have the patient imagine that he is involved in the deviant behavior; then, introduce some negative aspect, such as "you are getting violently ill as you begin to commit this act." This often creates a negative feeling toward the deviant behavior and a loss of desire to commit the undesirable act. This technique is called "Covert Sensitization."

### Alcoholism and Drug Abuse

The teenage alcoholic and the teenage drug addict are both commonly used terms to describe a young person who has found the effects of narcotics to be strongly rewarding. Recent statistics have indicated that about 6 percent of the nation's high school pupils have used heroin. One survey conducted by the National Committee of Marijuana and Drug abuse indicated that 39 percent of the high school students they questioned said they had used marijuana. Alcohol, society's legal drug, is widely accepted today. Of the 90 million Americans who use alcohol, 9 million of them are alcoholics. As you can see, alcoholism and drug abuse are widespread problems in our country.

Many people have asked "What causes a person to want to use drugs or alcohol in the first place?" Many theories have been suggested to explain the causes for alcohol and drug abuse. One theory suggests that abuse results from the inability of the person to cope with stress. In a tense situation, the person turns to alcohol to free him- or herself. For example, let's suppose that a young wife is having marital problems. She doesn't know what to do about her situation, so she starts drinking and finds she can escape her worries for awhile. Soon, her husband becomes more dissatisfied with their marriage because of her drinking, which causes her to drink more. Eventually, the couple gets divorced. The wife soon finds that when she stops drinking she gets very depressed, so she continues to drink. She begins associating with friends, who, like her, also drink and her drinking soon leads to alcoholism.

Another theory suggests that alcoholism is inherited from parents. If a person is born in a family where one or both partners are alcoholics, or heavy drug users, the person is more likely to be an abuser. Other psychologists have pointed out, however, that this tendency may be more from the example the parents set for their child rather than inborn characteristics. Still another theory suggests peer pressure to be one of the major causes of drug and alcohol abuse. When it is popular to drink kids will be inclined to drink in order to stay in the group. Generally speaking, one of the important factors behind drug and alcohol abuse treatment is to discover the emotional reasons behind the abusive behavior.

What happens when a member of a family starts abusing alcohol or drugs? What can be done on the professional level?

One commonly used technique is to treat alcohol and drug abuse by making the abusive behavior itself punishing or removing the rewarding qualities of the drug. The use of methodone in the treatment of heroin addicts is based on this idea. When given to an addict, methodone satisfies the withdrawal symptoms that follow heroin use, but gives the user no "high." When an addict uses methodone it is like he is taking heroin but getting no benefit from it. After a while, the addict no longer desires to use the heroin. Medication called "Antabuse" works in a similar way for alcoholics. The only difference is that once a person takes "Antabuse" if he even drinks a small amount of alcohol, he gets violently ill. Psychologists feel that these treatments are about 60 percent effective.

Another method for treating the abuser is centered around training the person to develop other means to handle stressful situations. Again, the old incompatible response idea says when a person is put in a stressful situation his new skills will be incompatible with his drinking and he will be forced to choose between the two approaches to solve his problem. It is the aim of the psychologist to make social skills the more rewarding of the two choices.

Finally, one of the more successful treatment approaches for the alcohol and drug addict is to get the family members involved. If family members are trained to provide support and strength to the abuser and withdraw their support from the abuser at certain critical times, they can decrease the abuser's unwanted behavior. It has been shown by experience that proper family love and concern can be very helpful in overcoming such behavior problems.

In summary, I have tried to show that childhood problems come in various types and forms. Some, like homosexuality, are serious in nature. Others, such as thumbsucking, are mild and could be handled by parents given proper direction, but could become serious in some unusual cases.

The list included in this chapter is not exhaustive by any means. It was the purpose of this chapter to give parents a feeling for various problems and to suggest times when a psychologist should be consulted. Perhaps, as awareness of parents in the psychologist's skills increases, many of our misconceptions about psychology will be dispelled.

# 14

# Types of Problems Parents Can Handle

Now that the tactics children use have been identified and the strategies parents can use to turn the tables have been explained, it might be helpful to discuss some of the more common behavioral problems parents can handle. Some suggestions as to how these problem behaviors would be dealt with by me or other psychologists who use the natural approach will also be given.

In essence, this chapter explains some of the effective treatments psychologists could prescribe if you told them your child had a particular problem. It is important to keep in mind that psychologists can do more. The psychologist can provide at least two valuable services to parents. One is to prescribe ways of handling well-identified problems in children such as tantrums, swearing, and selfishness. This is one service of this book.

The second service a psychologist provides is diagnosing what the problem actually is. Oftentimes we visit a medical doctor when we know the problem. The child has measles, has a large cut on her arm, or a snake bite. In many instances, however, we bring the child in not knowing what is medically wrong. In such instances, the medical doctor must probe to identify the problem before a treatment can be prescribed. Diagnosing problems from the murky thoughts and actions of children is possibly the most important service psychologists, psychiatrists, and social workers provide a parent. Without a doubt there are situations in which a child may commit undesirable acts because of a deep-seated psychological conflict within himself. In one case, for example, Carol and I had a teenage girl brought into our home who had repeatedly attempted suicide. The apprehension and uneasiness which repeatedly recurred in her actions made it apparent we needed to do more than just reward when she did things right or punish when she tried to kill herself. After a few months of probing past events in her life, which she repeatedly tried to avoid, the rest of the problem surfaced. One night as we questioned her during one of her uneasy moods, she recounted how a brother and friends had sexually used her. The incident started a tempest within her which led to her attempting suicide at times and acting as a rebellious child to her parents on other occasions. As was true with this girl, there are times where getting to the root of the problem is necessary, and a psychologist is needed.

There are psychologists and psychiatrists who treat tantrums, biting, not doing what parents request, and lying, as behavioral signs of turmoil within. Their approach focuses on the idea that "If I identify and remove some underlying psychological problem, the behavioral problems will disappear." In contrast, the approach in this book has been toward dealing directly with problem behavior and downplaying the idea that problem behaviors in children are mainly outward signs of inner conflict. There are two main reasons for this. First, there is little psychological research evidence to support the position that even one out of four problem behaviors in children is due to underlying causes. Psychologists and parents who use the strategies in Chapters Eight through Eleven directly on behavior problems show overwhelming successes without having to search deep in the child's psyche. Second, even in situations like the girl mentioned previously, helping her reestablish a good feeling about herself after an incident over which she had no control did not automatically eliminate the bad habits of throwing emotional fits and lying that she had developed. In addition, my wife and I had to use the strategies in this book directly on those problem behaviors to get rid of them.

In this chapter, several behavior problems are discussed which could be signs of underlying psychological problems. This should be kept in mind, and professional advice sought if that is the case. At least ninety-six times out of a hundred however, the problems discussed in this chapter are simply behaviors with which children have learned to manipulate their parents. Parents should not hesitate to try to deal with them.

What if the real reason of the behaviors is internal turmoil? Will my attempts to get rid of the problems cause irreparable harm to my child? As mentioned earlier in Chapter Two, children are very resilient. Attempting any of the strategies in this book will not make the problem worse. At worst they will simply not work.

Many parents have often heard there are critical actions a child must express to be psychologically well adjusted. These parents may hesitate in interfering with a child's offensive actions for fear of thwarting the expression of a possibly valuable inner psychological force. This chapter also addresses this issue to some degree, and hopefully convinces the parent that there is no psychological justification for believing parents must put up with the offensive actions of manipulative children.

## TANTRUMS

Temper tantrums come in all types and sizes, and can include angry outbursts of yelling, kicking, hitting, throwing things, and writhing on the floor. At one time or another all children throw a tantrum. While tantrums in younger children may worry the rookie parent, they are not indications of deep psychological turmoil or inherited tendencies. While the temperament of a child may be inherited to some degree, temper tantrums are not inherited behaviors. They are learned. Children who exhibit temper tantrums often model this behavior from parents who express tantrums on occasion to get their way. But temper tantrums may also occur in children whose parents do not use such tactics. In situations where tantrums occur, one thing is always present: the parents or people around the child respond to those tantrums! Some parents have the misconception that tantrums are psychologically necessary and beneficial for the child. While letting off steam can be psychologically valuable, this can be done in a variety of ways (for example, through physical games, work, exercise) without need for tantrums. Tantrums are logical extensions of the crying and banging strategies infants use to initially get their way with parents.

Two of the most effective strategies for eliminating tantrum behavior are *extinction* and *punishment.* Recall that extinction is a strategy for getting rid of an unwanted action by making sure it receives no pleasant payoff. Throwing a good tantrum takes quite a bit of energy and effort. So it does not take too many unrewarded tantrums before a child quits. However, keep in mind from earlier chapters that it will take longer to extinguish tantrums if, in the past, a parent has been inconsistent in trying to ignore the tantrum. If the parent not only makes sure the child does not get what he wants, but also judiciously *punishes* the child for the tantrum, the tantrums will cease much quicker, and the child is not left with a psychological scar. Just as we learn not to touch a hot stove because such acts are followed by something unpleasant, even a ten-month-old child will learn not to throw a tantrum if that tantrum produces something unpleasant.

The topic of tantrums is a good place to bring up a mistake most parents make without realizing it. Parents often let infants and young children get away with tantrums because they cannot bring themselves to use unpleasant consequences on an infant. We parents show no hesitation to reward infants with smiles, laughter, and affectionate caresses when they smile, say "dada," or take their first step. On the other hand, we are slow to reprimand them for actions such as an infant playing in her food, a two-year-old grabbing things off coffee tables, or an infant obviously throwing a tantrum for attention. We build in the child the incorrect perception of the world that only pleasant things happen no matter what you do. During the formative years even infants are very capable of learning right and wrong.

At birth the child's brain and nervous system are not completely developed. Over the first few months the finishing touches are completed on the nervous system as that system tries to make sense out of all the sights and sounds the infant is encountering for the first time. Once he begins to make sense out of the things he sees and hears, he begins to learn about his own actions. If he does such and such his right arm moves, while other actions of the mind create movement in the legs.

He is ready and able at this time to learn that certain actions produce pleasant consequences while other actions produce unpleasant experiences. A child is both physically and psychologically ready to associate his actions with the consequences of those actions. Parents partially realize this as they smile and react to get the young baby to smile. Such infants are also ready to learn not to do such things as throw tantrums through unpleasant feedback. But we parents resist letting infants experience unpleasant consequences and lose possibly the best time in life for such lessons to be learned.

But how can an infant cope with unpleasant and painful experiences? Don't we run the risk of overpunishing the child with consequences he cannot comprehend, thereby leaving irreparable psychological scars? When teaching a child to smile or walk we do not use the same intensity of hugs and other rewards we would be inclined to give a ten-year-old. The infant is more fragile, and we tone down the infant's handling by using softer, but still rewarding, hugs and other signs of affection. The infant is sensitive too, and can learn from these milder consequences that a five-year-old would not consider strong enough. The same is true for using unpleasant consequences with very young children. A mild but firm pat on the diapered area, or a scowl with the simultaneous sound of two hands slapping together often provides an unpleasant enough situation the child can easily cope with psychologically, and learn from.

The virtue of starting young with unpleasant experiences becomes more apparent when we recall the point made earlier that unpleasant consequences for a child's actions generally stimulate one of two reactions: (1) to keep the unpleasant experience from happening again by learning to *not do* the act again, or (2) to be aggressive toward the one administering the punishment. In a very young child this second choice is not usually seriously considered. The younger a child begins to learn from punishment, the more impact the punishment has on an effort not to repeat the wrong behavior. Mother Nature has endowed man with a natural tendency which has great survival value: "The larger the adversary (and the fewer the options), the more prone man is to comply rather than rebel." By waiting until a child is older before using punishment, we make it harder on the child (stronger unpleasantries are needed), and we increase the probability the child will be aggressive to the parent rather than comply. Starting young helps both the child and parent.

## RUNNING AWAY

Almost every child at some time or another reaches a point where running away is considered. Fifteen thousand children run away each week in the United States alone. In some cases running away means leaving one's parents to get away from a deeply disturbing, but difficult to identify, uneasiness within the child. When unexplainable fear and apprehension seem to be the motivating factor for running away, parents should seek the help of a trained professional to deal with the problem.

On the other hand, running away by children is often an attempt to try to punish the parent for making the child do something he did not want to do. Parents should not be too hard on children who try this, just make sure the child's expectations are not met. Parents are not easily controlled and intimidated by such threats, so children usually switch to something else.

If a child, particularly a three- to seven-year-old, repeatedly runs away from you in shopping malls or does not come home when called, his or her behavior is most likely the result of simply finding rewarding experiences from launching out on their own. They get to go look and touch toys in the stores without mother stopping them. They find more fun on a neighbor's jungle gym set than they do in their backyard. A twelve-year-old may get away with doing things at a friend's house that he cannot at home, so he fails to respond to mother's calls to come home.

For instances of running away just mentioned, using *extinction* or ignoring the behavior will not work. These experiences of running provide their own pleasant payoffs. Such incidences can be effectively dealt with in two parts. First, administer some form of punishment to make running away an unpleasant idea. Second, where possible provide for the times the child can properly experience the enticements wanted. For example, set certain times aside children can look at toys and other things of interest to them. For those bad activities (smoking, drugs, vandalism) that children run away to do, the parents should use punishment, stand firm, and work toward interesting the child in more appropriate activities.

## BITING

Biting is a behavioral problem that has very little chance of being caused by underlying psychological turmoil. Most young children bite because they have very few ways to retaliate to older brothers and sisters that gains them the respect biting does. Once a child learns that biting helps him get what he wants, he will use it again. Most children bite at some time or another because it is a natural extension of one of the strongest habits (eating) a young child has. Extinction is usually a poor strategy because the act of biting provides its own satisfaction. A child does not do it to get applause from his elders. Satiation is often a successful approach because the mouth area is sensitive and gets sore easily, plus the muscles for biting get tired and sore relatively quickly. When a child bites, make that child bite a medium-hard ball of practical size repeatedly in one sitting. The desire to bite will fade quickly. Properly used punishment can work also. Many parents let the child experience a bite themselves as a punishment. I have heard some positive reports with such retaliatory biting, but have not used or strongly pushed this approach myself.

## EATING PROBLEMS

Eating problems are one of the best psychological thermometers there is around the house. Most mothers learn to spot when something is bothering their children by the way they eat. A child who has lost his or her friend may lose their appetite. A ten-year-old who has done something wrong may be more quiet and cautious while eating. Many adults overeat when under some emotional strain.

Changes in eating habits can be behavioral indications of underlying psychological turmoil for the person. Many times, people lose their appetites, overeat, or pick at their food while attempting to deal with problems. Often these problems are solved in a day or two and the person is back to his or her old eating self. In cases where the changes in eating habits continue for weeks and months, yet the parent is unable to identify the problem, professional help is advised.

There are numerous occasions, however, where eating problems do not indicate underlying psychological problems, and the parents can deal with such cases by themselves. There are four major types of eating problems psychologists encounter. These are: (1) young high-chaired infants playing in their food; (2) overeating; (3) picky eaters; and (4) teenagers eating mainly junk food. Children can learn to throw food and generally create attention at mealtime with such activities. For the high-chair-aged child, such activity often is part of finding out what nonnutritive qualities food has such as spooning oatmeal to see how it falls to the floor. In such cases you have a situation where you want them to *not do* something. You may successfully implement some punishment procedure. For example, you may remove the bowl of food from the child for one minute each time he plays in the food. This would be a "time out" strategy and this can work on both children and pets. Or you may take the food away until the next meal as a punishment for playing in the food. There is an interesting relationship between children and food. The less hungry they are the more prone they are to play in the food. The more hungry they are the more serious they get about eating. Sitting a child in a chair with a bowl of food for twenty minutes is not a good idea. Do not require the child to eat a certain amount. Let him stop if he wants. If he did not eat enough, it will be evident at the next meal (assuming of course you did not commit the sin of letting him snack between scheduled meals).

Overeating is such a large concern of society that books and more books have been written on the subject. To solve the problem one obviously has to decrease consumption and increase exercise. There are no magical cures, but there are many effective programs for overeating. Some, such as *Weight Watchers,* focus on reducing intake and establishing healthy eating habits. Others, such as health spa programs, focus on exercise with nutritional eating. Check around to find the one that fits you or your child best. There is one important point about overeating that all parents should remember. Punishing children for overeating is an unwise strategy. In fact it can, and often does, fan the flames. You can help the problem child to some degree (along with total programs such as *Weight Watchers*) by using the strategies of physical restraint and stimulus change. Using physical restraint you may help the child by not having fattening foods around the house. Fruits and vegetables such as carrot sticks could take the place of candy and cookie snacks. If no candy is available in view of the child, there is less of a chance it will be eaten. Using stimulus change, you may focus the child's thoughts to activities other than food. Remove pictures and other items around the house that make one think about eating. Get your child busy in activities. A child is less prone to think of food if he is putting puzzles together, painting, or playing football.

Picky eating is usually one of the easiest problems to solve and is almost never due to underlying causes. Picky eating is a learned bad habit, which can be eliminated by not rewarding a child's efforts to get preferential treatment. I usually handle such problems with incoming foster children by saying "Well, this is what we eat around here. If you do not like it, you do not have to eat it. You may be excused from the table." Within a meal or two the child becomes quite reasonable. A good practice is to allow each child the right to have two foods he does not have to eat. Limiting, rather than totally forbidding a child from having the right to refrain from some foods, helps them make decisions, and usually solves the problem of picky eating. Remember, food preferences change as one grows older, so it is a good idea to have children try at least a spoonful of new or disliked foods once every few months or so.

The problem of junk food eaters is again a direct preference problem and not likely to be related to major psychological disturbances. Children who eat junk food are also commonly absent from family meals, or are in a family where the family members eat at different times. Making sure the whole family eats together at least once a day is one of the most powerful tools for a strong family. The key is to make that mealtime a rewarding experience for all members of the family. Good food and good conversation are natural partners. Do not make mealtimes a strictly biological affair. Plan family outings at mealtime. Talk of interesting things that could be done. Let children tell of their experiences for the day. Tell stories to your children about things that happened to you and your parents in years gone by. Make that meal an event the children do not want to miss.

## FEARS

Fears can be signs of underlying psychological problems, and in many cases parents need professional help to cope with a child's fears. But childhood fears may be handled by parents in most cases. And even if a parent's attempts to help the child fails, such attempts do not inhibit the ability of a professional to help later. So try and see if you can solve the problem yourself, before going for help.

Physical pain is Mother Nature's way of letting us know there is something physically wrong with our bodies that is threatening our health. Fears are Mother Nature's psychological indications of impending danger to one's self. Fear is an emotional reaction controlled by a special area of the brain and nervous system: the emotional reaction of fear is unpleasant and is a motivator within us to do something to get rid of the fear. The presentation of dangerous items such as snakes, cliffs, and spiders often naturally elicit fear in a child. Fear is so important in man's survival that the portion of the brain which can produce fear is always primed and ready to go into action at a moment's notice. Oftentimes the system is too ready and sort of jumps the gun by reacting to things that really are not dangerous themselves. For example, a woman was in a car accident. Her brakes went out on a hill in a city. She made it through two intersections before colliding with a parked car. After the accident, the feelings of fear she had before the impending crash recurred in her mind whenever she saw the color bright red. She had a bright red coat on in the accident. Apparently her mind's eye associated the coat with the other visual sights of cars flashing by and so on. Just as the visual sights experienced on a roller coaster can elicit fear, the coat became a visual cue which could elicit fear in this woman.

Psychologists have found from thousands of cases like this woman's that many nondangerous objects in our environment can come to elicit fear. The secret to an object gaining the ability to produce fear is to "pair" the object with a naturally fear-inducing situation, and the object can then induce fear. In many instances the pairing only happens in the mind. A child is bitten by a dog; now all the animals with hair on them frighten him. A horse he has seen for the first time may cause a fear reaction.

The key to getting rid of a child's fear is to have him experience the presence of the object without the feared unpleasant consequences happening. For example, a child will lose his fear of the dog after he has petted the dog and interacted with it long enough to realize he will not get bitten. There are three effective ways to accomplish this task. First, you can simply put the child in the fearful situation at full strength, and the fear will gradually subside. A young child fearful of school can simply be taken to school and left in the classroom. After hours or days the child will automatically lose his fear because nothing really bad happens. A child fearful of horses may be forced to sit on the back of a horse until the child quits crying and the fear gradually leaves him. Psychologists use this strategy of directly confronting one's fears to a degree in two therapeutic approaches called *implosion* and *flooding*.

A second, and possibly easier, approach to getting rid of fears is to use a gradual approach. A child fearful of school may be gradually prepared for the experience by first visiting the class with his mother for a few minutes. On a following day he may be left there with other children for just a few hours rather than a full day. Eventually he experiences being in school for a whole day. Using the first approach of just leaving the child in the classroom for a full day, the child will experience a strong fear reaction which will eventually subside. He may cry or wet his pants on that day, but such instances will fade. This second approach of gradually introducing a child to his fear can effectively rid the child of the fear without the child having to go through the total fearful experience in one or two big swallows. The second approach stretches the fear reaction into smaller bites which the child may take longer to experience, but the experience is less severe. A young child's fear of a dark bedroom can be handled by installing a six or seven dollar dimmer control switch and gradually dimming the light a small amount each night over several days.

The third approach entails putting the child in the incompatible response situation explained in Chapter Eight. Suppose a three-year-old child sees her grandparents for the first time but is fearful to run across the room and hug them as mother requests. The child may be too afraid to go. If, however, the grandparents are holding a chocolate bunny, the girl is in an incompatible response situation. The fear of people she does not know tempts her to stay away. The chocolate bunny tempts her to go. If the bunny is big enough so the desire to go is stronger than the fear, the girl will go. And once her mind realizes the fears are unfounded, the fears will fade. A young child will be more prone to approach a dog if mother holds his hand and gives him words of comfort in the process.

The key then to any of the three ways for eliminating a fear is that the child must confront the fear and let it dissipate. As the charged battery in a flashlight will lose its strength over time as it is called upon by the user, a fear reaction will fade as the child confronts the fear and negative consequences do not occur. All three approaches mentioned require the person to confront the fear, but in different ways.

## LYING

Lying is one of the more difficult problems to deal with because it is one of the more difficult problem behaviors to catch and treat immediately. Lying can keep children from doing work and from being punished. Lying can also help a child present himself to others as more than he is. If a child's face turned green every time he or she told a lie, few lies would be told because the lie would not help fool someone. Unfortunately, however, lying is often a rewarding way out of unpleasant situations, so lying continues.

The best way to deal with the problem of lying is to keep it from occurring in the first place. But once it occurs there are a few things which can help to get rid of this behavior. First, some sort of punishment (for example, spanking, time out, scolding, taking away something the child likes) is needed so that the lying becomes less attractive. But because the punishment for lying is often delayed and does not occur every time one lies, other actions are also needed to help reduce the attractiveness of lying. Be sure your child sees situations where you tell the truth when lying would let you off the hook. Later discuss the incident with your mate (in the presence of your child) while adding the point that telling the truth pays off in the long run. Emphasize the importance of a person's word. Also be sure to later approach a child who has told the truth and paid the price and let them know how proud you are for his accepting responsibility for his behavior. Stretching the truth and telling tall stories may be the first steps toward lying. When children tell small lies such as "I can drive a car," show some mild form of displeasure, indicating such actions are not appropriate. If your family likes to tell tall stories and joke around, be sure to emphasize on several occasions the distinction between stretching the truth for a laugh and stretching the truth to build one's importance or avoid responsibility for one's actions.

## STEALING

The problem behavior of stealing is handled much like lying because they have so many things in common. Stealing provides immediate rewards for the child, often occurs without being detected, and punishment for such actions is often delayed. When handling children who steal, we wait for its occurrence and emphasize the point that there is no possible justification for stealing. It is not funny, it is not harmless, and it is a totally unacceptable act. It is important to emphasize that such acts will not be tolerated. Many foster parents find it difficult to handle children who steal, and often solve their problem by sending the child somewhere else. Although a parent should stand strongly on the issue of stealing, it is important that the child realize the parent is very much against the act of stealing but not against the child who does it.

*Questions from Parents*

**Q:** I find myself trying to settle fights between my children and not being able to determine who was wrong. How does a parent handle this problem?

**A:** Many psychologists suggest the parent ignore such arguments and don't get in the middle for fear of incorrectly offending the wrong child. I, on the other hand, feel the parent should act as if there are two problems. First, fighting is not an acceptable behavior. The person who retaliates is as wrong as the person who starts the fight. Parents should use the strategies outlined in Chapter Eleven designed to teach children to *not do* things. Parents should also praise children on the occasions we see them deal correctly with such problems. Second, the parent should act like a judge who takes all facts into consideration (including eyewitness reports) and then make a decision. Keep in mind all children get emotional at times to use some discretion in dealing with these situations.

**Q:** Do parents have to be exacting and completely consistent to make the strategies work that this book talks about?

**A:** If that were a requirement of the strategies there would not be one successful parent. Successful parents make mistakes, are often inconsistent, and do not do everything as specifically as I have outlined in the book. However, the more consistent you are and do exactly what is outlined in the book, the more success you will have. A basketball team can make mistakes and still win the game. The more mistakes, however, the less likely they are to win. The same is true about parenting.

**Q:** I tried dimming out the lights in my child's room over a week and he still cried. What did I do wrong? Or doesn't it work all the time?

**A:** It works all the time. When using the gradual approach the child's fears may arise if you try to accomplish the feat too fast. Back up and start again, or back up more than once if you have to. Just be sure your child, if he or she is old enough, is not just trying to manipulate you when he realizes what you are doing. By the way, you do not have to back up and start at the beginning again. Just illuminate the light enough that the child is no longer responding fearfully, and start down from that point.

**Q:** I am a mother with twelve- and fourteen-year-old sons. I am concerned about trying to discipline them with spankings. What should I do?

**A:** Never try to discipline a child using an approach you cannot enforce! If they are as big as you, spanking is an unwise choice. Use the form of punishment in which you take away privileges and other such nonphysical strategies. I often use the incompatible response approach when I cannot spank a child because the child is not my own.

# 15
# Caring—The Family Adhesive

## THE ROLE OF CARING IN SUCCESSFUL PARENTING

> "My teenage daughter cannot seem to wait to get away from us to go with her friends."
> "I have tried to do things with my son, but he would rather be with his friends."
> "My six-year-old son does not do a thing I tell him to. He does not seem to care about how I feel."
> "My kids mock all that I value, and call me and my views outdated and old fashioned."
> "My daughter hates me. She told me so."
> "Our kids do not care about us. They do not show us any consideration. They come and go as they please without telling us where they are going. We tell them to do something and they do just the opposite."
> "My kids don't care about me. They just use me."

These types of comments made by parents seem to be on the increase. More parents are coming for help to find out how they can get their children to care about them. In Chapter One several incidents were mentioned that illustrated the lack of caring by children for adults. Danny did not care that his teacher wanted him to stay in class until school was out. He was going home when he felt like it. Lee Ann did not care how her parents felt concerning the trip to Hawaii. She did not want to be with them while touring the islands. She expected her parents to let her do what she wanted by herself although they were paying the bills. Phil's nephew did not care if his uncle was busy talking to someone else. He would hit his uncle in the groin to get him to pay attention to him *now.*

On the other hand, there are children who want to know how they can get their parents to care for them.

> "My dad has never come to one school activity with me."
>
> "My mother did not get my costume ready for our third-grade play, and the kids teased me."
>
> "My parents could care less that I am here in jail. They don't care where I go or what happens to me."
>
> "I got in trouble with the police to get back at my parents and they were just worried about how to hush up the incident. Why don't they care about me?"

Caring is the staff of life. It is one of the natural attributes of life which gives meaning and value to life itself. It is the reason for most unselfish acts. The hunter often uses the caring of a parent for its offspring. He stakes out the young bear cub knowing the mother will come to try to save her young. Because of caring, she unwillingly trades her natural habitat for a zoo. The mother rhinocerous stands between her young and the jackals because of her instinct to care.

Not too long ago a trained police dog had to be shot because he would not let other policemen get near his wounded master who lay unconscious on the ground bleeding to death. A classic movie was made several years ago about the true story of a man and dog that cared for each other. Eventually the man died. Every day the dog lay on his master's grave—until the dog finally died.

In the winter of 1980 Southern California was hit by devastating rainfall which produced mudslides and swollen rivers. A young newly married couple had recently moved to California from the East Coast. They took a walk along a swollen and turbulent river, absorbing the wonder of everything around them. Close by a little boy fell into the river and began screaming for help. The newlywed unhesitantly jumped in to help the boy. The boy was pushed to shore and lived—at the expense of the young man's life.

## INDICATIONS OF CARING

Each of us has been touched many times by the caring of others. That caring is the adhesive which keeps a family together. Oftentimes it is the reason we are willing to endure the many trials of life Mother Nature puts before us. Caring is such an important part of life that few parents need to be reminded of its role in successful parenting. However, there is an often unrealized dimension of caring which we sometimes forget. Caring often requires firmness. Leniency is not always received as an indication of caring by children.

Throughout this book I have suggested and emphasized an approach to childrearing which many readers may interpret as uncaring and noncompassionate. I have told about giving spankings to even teenage children, and advocated parents not to catch toddlers from falling down "one" carpeted stair. I have suggested the reader let children experience uncomfortable situations as they grow up. I even suggested some uncomfortable experiences the reader could devise for them. All of these things I have said because I care about children. While this may seem hard to believe, let me try to clarify by telling you of a past experience I had many years ago with one of the first foster children we took into our home.

As you may recall, Maria was ten years old when she joined our family. At the age of four her parents separated. Her mother did not want her so her father took her. He received much better welfare assistance because of her. One day he took her to the hospital emergency room because she was sick with a high fever. While examining Maria, the attending nurse spotted marks and bruises on Maria's back. The nurse called Social Services who told her to keep the frightened young girl there until they arrived. Realizing something was wrong when he could not get his daughter released, the father fled. After court hearings in which it was noted that many beatings had occurred, Maria became a ward of the court and was placed in the care of my wife and me. Feeling compassion for what had happened to her during her young life, Carol and I were extra careful about how we disciplined her.

As is the case in most families, children get into trouble together because of some unacceptable group activity. Such was the situation one day when two of our boys and Maria did something they knew they should not. Catching them in the act I spanked Kit and Michael before sending them to bed. I verbally reprimanded Maria and sent her to bed. Later that day all three were allowed to get up, and the boys went out to play as usual. Maria was unusually quiet and seemed to watch me whenever I entered the family room. "I was too harsh on her," I thought.

Just before bedtime Maria came quietly over to me and said "How come I didn't get spanked like Kit and Michael did?" Her question made me realize I had made a mistake. I had committed the most serious mistake any foster parent or adoptive parent can make. *I had not treated her the same as our other children.* And what I had done indicated to her that I did not care for her as I did the other children. From the ten-minute talk we had, it became apparent that because I treated her different, she felt I perceived her as different. And to foster kids, being treated different means you don't care as much for them. Even though my "different" discipline for her was milder than for the rest, it meant I did not care as much.

As I later thought over what had happened, my only defense for not spanking her was my concern over what a spanking might do psychologically to a child who had been beaten many times. Not having previously experienced such a situation I had convinced myself that scolding her and sending her to bed would be best for a child who had been physically abused. That experience, and more successful ones which followed has convinced me that the rule *treat all children the same* is important in showing those questioning children you care. And if the child does not feel you care, the value of what you do for them is greatly diminished.

## Rules and Limitations Often Signify You Care

Oftentimes children sense a parent's failures to enforce rules and regulations as an indication that they do not really care. Several years back, Morgan, a foster parent, was being sued by a civil liberties group because he was "violating the civil rights" of the children put in his care. Morgan had been a boxer in his younger days and was quite firm in his beliefs. Older boys were put in his care at his ranch, and often he had struck them for not doing what they were told. The case was never brought to trial, however, because the prosecution could not get any of Morgan's wards to complain about him. In fact, one young man who had been sent to Morgan's ranch when he was younger returned to help Morgan when he heard of the possible trial.

"I was sent to several foster homes before I ended up at Morgan's ranch," the young man told me. "I did not last long at any place. I did many things to upset my new parents. But they never cared enough to take the time to deal with me. Morgan would not let me get away with the things I did at the other places. He swatted me many times and I repeatedly told him how I hated him. But Morgan was the only one who really cared enough about me to not let me get away with things. Many times he'd tell me what he was doing was because I meant something to him. At that time I felt he really meant what he said—but I didn't tell him that."

I have had several similar situations with teenage girls. Many times they have broken rules of the house to see if they could get away with the act. Once, as one of our foster daughters was getting ready to return to her parents, Cindy reminded me of the importance of rules and discipline in caring.

"I can still remember when you caught me cruising Main. It was the first time you let me take the car alone and I was supposed to go to a meeting. You grounded me for two weeks and gave me extra work to do at home. I remember you told me you were mostly mad because I did not do what I was told. You said you had to be able to count on me so that I would be able to count on you when I needed help. Ever since then I knew you and Carol cared about me. I meant enough to you to make you mad, yet you did not just send me away."

Many times parents care for their children by enforcing rules and discipline. Children often see our failure to enforce rules and regulations as signs that we do not care. And there are times that we have to admit it could seem that way. Disciplining children is uncomfortable for most parents (those that enjoy disciplining should seek help). And most of the times we do not discipline it is because we find it easier on ourselves (not the children) at the moment. We may not accept the responsibility our children expect—unless we really care.

### Positive Signs of Caring

A second and more recognizable form of caring relates to showing interest in others. We care about scouting if we get involved in the Boy Scout and Girl Scout programs. We care about our mates if we show interest in their welfare and show appreciation for them. We care about our children if we listen to the illogical questions of a three-year-old. We care about our children if we take time with them. We care if we go to their school activities.

When someone begins to receive less attention, that person takes that reduced attention as a sign of lack of care and concern. One may argue that he cares as much, but other things just need to be done. Most of us must admit, however, that this is a rather empty contention. The busy executive can always find that extra time in the evening to watch the basketball game while not finding time to fix the back door as his wife requested. The uncaring daughter may not find time to help mother, but has time to go over to her friend's house.

Answering questions, taking time to talk, doing favors, expressing appreciation, and showing consideration are all positive signs of caring. Ignoring family rules, avoiding someone, throwing tantrums, and being inconsiderate of others, are all signs that one cares little. And more parents are seeing those signs of uncaring in the actions of their children.

## GETTING CHILDREN TO CARE ABOUT PARENTS

### The Parent–Child Bond—a Special Gift of Nature

One of the nicest things Mother Nature does for parents is send them infants who are prewired to believe their parents are the most important objects of life. This is true even in the animal world.

The Nobel Prize-winning naturalist, Konrad Lorenze, made an interesting discovery with baby ducklings. He hatched eggs with the help of an incubator and found that the ducklings entered the world believing he was their mother. They followed him everywhere. Even when their natural mother was brought to where he and the ducklings were, they continued to stay with Lorenze and treated her as an undesired stranger. When seperated from Lorenze they would quack the same as other ducklings who were separated from their mother. They would try to overcome impossible obstacles (for example, deep ditches, fences) to reach him if he could be seen in the distance.

While newborn children differ from ducklings in many ways, they also come prewired with a strong, somewhat mysterious, disposition to strongly want and love those people they first come in contact with who provide for their needs. With ducklings Lorenze found this bonding would occur to the first moving object the ducklings encountered after being hatched. In the natural setting the mother duck is almost always that object. In the laboratory Lorenze bonded (or *imprinted* as it is more commonly called) newborn ducklings to either a bouncing ball, a moving beer bottle, or himself.

With human infants the bonding process is not quite so quick. While ducklings bond within a few hours, the bond between parent and child strengthens over weeks, months, and sometimes years, as the mother comforts, suckles, and protects her offspring. However, the result of the special human child–parent bond is just as remarkable as for the ducklings. The parent becomes the most valuable object in the world to the child. No king or queen can take the place of a child's father or mother. No woman is so loved as a child's mother. A plumber is the wisest man in the world—in the eyes of his four-year-old son.

I am often surprised by the strength of this bond as I am confronted with situation after situation where children continue to love even undeserving parents. I have seen four- and five-year-old children in the hospitals all brusied and battered who cry until they are returned to the parents or parent who injured them. I've seen uncared-for children standing in urine-soaked carpets in filthy apartments crying as they are taken from their alcoholic parents. In 1977 a Pennsylvania woman with a bruised forehead offered to sell me her eight-year-old son for two thousand dollars so she and her husband (who had beat her up the night before) could move to Florida. In talking to the boy he said he was willing to be adopted—if that was what his parents wanted.

Karen was a pretty, dark-haired girl, who, at the age of fourteen, was brought to our home. When she was eight years old Karen's mother used her in a shoplifting ring. One night when she was eleven, her father slipped into bed and took advantage of her. Frightened, and not knowing what to do, she tried to ignore the problem by pretending she was sleeping through the ordeal. He returned on two other nights. Both her uncle and father used her one day in Boise at her uncle's home while the aunt was shopping.

Feeling ashamed and unclean Karen tried to take her own life. She was admitted to the youth center of the State Mental Institution as a maladjusted child with strong suicidal tendencies. The state revoked both parents' rights and took custody of Karen. She adamantly refused to testify against her father or uncle. After a few months she was placed in a foster home, but had to be removed because of fighting with the mother and other children. Over the next two years she lived in seven different foster homes, always successfully doing something to upset the foster family.

While staying with our family, she continually wrote to her then separated parents telling them how much she loved them. They seldom wrote back. Hearing her mother was in the hospital for a serious operation, Karen asked to go see her. My wife, Carol, drove Karen, age sixteen, the hundred miles to the hospital.

Karen's mother had seven children, as far as we could determine. She enjoyed making love with any man (a nymphomaniac as psychologists label such women). The children that she had not given away were wards of the court in several states. When Carol and Karen entered the hospital room, her mother was talking to a woman visitor seated in the corner of the room. Karen gently sat on the bed and held her mother's hand in both of hers. Except for a short "Hello, how are you?" her mother paid little attention to her daughter and continued talking to the other woman. Karen started several conversations, but her mother always returned to the conversation she was having with the woman.

For over an hour Karen held her mother's hand and stroked

her arm. Realizing Karen was being ignored, Carol finally said it was time to go. The walk back to the car was quiet, something unusual for Karen.

"My mom was really glad to see me, wasn't she," Karen said in an insecure tone with a sheepish, half-questioning smile on her face. Trying to keep her composure, Carol searched for something positive to say.

My wife recounted the whole story to me as soon as we were alone, and ended by saying "How is it possible that she can still love her parents after all the things they have done to her?" With such a strong bond of love and dedication for parents instilled in our next generation it makes one wonder what events along life's highway are so powerful and serious that parent–child conflicts are occurring in epidemic porportions

## Parent–Child Bonds Are Not Built in a Day

Unfortunately that child–parent bond instilled by Mother Nature is not indestructible. There are a number of forces in this world which try to disrupt and destroy her handiwork.

Before discussing these factors, however, it is important to point out something we parents often fail to consider. *Parent–child relationships are not built or destroyed in a day.* Most parents who have decided to correct the problems that have grown between them and their children act as if there is an opponent to be conquered. Like a wounded animal, they want to strike out at whatever it is that is causing the problem and defeat it quickly. They act as if causes of problems are like weeds which can be plucked.

Unfortunately the forces which destroy parent–child relationships do not strike with such quickness and strength. Instead these antiparent-child forces come like thieves in the night who repeatedly take a little at a time without being caught until it is too late, and almost everything is gone.

And even if the forces are discovered, they cannot be defeated with one quick stroke. Like a swarm of mosquitoes they return again and again, knowing that your attacks against them will not persist. Eventually they reach their desired ends. Fighting the forces against a good parent–child relationship is like fighting obesity or alcoholism. It's a battle which must be fought every day. It is like a long contest won through endurance and stamina rather than quick strength. While this idea of a day-to-day encounter may discourage you, keep in mind the positive aspects of the situation. This means the force behind the mistakes you and your child make cannot destroy the parent–child relationship quickly either. And this allows parents the luxury of making mistakes without causing irreparable damage.

A second point to keep in mind is that parent–child problems can be healed. The relationship between parent and child is a living thing. And like a living organ that becomes damaged, it can be healed as good as new. A child who has come to take advantage of his parents can be returned to the state of loving and respecting his parents which Mother Nature initially intended him to have.

### Ways to Tell If Children Care

Generally speaking there are two times in the life of a child when the signs of an uncaring child become apparent to the parent. First there are children who do not develop the strong bond for the parents which most children develop. Angie, the fourteen-year-old Indian girl referred to in Chapter Nine is an example. Recall that she was adopted at age five and intentionally broke every present the members of her new family gave her. She had never really formed a bond with her natural parents or her adoptive parents. In Chapter One, the case of Harold was mentioned. At four years old he flooded the toilet, started the fire in the kitchen, and tore down the ceiling tile. This child also had not formed that special bond with his parents. Both Angie and Harold cared little about their parents. They unconsciously viewed their parents as objects to be used for their own gratification. They had never developed an appreciation for their parents.

There are a few simple and easy checks parents can use as indications as to whether their child (or children) has developed an appropriate attitude of caring for their parents. Ask yourself the following questions.

Does your child seem to be going through a phase of acting in a way that you do not like?
If your child is over four years old, do you consistently have to chase after or go find him/her while shopping?
Does your child consistently talk back to you?
Does your child frequently ignore instructions you give?

If you answered "Yes" to any of these questions, it is a good indication that the caring relationship between you and your child needs to be strengthened. As mentioned in Chapter Four, children do not naturally go through phases of disruptive or antisocial behavior which the parents should ignore. The terrible twos turn into the terrifying teens if things are not done to correct the child's actions. Obviously no child does everything his parents say. If, however, the child "frequently" ignores parents' instructions, frequently talks back to parents, and frequently goes and does what he/she wants when parents shop, then these are subtle indications that the child is not developing a proper caring attitude for parents.

The second time indications of an uncaring child may appear is when the child becomes a teenager. In many cases the parent–child bond forms naturally, but for some reason it becomes weakened. Children may have a strong relationship with their parents when they are young, and then seemingly "drift" away from it as they grow older. Ask yourself the following questions if you have a teenager.

Were you close to your child at one time, but now he/she argues with you frequently?
Were you close to your child at one time, but now he/she no longer wants to do things with the family?
Does your teenager avoid asking you to school activities and prefer to go with friends?
Does your teenager seldom ask your advice?
Does your teenager spend most of his/her time alone when just the family is around?

If you answer yes to any of these questions, you should take a closer look at what is happening between you and your teenager. There are those people who will argue that teenagers naturally draw away from their parents and closer to those of their own age as they mature. Even though it is true that teenagers strengthen their relationships with other teenagers, it does not automatically follow that the teenager's relationship with their parents must weaken. This position implies there is a limited amount of love and caring a human can have in his life space. And if more love is devoted to one person, that love must be taken from another. Must a girl care for her sister less when a second sister is born? Does a mother love each of her four daughters only half as much as the mother who has two daughters?

Parents should expect their growing children to spend more time with persons their own age, but it does not automatically follow that the bond between the parent and child should suffer. Teenagers should be spending more time on school activities, but should not be withdrawing from family activities when they are home. Teenagers can expand their horizons with friends and schoolmates without having to complain about having family responsibilities. Those close talks between parent and teenager should still occur (though less frequently perhaps) as the teenager strengthens his/her commitment to jobs or a person they view as a potential partner of life. While teenagers may naturally spend less time with parents, they need not show less respect and concern by avoiding their family, ignoring advice, or increasing their complaints about their parents. Parents should be having positive and rewarding experiences with their teenage children—or something is wrong.

## BUILDING THAT BOND

Once parents determine that their child seems to show little concern for them, there are several tactics which may be used to strengthen the child's concern.

### Let Your Child Experience Life

There is sound reasoning in Mother Nature's plan of sending parents children during the busy years of their life. Children most frequently join their parents during the years parents are busy trying to establish themselves. Long work hours are required to cope with the financial needs of getting started. Each parent is busy learning how to deal with the day-to-day problems of having a mate. Many mothers are changing the diapers of Child Number Two while having to deal with the morning sickness of future Child Number Three. All of these daily trials and tribulations make it almost impossible to meet all the demands of the infant. And rightly so. The child needs to learn there is more in life than just itself. Sometimes it won't be fed when it starts to get hungry. Sometimes it cannot have the toy it wants immediately. Children then begin to realize "I should be careful what I do because falling down can hurt." "I have to wait my turn." "If I take from others I must suffer the consequences."

Too often parents unknowingly interfere and spoil Mother Nature's intended plan. They respond to all the wants and wishes of the child, building in that child false expectations of life.

> "I get what I want."
> "Everyone should look out for me."
> "I am the only one who really counts."
> "I don't have to be careful or considerate."
> "What my parents warn me about never really happens."

There are false ideas children tend to develop when parents do not allow their children to experience many of the natural consequences of life when they are young. In spite of the many obstacles Mother Nature places before parents to keep this from happening, many of we parents and grandparents cannot restrain ourselves. We overlook the long-term effects and rush to almost every crying child. We step in to help our children having squabbles. We make allowances when our children are rude and overbearing. As a result the child does not get an accurate picture of life and learns to use parents at will with little care or concern. Appropriate development of the parent–child bond requires parents to let children get a true picture of life. In a semiprotected environment the child needs to get an awareness that his or her environment (which includes parents) can provide many rewarding things and experiences when treated with respect and consideration.

## Help Them Build Self-Confidence

As the child becomes aware that life has both pleasures and pitfalls, he/she will consciously develop a special place in their hearts for those people who show them how to succeed in the world. Many times the child learns this through modeling his parents, so time spent with children is important. A second important ingredient for building self-confidence in a child is to provide for success when the child tries. As adults we realize how important success is to us, but often we fail to realize how important it is to children. I watched a father once wrestling with his four-year-old son. The father wanted to find out why his son avoided physical activity. "I spend a lot of time rolling around with him," he told me. Upon going to his home to casually observe the situation, I watched the father pin the boy time after time as he smilingly told his son "This is what you do in this situation." Unfortunately the boy was always the one being pinned. Teaching boys to enjoy wrestling, or any other activity for that matter, requires *them* to experience success. As the father and son roll around, a father can sense when the boy is about to give up. Then is the time the father should pretend to give in and say something like "Oh, I give up. You're too tough." It is surprising how much harder the child will try next time. Too often we fathers sacrifice our child's need to succeed with our own desires of winning.

Frequently children fail to succeed because the tasks put before them are too difficult. Sometimes we parents unknowingly thwart a child's chances to experience success by placing situations before the child which are too difficult for his or her age. One father was disappointed with how his four- and five-year-old sons failed to appreciate a particular Christmas gift. He spent over two months building a rather scenic and elaborate train setup with tunnels and tressles. Unfortunately he built a system for very small and delicate trains. The boys were not old enough to work the train correctly. It kept going off the track, and they were unable to put it back on properly. Soon they became frustrated and left it alone.

A major percentage of teenagers who consistently skip school and get into trouble do so because they are not successful in their schoolwork. Many of them were passed from grade to grade, each year dropping a little further behind their classmates. Tim was sixteen years old and ran with a group who skipped school day after day. Both parents worked and could not control his leaving school. After getting in trouble with the law, he was sent to a foster home. Tests revealed he had the reading and math skills of a ten-year-old. When sent to school he could not even understand the materials in the assignments. He tried to cover up his inadequacies like so many children do by acting out in class. If the teacher asked him a question concerning math, he hid his lack of knowledge from his classmates by giving some smart remark in reply. With special tutoring the foster parents helped him catch up. One year later his unruly behavior was almost completely gone. He was succeeding in class.

Whenever lack of success is a problem, there are a few things a parent can do to reduce the problem. For example, it is important to remember starting or re-starting children is like planting or re-planting trees. The beginning tree needs extra helpings of water and nutrients to get started. The re-planted tree also needs extra amounts to properly take hold and grow. Children learn to take hold and care about things when their initial experiences include a high density of successes. A young child learning to bat may become frustrated and not develop a caring attitude about baseball because the frequency with which he connects and hits the ball is far outweighed by his unsuccessful misses. The wise father will take his four- and five-year-old sons to a toy store and buy an unusually large (but full of air), lightweight, plastic bat. Using a large plastic ball, he pitches slowly to his son. After the child has experienced many successes, the father switches to smaller and smaller bats and balls.

A father has a greater chance of his son learning to care about fishing if the child meets with a high frequency of success at the start. When I started my four sons fishing, I took them to a nearby Indian reservation which allows young children to fish in a series of well-stocked ponds. Later they were taken to less promising areas, but their initial experiences instilled in them a strong love for fishing. Just like fishing, children learn to enjoy doing things with parents when they have shared successful and enjoyable experiences with them.

**Share Your Life**

One of the best things parents can do is share their life with their children. There is no greater gift a parent can give a child than some of his or her time. And it is a gift all parents may give. It is not necessary to set aside particular times to be with children. You may incorporate them into your schedule. You may include them in your work, your hobbies, or in the chores which must be done around the house.

Not all parents may take their children along to work, but some can. In those cases where it is possible, most children find it a rewarding experience. Often I ask students what they like to do best with their parents. A frequent answer is "Go to work with my Dad." One college student explained his father delivered milk when he was young, and he used to go with him on the route.

"My Dad delivered milk to apartments and I helped him put the milk in front of the doors. I enjoyed riding in the truck. It seemed special, and I could ride along standing up. We would stop at a park on his route for lunch, and I could drink as much chocolate milk as I wanted . . . he taught me my times tables on the route. I remember him telling me to just add a zero behind a number when you multiply that number by ten."

A ten-year-old girl said her parents were divorced. As a second job her father refereed high school and college basketball games and would often take her and the other two children with him. One boy's father was a traveling salesman and sold farm products. "I enjoyed going with him and meeting the Hutterites, communal-oriented groups of people with large farms who originally came from Germany."

Hobbies and recreation provide great opportunities for developing parent–child relationships. At my suggestion, an aeronautical engineer began taking his nine-year-old stepson with him to race go-carts on weekends. The man and his son became very close as the boy became actively involved with his new father. It gave them a common interest to work from. Allen, a director of recreational therapy at a state hospital loves to go "dump hunting." Almost any Saturday morning you will find him at the county dump scavenging through the trash. His three boys, and all the neighborhood kids, love to go with him. What he brings home constantly amazes his wife (who secretly takes most of it back).

House duties always provide a good background for parent-child interaction. It differs from the first two in that the tasks involved are not so rewarding in and of themselves. Visiting Hutterite colonies, riding in trucks, going dump hunting, and fishing are inherently more interesting than cleaning rooms, washing cars, cleaning garages, ironing, weeding, and lawn mowing. But it is important that children learn to work and accept responsibility. And a large portion of the experiences a child affectionately remembers through the years involve everyday house chores.

Sharing your life with your children is perhaps the most important single ingredient in raising children. Children with criminal records typically spend one third the time with their parents that other children do. It is important to remember that children learn a great deal just being with their parents. Observing parents, they learn how to express joy, how to have fun, how to cope with problems, how to handle mistakes, and how to be considerate.

### Listen

There is a cute little advertisement which is played on television showing a little girl who comes home from a birthday party and tries to tell her parents and sister about the party. Mother tells her "Not now. I am watching my favorite soap opera." Father says "Tell me later. I am busy fixing this radio." Her older sisters ignore her. The little girl then goes outside and tells her dog who wags his tail and listens to every word. The advertisement ends by saying "Children go to the dogs when parents do not listen." Children typically begin life by talking and asking questions that are quite bothersome to us, so children seek out those people who will listen to what they have to say. An interesting thing then happens. Children listen to those who listen to them. Later on when our children are young adults and on a higher intellectual plane we parents are willing to talk and listen. By then, however, they do not want to listen to us.

### Take Time

So often we get so wrapped up in the problems of our work or our own interests, that we put off doing things we should. "I'll get caught up with my work this year and next year we will take lots of family trips." "Next year we will have the money to really enjoy ourselves." "Someday we will get around to it." "Soon I will spend more time with those I love."

Most of us have our nose so close to the grindstone in order to stay ahead of the daily vocational and financial problems, that we fail to see life is passing us by. Someday we will realize our child is fifteen years old and we did not do half the fun things we said we would. And then it is too late.

## REKINDLING THE CARING IN CHILDREN

How does the parent go about rekindling that sense of caring for parents once it has gone out in children? The first step is to keep strongly in mind that it can be done. Too often parents make only half tries at the problem because they are not sure within themselves that it is really possible.

One of the most effective ways of rekindling a teenager's interests in the parents is for the parents to approach the problem by finding out what interests their daughter or son and incorporate those interests into what the parents want.

Lisa was fourteen years old when she joined our family. She had been in four foster homes before she came to us. Initially at each home she fit in nicely. She got along well with other children in the families and gave a good first impression to the new parents. Within six months, however, she would have to be moved. Her case history indicated she never really acted as an accepted member of any family. In talking to a few of her previous foster parents, they all commented that their problem with her mainly stemmed from their inability to make her feel part of the family. They reported she always wanted to be at a girlfriend's home rather than the foster home. Whenever disagreements broke out, she had a tendency to go tell her classmates all about it. She would gain sympathy from teachers and friends by telling rather distorted versions of what happened. Lisa also had a stronger-than-average interest in boys, something quite common for teenage foster girls.

In analyzing the situation I concluded that she would most likely react to disputes in our home the same way she had in previous foster homes. When our first major disagreement would come I expected she would try to play her friends and teachers against her new family. To counter her rather successful tactic, I set out to get to know her friends and teachers quite well, and let them come to know Carol and me. Right after she joined our family, we suggested she throw a slumber party or two for her new girlfriends. We helped her plan two parties, inviting many of her friends from the school she went to before coming to our home. My wife and I mingled with all those who showed up.

After the parties I told Lisa I wanted to hire four or five fellows to help me work around the house (that is, putting in a cement patio, painting trim). She asked to select the boys (something I hoped she would volunteer to do). As we worked, I came to know the young men pretty well. We also had many enjoyable experiences together. One of the boys became Lisa's boyfriend. I went to school several times to get to know her teachers.

About four months after her arrival, the first major disagreement occurred. I reprimanded her for giving one of the other foster girls an undeserved hard time. She responded by calling her friends and complaining that the whole family was picking on her and were insensitive to her problems. But none of her friends would believe her story. Due to their many positive experiences in our home she was unable to drive a wedge between her friends and her new family. Her friends did not give her the sympathy she had learned to expect from past situations. Even her boyfriend told her he felt we really cared about her.

We continued to include her friends in our family activities. We initially took at least one of her friends when we went fishing or picnicking. My wife and I went to our first stock car race with

Lisa and several of the boys and girls her age. It was something the boys really wanted to do. Through combining her interests and friends with our activities we were able to rekindle Lisa's care and concern for families. She ended up staying with us until she turned eighteen and was married.

## GETTING PARENTS TO CARE ABOUT CHILDREN

Getting parents to care about children is often more difficult than getting children to care about parents. While parents are generally the focal points of a child's world, the opposite is not true. There are a host of things with which a parent may occupy his/her time. And more parents are asking how to get kids to care than vice versa. One reason fewer children ask for help is because they often feel they are the ones responsible for their parents not caring. They feel their parents do not care because of something they have done. Let's take a look at two reasons parents cease to care about their children, and how to rekindle the parent.

### Lack of Success

More and more parents withdraw from their children because of their feelings of failure as parents. It is not an enjoyable experience for a parent to deal with a child who continually throws tantrums. It's not pleasant to be around a demanding teenager who will not listen. It is natural for people to want to avoid unpleasantries of life. You do not go visit people you hate. When given the choice, we do not eat food we dislike. We typically avoid things we dislike, and the more we dislike something, the greater is our tendency to avoid it.

People tend to draw toward their successes and shy away from their failures. A woman who likes to read, but cannot paint, directs her energy toward reading. A parent who is successful in her career will focus more of her attention in that direction, particularly if dealings with her children have been relatively unsuccessful. Many mothers refuse to discipline their children because it results in an unpleasant experience for them. And over time they may begin to rationalize in their mind about having to discipline at all.

In Chapter One, Ann wanted to give her son up for adoption because of her lack of success in raising him. After finding out she could be an effective and successful mother, her attitude about her son changed. She even began enjoying doing things with him.

Few things can rekindle a parent's love for his/her child more effectively than a parent experiencing success in childrearing. And hopefully this book has given the reader ideas as to which tactics can be used to make them more successful with his/her child.

### Loss of Interest

It is not uncommon for a child to lose the interest of the parent because of competing demands. Often the failure of parents to show concern for their children has nothing to do with the actions of the child. All of us experience times in our lives when we quit doing certain things we enjoy because other events get in our way. We may get so involved in striving for certain goals in life that we fail to find enjoyment in doing things we used to enjoy.

A rather strong illustration of this problem concerned a rising young business executive who had lost interest in having sexual relations with his wife. They were an attractive couple, both professionals, intelligent, socially well at east; and Roman Catholic. Both wanted to maintain the marriage, but the wife thought she might be driven to extramarital relations. Sexual contact had only occurred twice during the last twelve month period. Both husband and wife agreed that the problem was due to the husband. Although his wife was rather shapely and attractive, his attention and energy was so focused on his business aspirations, their sexual encounters were relatively quick and unrewarding. She bought him an issue of *Playboy,* but he fell asleep reading it.

"I'm at my wits end as to what to do," she complained. "I cannot use deprivation like other wives because that is my problem."

Parents may find themselves in a similar type of situation with their children. They get so involved in politics, social clubs, service organizations, or their professions that the memorable experiences they have had with their children fade. They show less and less care and concern for their children. In many such cases (as was true with the young executive) reactivating the interest occurs by returning to those somewhat forgotten activities and savoring the experiences. For many of us, it has been so long since we went on a Sunday picnic that we have forgotten how enjoyable such excursions may be.

*Questions from Parents*

**Q:** I have a seventeen-year-old daughter. She throws fits to get her way, and has not developed the values I feel she should have. What can I do to get through to her?

**A:** As mentioned earlier in the book children are just apprenticing under their parents. By the time a child is seventeen you have very little time left before they will be on their own. So you have little chance of making a quick dramatic change in her. If you do not want to try to "reach" her in a short time, your best bet is to get help from a psychologist. They are trained to be more likely to have a faster effect than most parents. A second important point to remember is *do not live with a feeling of failure.* As your child nears the time of going out on her own, do not mentally whip yourself as a failure. If you gave it your best, be satisfied with that. Enjoy your life as you should. Older teenagers who seem to strongly disagree with mom and dad generally become more appreciative of their parents after two or three years of being on their own.

# 16 What to Do with a Bad Apple

## REMODELING THE HALF-GROWN CHILD

The approaches needed to remodel or change the half-grown child can be quite different from those approaches which can successfully be employed to raise and mold a naïve child from birth. The differences between starting at birth and attempting to remold an older child is comparable to the difference between building a home from scratch and remodeling an existing home. The carpenter remodeling a home must work within certain limits. In putting in new kitchen cabinets, for example, he is somewhat restricted by the existing arrangement of the walls. And it is more expensive and time consuming to put in new cabinets, because there are already old cabinets there which must be removed first. In remodeling children you have a similar task. You are faced with undesirable attitudes and habits which must be removed and replaced with proper habits and attitudes. The task is generally more difficult than instilling proper habits and attitudes in the first place.

Does remodeling always take more effort? In refurbishing the home, the carpenter must take out the old, possibly rotten wood and put in new and sound replacements. The amount of time and effort he must put in depends on the amount of wood finishings which must be replaced. If only the kitchen needs changing, his task is simpler and quicker than if he has to change the bathrooms also. The same is true for remodeling children. The fewer things that need to be changed, the less time and effort required. And, conversely, the more that must be done, the more time and effort required.

More and more parents are finding themselves with what is often referred to as a "bad apple," and search for help in remodeling their child. Chapter Twelve was all about sources outside the family that parents can go to get assistance in raising their child. However, when the child is half-grown or full-grown, with socially unacceptable habits and attitudes, there are three main approaches to the problem. First, the parents may decide to send their son or daughter to one of the many private schools designed to handle problem children. There are a number of these schools that do an excellent job. As mentioned in Chapter Twelve, however, these schools are quite expensive and may charge fifteen hundred to twenty-five hundred dollars a month. A second approach is to contact the Division of Social Services for your state and see about their foster care program. Most states have a voluntary program where parents requesting help can enroll their child in the foster care program for a time of one month to however long it takes. This program may cost the parents anywhere from one hundred and fifty dollars to four hundred dollars a month. Most states have specialized foster homes designed to handle different types of children according to their bad habits and attitudes.

The third approach is for the parents to decide they will solve the problems themselves. This is a fine idea; and has a good possibility of working if several things are kept in mind. First, the problem the child has is not just inside the child. There are aspects of the environment which are partially responsible for the child's actions. While some psychologists may tell you that something in the child's past may have triggered a traumatic experience which is now at the root of the problem, you are not going to hear that from me. The philosophy underlying the tactics presented in this book is based on the idea that our actions are influenced not only by our internal feelings, but also by things around us. With this approach it is important to keep in mind that the atmosphere the child is in produces the problem. So to solve the problem, one needs to change the environment. This means that parents should not only look at the child but also the whole home environment. When changing our children we parents need to realize that we need to change ourselves also. We more than likely need to become more attentive to the child and to what is going on in the family, become more consistent with our dealings in the home, and more serious about devoting time to the problem. Children are not changed in a day. They did not develop their bad habits and tendencies in one day; and they certainly will not get rid of them in a day. The real secret to success is to remember that almost any mountain can be climbed, but success only comes *one step at a time.* The process does not require superintelligence, untold wealth, or physical superiority. Any average parent, or even below-average parent, can be successful at remodeling if they can be *persistent* and *consistent.*

There are a few basic principles to keep in mind which will help in dealing with the remodeling of a child. The first has to do with special treatment. Almost every foster child brought into our home has been receiving special treatment. Parents sensitive about the problems they are having with their child tend to be giving that child special treatment. In many cases parents have come to let problem children bend the rules of the home in an effort to solve the problem. A mother might not remind her problem daughter to do the dishes because that seems to provoke an argument from the girl; so mother does the dishes herself. The home rules have been bent in an attempt to keep a more pleasant atmosphere going. What happens when you go to pay a traffic ticket which you justly deserved and the clerk reduces the fine after you complain about the ticket. Right! That is why most offices do not allow that option to clerks who collect ticket fines. More people complain when complaining works. Giving problem children special treatment generally leads to more needed special treatment. Look at the rules of the home, and either change the rules or require the existing ones be kept. Bending rules leads to breaking rules.

When children with problems were first brought into our home years ago, Carol and I had a tendency to be more sympathetic to new members of the family. We felt we would be more successful in the long run if we were extra considerate at first and bent the house rules for newcomers. We found from experience children adjust to new surroundings better when treated like everybody else. As soon as they arrive in our home they are treated equal with everyone else. No special announcements or introductions are made. We greet them and assign one of the children to show them around. At the first meal no special topics are discussed. The newcomers learn from being with the family.

To children with problems, talk is usually cheap. What they have experienced prior to coming to us is that people often do not do what they say. In desperation their parents have threatened certain actions, but not followed through. Frustrated teachers have done the same. We waste little time making promises or claims; and we follow through with whatever we say we will do. Threats and promises tend to be ineffective with children needing to be remodeled. Do what you say you will, and you soon find they begin listening to what you say.

Structure and rules are an important part of any well-run business or family. Choose your rules carefully and abide by them. Rules should be informative signposts which signal avenues of actions that are rewarding. Sometimes we are inconsistent in enforcing the rules, so children become inconsistent in complying with rules. I have yet to have a foster child come into my home who cannot live by the rules of the house. And most foster children we have did not live by the rules in their previous homes. Rules should not be hindrances to personal growth, but helps. Rules on going to bed, doing house chores, getting to go places, and being considerate of others, should be presented in the spirit that such rules are there for the benefit of "everyone." And if those rules are met, certain rights are guaranteed to the child. Carol and I emphasize that obeying the rules leads to expanded opportunities for the whole family. All do their work and all have times to play. Rules are never discussed in the heat of battle. If a child complains about having to do a certain chore as he is doing it, no one listens to the complaint. Once a week, however, a family meeting is held and complaints are then heard. Constructive suggestions from all the children in the family are encouraged. And rules are changed when changes are needed. Children can be quite reasonable in terms of complaints when the complaints are discussed at the right time, and a proper avenue for complaints is open in the family.

Develop standard routines and responsibilities. Children create fewer problems in the home when certain routines and responsibilities are specified. If members of the family get up at certain times, go to bed at certain times, do their household duties at certain times, it has the effect of reducing problems. Having a certain amount of stability in the home functions has a positive effect on a child's psychological stability. The less stable and more whimsical family operations seem to be, the more uncertain and unstable the child is. Responsibilities and routines can often help, not totally control, the behavioral beast in children needing remodeling. Security is an important thing even to teenage children, and routines often help to instill a feeling of security.

## WHEN IS IT TOO LATE?

When is it too late for parents to be successful in remodeling a child? That is a question some people would feel should be answered "never." All through the book I have repeatedly emphasized that something can be done to deal with any behavioral problem a child may have, so you might conclude that "never" would be the answer I would give. It must be remembered, however, that while psychologists may sit in the office and theorize how life should be, we must realize there is a practical side of life. There are limits to what a parent can do. Parents cannot devote one hundred percent of their time to a problem child. Time must be spent earning a living. Time must be given to problems of other members of the family including the parents' personal problems. Parents do not often have the training required to handle problems that become severe. And, even if they did, they often do not have the time to do what has to be done.

Oftentimes Mother Nature deals us a hand which places us in circumstances where we parents are unable to cope with a problem child. Beth was a somewhat heavy-set woman in her late thirties. She married soon after she graduated from high school. Although planning to go on to college, Beth had become pregnant. She and the child's father then married. Her husband was a free spirit and had difficulty keeping a job. After two or three years he had the good luck of becoming a longshoreman. It was a good job and solved many financial problems which, in the past, seemed to bother Beth much more than her husband. Over the next fifteen years her husband was in and out of prison for theft and burglary. He and some of his drinking buddies formed a car theft ring, after getting out of prison for three burglaries. Within two years he was back doing time. Beth's son, Duane, only had the opportunity of having his father around for three years from his tenth to eighteenth birthday. The remainder of the time his father was in the state prison. Duane loved his father and was greatly influenced by his father's carefree ways. While Beth tried to get Duane to go to church and mingle with the right kind of friends, she wasn't very successful. She was sick a great deal, and on welfare. Being large for his age and on his own a lot, Duane became much like his father. He stole when he felt like it, beat up those who got in his way, and had no fear of the law. The stories his father told about being in the "joint" excited him.

Caught between the love of her child and the realization that she could no longer control him, Beth reluctantly chose to keep her son rather than place him in a foster home. She realized he was unruly and could get in serious trouble, but held the hope that somehow everything would work out. It did not. Breaking into a home at age seventeen, he encountered a thirteen-year-old baby sitter. He raped her and then threatened bodily harm if she did not keep the incident to herself.

There are two important points which should be considered when asking the question if it is too late for your child. First, whether it is too late for you as a parent to handle the problem yourself depends on whether you are still in control of the situation. If you cannot physically handle your child, or if you have so many other responsibilities to cope with that you cannot address the problem, or if because of poor physical health or emotional problems you cannot handle your child, then it is too late. *Control* is the issue you should be concerned with when trying to determine whether it is possible to remodel the child. "Am I in control of what does and can go on around my home?" is the question the parent has to answer. What problem the child creates is not so important as what is my ability to handle it. For some parents, dishonesty and thievery is something they find difficult to deal with, while tantrums is the Achilles' heel for other parents. Realistically, look at your situation, seek professional advice if needed; and make your decision.

The second point to consider when asking whether you should try to remodel your child is "Will other people have to pay if I am wrong?" In the case where Beth decided to keep her uncontrollable son, the baby sitter paid a price for Beth's decision. If Beth had sought and received help for Duane the baby sitter would not have had to pay for something she had no control over. The less a child respects his parents, the more self-centered and obnoxious a child is, the greater the probability that some innocent person will pay for the actions of a misbehaving child. Stealing a car and going joy riding will likely cost the parents, the person who owns the car, and any unlucky pedestrian who may get in the way. Teenagers who go joy riding are thrill seekers and risk takers. Their actions frequently result in the physical injury and financial pain of others. Parents should ask themselves whether their decision not to seek help can lead to situations where innocent people have to pay for their child's misbehavior. We need to remember that we live in an interdependent world where our decisions affect others.

## HOW DOES ONE GO ABOUT RETURNING THE MERCHANDISE?

Many parents realize they need help in handling situations, but do not seek such help. Most are afraid that the psychologists and social workers they approach about their problem will view them as failures. These parents feel a stigma will be attached to them. Actually just the opposite reaction is more likely. I, like most other psychologists and social workers engaged in working with parent–child relationships, am impressed when we come across that parent who comes for assistance. Parents show wisdom when looking for help with a particular problem. Suppose your car broke down. Few people would consider you very smart if you decided to stay and fix it yourself rather than seek a trained mechanic. Seeking experts to help solve problems is exactly what wise and successful individuals do. The unintelligent try to live with problems they cannot handle. The wise person is not the one that can do everything himself, but intelligently uses others who are in the know. Most parents are pleasantly rewarded once they get by that first step of overcoming their fears concerning getting help.

The issue of returning children is much like the issue of returning a sofa which somehow does not fit in with the home scheme. We are often hesitant to even consider going back to the furniture store to say it is not working out. After we acknowledge, however, that something is wrong and needs to be done about the couch, we have three major options. First we can simply take it back. Second, we can trade it in on another sofa. Or third, we can remodel the sofa so it fits in the room.

Those options are also open to parents with problem children. As pointed out earlier, there are times when parents may find themselves in situations where things cannot be worked out. Sometimes conditions have grown to the point that an adoptive child or a natural-born child becomes too much for the parents. These situations happen, and must be accepted. It is the kind of decision, however, that is very serious and must obviously be done with professional consultation. It is not the kind of thing you can change your mind about a week or two after you make it. And one of the reasons psychologists are so hesitant to advise parents to give up a child they have, is because experience has taught us that most parents later change their minds and want their child back (besides the fact that such a separation can be so emotionally expensive to all parties involved).

In most problem situations the answer does not have to be that parents should turn their child over to state social services. In many cases a good approach to take is to remove the child from the home for a month or two relieving pressure of both the parents and child. Most states have what is called a voluntary placement program which allows parents to place a problem child temporarily in a special foster home designed for such situations. After consultation with psychologists and social workers from Social Service offices, such an option may be taken during which time caseworkers are available to both the parents and child so the problem can be effectively resolved. Parents may use these existing available services to permit themselves to get a surer footing for handling such incidents, as well as using the knowledge of the social service workers to upgrade their own parental skills in dealing with their child in the future.

The Department of Social Services, which is usually listed under county offices in the telephone book, is an excellent place to go when you are having problems with your children and need help with the merchandise. Most parents identify social services with welfare cases and fail to realize that the social service office (provided by your tax dollars) is also well trained for, and has programs for, parents in all financial brackets to help with problem children.

In many cases they will help you decide that your problem can be handled without removing the child from the home at all. Being in the business they can direct you to the most effective psychologists in the area, if that is all you need.

## ADOPTIONS—ARE USED MODELS ANY GOOD?

One of the most enjoyable sections of the whole book to write was this section on adoption. Having been personally involved in many child adoptions, including several of my own, I can say that children are one of the few commodities which are very likely to be better used than new. This statement is directed mainly to the older children available for adoption. Most prospective adoptive parents worry about the past history of children up for adoption. They are concerned that the experiences the child has already had may have left psychological scars which will make it difficult to fit in to their family. The pleasant surprise parents get is finding out that almost any experience those children have had prepares them to be better sons and daughters than ones we bring into this world ourselves. Most adopted children will do anything they can to please their new parents. Having no parents at all, or poor parents, has made most of the children more attentive to parents. They watch you closer and are more careful in what they do. This does not mean they do not come with a sense of humor, or necessarily have a poor disposition.

The most important point to keep in mind about adopting a child is that bringing an adopted child in your home will accentuate the problems in a weak marriage and will magnify the strengths in a strong marriage. An adopted child will not save a poor marriage nor destroy a good one. Like a reflecting mirror, that child will feed back into a family whatever that family radiates. This point is exemplified in the case of Terra.

Terra was a young girl who came to the United States from an orphanage in southeastern India. She was one of twenty young Indian children who had been adopted by United States citizens through a private adoption agency. Terra was brought to the orphanage by her mother because life in her part of the world is cheap and her father had attempted to drown her. Knowing future attempts by her husband might be successful, Terra's mother took her to the orphanage. Terra was the product of infidelity on her mother's part, and the father could not accept her.

At the age of four she was placed on a plane and flown to California to her new parents. Not knowing for sure what lay ahead, she became sick and threw up repeatedly during her plane ride and would not eat. Her new parents reported she seemed to be smiling when she first met them. The mother had coaxed her husband into trying to adopt. Their marriage was not very stable and she felt a child, which she and her husband could not have themselves, would help the marriage. After Terra arrived the marriage deteriorated rapidly. Within six months the parents filed for divorce.

The county attorney called my wife Carol and said there was a problem. An adopted child had been placed in a home where divorce proceedings were now going on. It was somewhat of an embarrassment because caseworkers should have detected the instability in the marriage. "Would we like to adopt her?" he asked.

Two days later we were on our way to the county attorney's office to pick up our new five-year-old daughter. Prior to our arrival the mother had brought Terra and all the things they had bought her (new bike, big doll house, new dolls, expensive new clothes) to his office and left in tears.

When we first saw Terra standing in a room with all her things around, she was in a pretty yellow lace dress with matching stockings and black patten shoes. For a child just losing her second set of parents she seemed to be holding up pretty well. She had a smile on her face but it was a shallow, searching smile. She let both of us hug her and sat on Carol's lap for most of the journey home. As we pulled up our long driveway, she spotted some of our children playing. She quickly joined in as if other children around gave her a feeling of security. Watching her from a distance, we noted she giggled and laughed as they played some type of tag which included the dog.

Over the next few months we never saw her in a bad mood. She never complained, threw a tantrum, or cried except when hurt while playing. She took to her chores of cleaning her room, making her bed, and setting the dinner table like a duck takes to water. Each night she gave us a hug on her way to bed. I could sense slight uncertainty in her actions around me. She often asked Carol questions about Carol and me. On several occasions while the family watched television Terra would spontaneously say "Dad, why don't you give Mom a kiss?" She enjoyed seeing us show signs of affection to each other. Later we found out her first adoptive parents fought quite a bit in front of her; and she saw her first adoptive mother hit by her husband on several occasions.

While Terra is a bubbling, happy, unmoody girl of eight years old, not all her experiences in our family have been enjoyable. People often stare at her when the family goes downtown shopping or on some family activity. In Utah we live in an almost totally white community, and Terra's skin is as dark as anyone's can be. After her first few days of going to first grade she came home and casually said some kid called her a nigger. "So I called him a nigger back," she said. She did not know what the term meant, so the remark had little effect on her. A few weeks later she came home in a mood I had not seen in her before.

"I know what a nigger is," she said in a slow quiet way.

"What?" I inquired.

"I'm a nigger," she continued in a tone as if she had just found out she was a leper.

In a small way Carol and I experienced what many black parents and other minority parents face with their children. She had been teased and degraded because of the color of her skin. Her new brothers were also affected. Some schoolmates asked them why they had a nigger for a sister. Somewhat enraged by these comments, Terra's older brothers finished several of those discussions by making a few kids eat their words. Her three older brothers at that school, one of which was voted vice president of the whole elementary school, gave her great support. And once the students at the school realized what was happening, almost all of them rallied around Terra, and she became somewhat of a celebrity.

While we, as a family, weathered the storm pretty well, it still brings back unpleasant memories remembering a young girl many times saying to her parents "I wish God didn't make be black." On one occasion I won't forget, she came to Carol and said "Can I go inside your tummy, so I can come out white?" And Terra's tribulations over her color are not over. But she is a constant joy to the family. She shares whatever she has with others, she has a way of laughing that touches anyone near her, and she is able to make a game out of almost any work she is given to do. If Carol and I had the power to mold the personality of a perfect child, it would be in the image of her personality. Sometimes I get the feeling Mother Nature instills the choicest human spirits into the children other people view as handicapped because such handicaps provide the medium through which choice people reveal themselves.

It is important to remember you can have good and bad experiences by adding an adoptive child to your family. But the possibility of positive experiences are much higher than negative experiences. And the statement made previously that adopted children almost always reflect what is already in the family is worth repeating again.

If my child was an infant when adopted, when do I tell him he was adopted? The way that question is answered by psychologists seems to have changed over the years. Twenty years ago most psychologists suggested parents tell their child as soon as he can understand. Within the past few years more psychologists have been advising parents to wait until close to the teenage years. My own experience suggests it is not when you tell them but how you tell them. I advise parents to tell their child they are adopted in a matter-of-fact way when they are young. Make the situation as normal and uneventful as possible. Perhaps a show about adoption is on television. Work in to the conversation the fact that they are adopted in a tone suggesting it makes no difference to you as a parent. The parent might even discuss how the adoption came about without identifying people involved. Do not tell the child he or she is special. As the child realizes he is no different from the kid next door, your story of him or her being special may lead him to question your sincerity. Keep in mind the important thing is not what you say, but how you treat and continue to treat that child. No words of love will ever have more effect than how you interact with your adopted child. If your child wants to know more about his real parents act in a matter-of-fact fashion in giving what information you feel good about sharing.

# Epilogue

Now that the final chapter of this book is completed, I, like most authors, wonder whether those reading this book will benefit from what has been said. In looking back at the completed work, I find I included many more stories and references to personal experiences than I intended to include at the beginning of the project. I originally planned to cover more specific topics and psychological principles concerning child-rearing strategies, for that is the type of format most books on child rearing have. However, the many parents I engaged to read this manuscript as it developed repeatedly expressed the opinions that they learned more from hearing about actual experiences than they did from the basic facts and principles approach used in most child-rearing books. I therefore was influenced to include many more true incidents in the book, and hope future readers also benefit from these stories.

In retrospect, I must admit it is possibly these stories, and others left untold, that convince me that the natural parenting approach is an effective approach for raising children that anyone can use. My father-in-law, Harold Spackman, and his wife Millie, raised nine children, all girls, the last of which was married in 1980. Harold and Millie are farmers who have never read a book on child rearing, nor have the faintest idea what the terms "proper psychological adjustment," "emotional maturity," or "cognitive insights" mean. Yet, they now have nine married daughters, none of which were unwed mothers, had used drugs, or were in any trouble with the police. Several of them have been in, and won, beauty contests, almost all were superior school students, and each is actively engaged in community affairs as adults. Harold and Millie's success as parents is truly an amazing feat, particularly in this day and age; plus being in a state where drug problems and unwed mother rate is above the national average. They now also have nine sons-in-law, most with much university schooling, who love and respect those seemingly uneducated but "wise" parents whose success came from following Mother Nature's natural approach. They, like so many other successful parents, maintained the five conditions for the home discussed in Chapter 7—namely accountability, responsibility, sensitivity, words with action, and family unity.

The intent of this book has been to sharpen the reader's understanding of some rather powerful tactics for manipulating children whose beauty lies in the fact that they are so easy to employ that even children are successful with them. And yet they are the same tactics that psychologists use to get not only animals to do super feats (for example, ride bicycles, play baseball), but also to successfully treat the most difficult behavior problems in children. My wife and I are so confident in the tactics discussed in this book that for years we have taken children with almost every type of behavior problem into our *own home.* I know of no other author of a child-rearing book who has taken several problem children at a time into their own home for over ten years. The tactics discussed in this book have worked well for my wife and me. I hope the information in this book has been presented in such a way as to allow these tactics to work for many other parents also.

Parents should be enjoying life. As adults it is their turn to become what they want. Raising children should add a positive dimension to, not take over, our lives. Children manipulating parents is a natural part of life that many of us find difficult to handle. In many instances such manipulating children make our lives as parents seem unbearable. I hope this book has provided insights and strategies for parents so both their lives and the lives of their children will be enriched.

For those parents seeking more help using the *Natural Approach to Parenting* (the NAP system) upon which this book, *Manipulating Parents* is based, more information is available. Workshops for parents and additional books are available through NAP Enterprises. Some of the books available include:

*Manipulating Children: The NAP Handbook.* The handbook alphabetically lists almost every type of behavior problem a parent can run into. These include problems of fighting, tantrums, cleanliness, disobedience, crying, shyness, thumbsucking, and bedwetting to mention just a few. Parents are given at least three different ways of handling each problem. Parents can pick the one best suited for their circumstances.

*The NAP Principles for Training Children.* This paperback book discusses the basic philosophy underlying the NAP system. It provides the explanations as to why the strategies presented in the *Manipulating Children Handbook* work. It also provides the parents with principles from which they can devise their own strategies for problems not listed in the Handbook.

*The NAP Training Manual for Parents.* This manual discusses the specific steps a parent should go through when setting out to get rid of a problem behavior in their child. The manual discusses how the parent can pick the best time and place for changing their child's behavior. Feedback charts and other support aids are included to make the task as easy as possible for parents.

For more information concerning these books and workshops write to:

Dr. P. W. Robinson
Department of Psychology
Brigham Young University
Provo, Utah 84602

# Index


A

Accountability, 94–96
  infant, case, 96
  Kit, case, 94–95
  and nature, 95–96
  and problem children, 95
Adoptions, 262–66
  attention to parents, 262–63
  race problems, 264–65
  revealing of to children, 265–66
  Terra, case, 263–65
Alcohol and drug abuse, 215–17
  Antabuse, 216
  rate of use, 215
  and behavior modification, 217
  reasons for, 216
Ask for more—settle for less tactic, 43

B

Biting, 224
Bonding, between parent and child, 237–44
  constant struggle for, 241
  durability of, 240
  in human infant, 238
  imprinting of ducklings, 238
  strength in bad families, 238–40
  Karen, case, 239–40
Books of remembrance, 102–03
  and home movies, 102
Budget, restrained, parenting on, 105–06
  and challenge to children, 106
  and life cycle, 105

C

Capacity, lack of, 173–75
  cases, 173, 174
  molding of, 174
  rat, jumps of, paradigm, 174, 175
  skiers, jumps of, 174
Caring in children, rekindling, 249–51
  Lisa, case, 249–50
Caring, indices of, 234–35
  distinguished from leniency, 234
  Maria, case, 234–35
  and treating all alike, 235
Caring, in parents for children, rekindling of, 251–53
  discussion, 241
  lack of success, withdrawal from, 251–52
  loss of interest, competing demands, 252–53
  married couple, loss of libido in, paradigm, 252
Caring, positive signs of, 237
Caring, and successful parenting, 232–33
  in animals, 233
  case, 233–34
  and uncaring children, 232, 233
Child 'enemies,' changing to allies, 111–12
  and questions of parents, 111, 112
Children, caring of, indices, 242–43
  discussion, 241
  and independence, 243
  questions to ask, 242
  teenagers, 242–43
Children, control of parents by, case, 1–2
Children, help from to parents, 196–98
  advantages, 196, 198
  Benny, case, 196–97
Childrearing, right to enjoy, 24–27
  and child, helplessness of, 25
  child, selfishness of, 25
  parents, guidance by, 26–27
  and sacrifice of parents, 24–25
  socialization, 26
Children, responsibilities, at home;
  age, 203
  and asking children, 203
  and children of other families, 204
  overdemands, 203–04
  speedups, 203
Community, aids in, 107–08
Consequences as key to shaping, 166–67
  and avoidance, 167
  cause and effect, 166, 167
Coverant control therapy, example, 212
Covert sensitization, 215

D

Depression, 210–12
Direct method, 54–56
  and excuses, use of, 56
  Harold, case, 54–55
Diversions:
  Jeffry the helper, 47
  Malcom the horsetrader, 47–48
  while mother gets a nap, strategy, 46–47
Divide and conquer, against parents, 48–49
Divorced parents, setting up of, 49–50, 68–69
  dad lets me do this, 50
  killing with kindness, 49–50
Do—give what they like, method, 177–79
  autism, 178–79
  bribery, technical difinition, 177–78
  distinguished from bribery, 177
  and material rewards, 178
  and reward hierarchy, 179
Do—take away what they dislike, 179–80
  nature, 179
  and parents, 179, 180
Drug abuse. *See* Alcohol and drug abuse

E

Eating problems, 224–27
  as emotional indices, 224–25
  junk food, 226–27
  overeating, 225–26
  picky eating, 226
  playing with food, 225
  and punishment, 225

Everybody is doing it, 65–66
  case, 65
  nature, 66
Expectations, reasonable, 103–04
  children, 103
  mother-in-law, 103
Extinction, 119–24
  bootleg attention, 122
  dirty talk, case, 119–20
  discussion, 119
  disruptive classroom behavior, 120–21
  and ignoring of behavior, 121
  implementation, 122–23
  points to remember, 123–24
  prediction of effect, 121–22
  reverse training, 123

F

Failure, avoiding feeling of, 253
Fears, 227–29, 231
  case, 227
  compared to pain, 227
  confrontation, 228
  gradual reduction, 228, 231
  incompatible response, 229
  induction of, 227, 228
Fights, 230–31
Followthrough, of parents, 99–101
  discussion, 99–100
  and problem children, 100
Foster care programs, 200–01
Foster homes, placement of problem children in, 260–62
Friends, checking out of by parents, 106–07

H

Half-grown children, remodeling of, 254–60
  author, practice of, 257
  and control, 259–60
  foster care, 255
  late, case, 259
  by parents, 256
  points to remember, 256
  private schools, 255
  rules and responsibilities, 258
  structure of family, 257–58
  and third parties, harm to, 260
Hand not quicker than eye, repeating tactic, 44
Hand, quicker than eye, tactic, 43–44
Help from mate, 193–94
  full responsibility, load, 194
  and inconsistency, work with animals, 194
Help for parents in family, 190–93
  Army couple, case, 191–92
  parental mutual support, 192
  quality time, 192
Hidden defeaters, 168–73
  action and reward, connection of, 172
  adaptation, 169
  attention, attempts to get, 169, 170
  and child's mind, 171
  consequation, 168
  immediacy, 172–73
  inconsistency, 171–72
Hidden defeaters *(continued)*
  masochism, case, 168–69
  masochism, induction of, 170
  pigeons, conditioning of, 170, 171–72
  shocks, to disrupt masochism, 169–70
  value, failure to see, 168
Hyperactivity, 212–13
  disappearance of with age, 213
  drugs for, 213

I

Incidents, views of as success or failure, 5–6
Incompatible response, strategy: and baits, use of, 116–17
  good activities, arranging of, 118
  meals, case, 117
  overdressing, 117–18
  prediction of usefulness, 116
Incompatible response tactics, parents susceptible to, 72–73
Independence, developing of, 108

J

Johnson, W.G., 212

L

Learning disabilities, 210
Life, allowing child to experience, 243–44
  false expectations, 244
  and limits of reality, 244
Life of parent, sharing, 247–48
  hobbies, 247–48
  house duties, 248
  and parent's work
Life style, right of parents, to, 36–38
  case, 37
  children, as apprentices, 36, 38
  vacations and children, 37–38
Listening to children, 248–49
Lorenz, Konrad, 238
Lying, 229–30

M

*Manipulating Children: The NAP Handbook*, 269
Manipulating children, right to, 27–31
  and children, natural preferences of, 31
  children, need of to learn, 27–28
  and learning from parents, 29
  questions to ask, 28–29
  and sex in teenagers, 30–31
  and technical progress, 30
  values, questions of, 29
  wolf children, case, 28
Manipulation, success of vs. 'wrongness,' concept, 2–3
  Danny, 3
  examples, 3
  Harold, 3–4
  Lee Ann, 4
  Todd, 4–5
Marriage, stopping by parent, 114–15
Mistakes, in behavior modification, 231
Mistakes, right to make, 38–40
  case, of instilling courage, 38–39

Mistakes, right to make *(continued)*
trauma, responsibility as block to, 39–40
universality of, 38
Motivation, four ways of, discussion, 175–77
Motivation, four ways of, effectiveness, 181–89
ages, range, 186
allowances, demands for more, 186–87
in animals, 181
diversification, 185
fading to internal rewards, 196
immediacy, 187–88
inconsistency, 187–88
Maria, case, 182–84
pleasure-pain axis, 181–82
priming the pump, 186
reminders, 188–89
rewards, 189
room cleaning, 187
shaping, 186

N

*NAP Principles for Training Children, The,* 269
*NAP Training Manual for Parents, The,* 269
Nonjob activities, involvement of children, 106–07
Not do—give something they dislike, 180
Not do—take away something they like, 180–81

O

Overpowering of parents, physically, 57–58
Ellie, 57–58
Leon and Louise, case, 57

P

Parenting, effective, natural approach, 8–12
adoptions by author, 10–11
author, experience of, 9
books, value of, 9, 11
and children as 'enemy,' 8–9
socially deprived, example, 9–10
Parenting, natural method, 88–94
foster children, manipulation by, 88–89
inadequacy, feelings of, 89
manipulation, as natural, 91
manipulation, neutrality of, 90–91
muddling through, 90
and psychologists, 92
spoonlifting, as paradigm, 91–92
Willie, case, 93–94
Parents, divorced and single, effectiveness of, 108–10
and grief, 109
and housework, 109
and self-pity of children, 110
Parents, rights of, 19–21
and childish misdeeds, 19–20
prior anxiety of mother, 19
Parent shaping by children, 6–8
as natural behavior, 7
Parents, type susceptible to superthreshold tactics, 61–63
and children's valuations of parents, 62–63
infant's cries, example, 61–62
Parents, type susceptible to superthreshold tactics *(continued)*
and self-confidence of parents, 62
and shy parents, 62
Physical restraint, 124–28
Hershel, case, 124–25
leash and halter, 126
questions of parents, 127–28
types, 125–26
use, 126–27
Presiding over family, right of parents to, 22–24
brats, case, 22–23
parents, advantages of, 24
Private schools, help from, 199–200
and class conditioning, 199, 200
Problems, of other parents, ease of seeing, 1–2
Problems, rarity of need for professional help, 208–10
childhood fears, 208–09
incompatible responses, 209
smoking, 209–10
Problems, types handleable by parents, 218–20
case, 219
and psychologists, services of, 218
tantrums, treatment of, 219
Professional care, discussion, 205–06
Professional care, recognition of need form in children, 206–08
retardation, 206
hyperactivity, 206–07
thumbsucking, 207
Psychologist as pawn, 82–87
discussion, 82
Kent, views of three psychologists on, 82–85
*Punishment,* Walters and Grusec, 142
Punishment:
absence as cause of child abuse, 143–44
arguments against, 142–43
Azrin and Holz, work of, 142
Boe and Church, work of, 142
example, 133–38
as molder, 143
and psychological research, 140
and questions of parents, 137–38
Schwartz, work of, 142
statements against, 139
and undesirable behavior, stopping of by, 144
Walters and Grusec, work of, 142
Punishment, fallacies about:
aggression in child, 151–52
and cause and effect, 152
hate, problem of, 155
inconsistency in parental response, 150–51
learned helplessness, work on in dogs, 154
more-the-better fallacy, 154–55
as negative feedback, 154–55
overprotectiveness, effect of, case, 152–53
pain, psychological arousal by, 150
planned disappointments, 153

Punishment, fallacies about *(continued)*
ratio of to rewards, 155
and retaliation by child, 151
trauma from, 149–51
'unnaturalness and ineffectiveness,' 152–53
Punishment, scientific look at, 144–49
associationism, 145
aversive experiences, 148–49
brain centers, 149
defined, 146, 147
hedonistic principle, 145
Mendel, Gregor, work of, 146
Olds and Milner, work of, 149
pleasurable experiences, 144, 149
pleasure-pain axis, 145–46
punishers, objects and acts, 147
reinforcement, defined, 146, 147
smoking research, as paradigm, 148
Thorndike, Edward, work of, 146–47
unpleasant experiences, 144–45
Punishment, tactics for effective, 155–63
alternatives, 160–61
association, 158
Biblical references, 164
and brainwashing by child, 159, 160
child abuse, 162–63
dislikes of children, case, 156
escape, prevention of, 159–60
hyperactivity, 160–61
immediacy, 158–59
intensity, 157–58
mule, parable of, 157
prolongation, avoidance of, 159
relativeness, 156–57
and situations, 160
spanking, questions about, 161–62
stealing, 161
Thorndike, work of, 158
timeouts, 156, 162
Putting parents over a barrel, strategy, 67–68
Audrey, case, 67
stepdaughter, 68

R

Raising children, right of parents to, 21–22
new laws, 21
and parental malpractice, 21–22
and social change, 21
Relatives, help from, 195–96
Responsibility, 96–98
byproducts of, 98
in home, 97
and society, as market trading of responsibilities, 97
Robinson, Dr. P. W., 269
Rules and limitations, as signs of care, 235–37
Cindy, case, 236
Morgan, case, 235–36
enforcement, 236–37
Running away, 223–24
reasons for, 223
treatment, 223–24

S

School, help from, 198–99
Satiation, 129–31
biting, pinching, kicking, 130
points to remember, 130–31
smoking, 129
School sluffs, stopping of, 115–16
Schoolteacher, help from, 199
Self-confidence, building of, 245–47
baseball, example, 246
excess difficulty of tasks, 245
fishing, example, 246–47
school trouble, 246
wrestling, example, 245
Seligman, Dr. Martin, 154
Sensitivity, 98–99
and feedback, 98
lack of, 99
Service from children, right to expect, 32–36
allowances, 33
discussion, 32
duty rosters, 32–33, 34–35
involvement of children, 33, 36
tantrums, 32
Setting up, of parents, 64–65
content, 65
defined, 64
Sexual deviancy, 214–15
homosexuality, 214
inherent reward of sex act, 215
premarital sex, 214
treatment, 215
Shaping, case, 6
Singh, Rev., 28
Social worker as pawn, 78–81
discussion, 78
hyperactive boy, manipulation by, 78–80
Society against parent, collisions between, 74–78
discussion, 74
Eddie and Karl, manipulation of society by, 75–77
Soft spots, finding in parents, 70–72
by children, 71
examples, 71
incompatible response situation, nature, 70–71
Spackman, Harold and Millie, 267–68
Stealing, 230
Stimulus change, 131–33
discussion, 131
points to remember, 132–33
stopping arguments, 132
stopping a marriage, 131–32
Subliminal conditioning of parents, 41–43
car repair, case, 42
use, 42–43
vacuum cleaner salesman, case, 41–42
Subliminal tactics, parents' susceptibility to, 52–53
children, awareness of parental weakness in, 53
times to ask requests, 52–53

Subliminal tactics, types of, 50–52
  and common interests, 50
  diversions, 51
  propagandizing, 52
  shaping, 51–52
Superthreshold, defined, 55
Superthreshold tactics, effect on parents, 58–61
  adaptation phases in parents, 60–61
  Bernie, case, 61
  case, 58–59
  and parents' blaming of child's behavior, 58
  problem neutralization, defense mechanism, 59, 60
  shock, paradigm, 59–60
Surprise, element of in family life, 104–05
  children, 104–05
  discussion, 104

T

Taking time, 249
Tantrums, 220–23
  and cause and effect, learning of, 221–22
  and extinction, 221
  and plasticity of infant, 222
  and punishment, 221
  and tendency to comply with superior force, 222–23
Teenagers, strategies of, 12–19
  child, separation anxiety of, 12–14
  childraising, unconscious, 18
Teenagers, strategies of *(continued)*
  extinction, 14–17
  fun, 18
  help, search for by parents, 17
  manipulation, naturalness of, 17
  manipulation, unconscious, 17–18
  points to remember, 18

U

Unity of family, 101–02
  discussion, 101
  lack, effects, 101
  steps to enhance, 101–02
Unsuspecting parent, unconscious molding technique of, 44–46
  case, use of on child, 45–46

W

Wearing down, of parents, 56–57
  avoidance of quick relief, importance of, 57
*Wolf Children of India*, Singh, 28
Wundt, Wilhelm, 181

Y

You don't love me as much because I am adopted, tactic, 69–70
  use, 70
  and verbal retaliations, 69
You like her best, tactic, 66–67
  case, 67
  nature, 66